# AUDUBON'S
# BIRDS
# OF AMERICA

# THE TINY FOLIO

# AUDUBON'S OF AMERICA

EDITED BY ROGER TORY PETERSON
& VIRGINIA MARIE PETERSON

ABBEVILLE PRESS
NEW YORK   LONDON

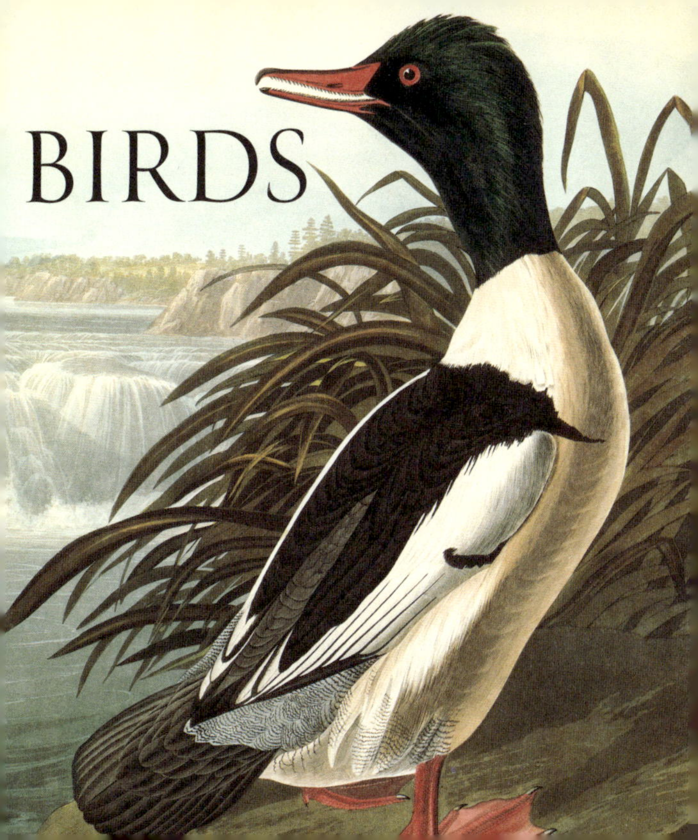
BIRDS

In this edition, Audubon's plates are presented in a modern ornithological order, rather than the order in which they were originally published. Audubon's original common names, where they differ from the modern ones, are given in brackets, with their original spelling and capitalization.



Second edition
Flamingo cover: ISBN 978-0-7892-1509-3
10 9 8 7 6 5 4 3 2

*A previous edition of this book was cataloged as follows:*
Library of Congress Cataloging-in-Publication Data
Audubon, John James, 1785–1851.
[Birds of America]
Audubon's birds of America / [edited] by Roger Tory Peterson &
Virginia Marie Peterson.—Rev. ed.
p. cm.
At head of title: The Audubon Society baby elephant folio.
1. Birds—North America. 2. Artists—United States—Biography.
3. Ornithologists—United States--Biography. I. Peterson, Roger Tory, 1908–1996. II. Peterson, Virginia Marie, 1925–2001.
III. Title. IV. Title: Birds of America.
QL681. A97 1990 598.2973—dc20
90-31607

# CONTENTS

# INTRODUCTION



*The Audubon Saga*

THE SAGA OF AUDUBON has been told many times, with variations. It is
not exactly a Horatio Alger tale of rags to riches, because the fledgling
Audubon, born out of wedlock, was given a young gentleman's tutoring
and was all but spoiled by an indulgent stepmother.

Jean Jacques Fougère Audubon was born in 1785 on the island of
Santo Domingo, now Haiti, in the West Indies. He was the son of an
enterprising French sea captain who, after reverses in Les Cayes, where
he owned property, returned to France with the boy. His mother was
a young lady, Mademoiselle Rabin, originally from Nantes, who died
before the captain returned to his home and legal wife in France. How
he explained his transgressions to Madame Audubon is not known, but
she took the four-year-old boy to her heart as her own as she did his
sister, also born out of wedlock.

Perhaps to enable his son to escape conscription in Napoleon's
army, or perhaps to help him avoid the stigma of illegitimacy, Captain
Audubon sent Jean Jacques at the age of eighteen to Mill Grove near
Philadelphia where he owned property. The birds of America fascinated
young Audubon, and drawing them became an obsession from which
he never freed himself.

Audubon performed an experiment at Mill Grove that marked a
"first" in the history of ornithology. He was fascinated by the phoebes
that lived along the creek near his home. By placing silver threads about
the legs of a brood of young phoebes to see whether they would return

the following year, he became the first bird bander (or "ringer," to use the British term).

At Mill Grove Audubon married Lucy Bakewell, the daughter of a neighbor. Shortly thereafter the young couple moved westward to Louisville, Kentucky, where Jean Jacques's father had set him up in business. But business was not in his blood, or so it seemed. It must be admitted that times were uncertain and investment risky on the frontier in those days. Moving farther west to the Mississippi and then down to New Orleans, Audubon met successive reverses until he was almost reduced to penury. In reviewing this difficult period Audubon wrote, "Birds were then as now I drew, I looked on nature only; my days were happy beyond human conception." He had conceived a grandiose plan of painting all the birds of North America—at least all then known—and at no time did he lose sight of this goal. He may have harbored the idea of eventual publication from the start, but it seems that an unheralded visit by pioneer ornithologist Alexander Wilson stirred his competitive spirit to action.

Audubon was often away from his family for months, exploring the wilderness, painting, and pursuing his dream. His devoted Lucy, who had borne him two sons, Victor and John, kept home and hearth together by teaching. He himself eked out a living as an itinerant portrait painter and as a dancing and fencing instructor.

As his portfolio bulged he began to look for a patron or a publisher, but he could find none in New York or Philadelphia. No one would risk the capital in those difficult days. Audubon decided that there might be a better chance of success in England, so with Lucy's savings as a teacher and some money he had managed to acquire by painting portraits, he set sail in 1826.

Abroad he was acclaimed immediately. Although he had been a nobody on his home turf, the rough, colorful man from the American frontier was a sensation abroad. He fascinated the genteel patrons of the art salons in London, Edinburgh, and Paris. Madison Avenue would have admired his public relations techniques. Long ahead of his time in the art of showmanship, he played his part well. To fit the image of the American woodsman, he wore buckskin and allowed his hair to grow long over his shoulders. The former bankrupt businessman became a supersalesman, traveling from city to city to secure subscriptions. Meanwhile, as a sort of production manager, he monitored with infinite care the work of the engravers and a corps of colorists. He was not only artist, author, and scientist but also publisher, business manager, treasurer, and bill collector. How could he have been "irresponsible" or "impractical" if he could do all this?

William Lizars of Edinburgh agreed to engrave and publish his work, but when only ten plates had been finished the colorists went on strike and Audubon was forced to find another engraver. This was Robert Havell Jr. of London. Audubon was fortunate to be in the hands of such a skilled craftsman and artist. Havell's accomplishment in etching the copper plates was as much a tour de force as the original paintings. It is instructive to compare the watercolors that hang in the galleries of the New-York Historical Society to the Havell prints with which most of us are familiar.

In his 435 colorplates, Audubon depicted the birds exactly the size they were in life. Even the oversize format, 29½ by 39½ inches (known as "double-elephant folio"), the largest ever attempted up to then in the history of book publishing, was insufficient to accommodate the largest birds comfortably. Tall birds, such as the flamingo and the great blue heron, were fitted in by drooping their long necks toward their feet. On the other hand, tiny birds, such as kinglets and hummingbirds, are all but lost on the page.

Among the last few plates in the Elephant Folio and the 65 additional ones in the smaller octavo edition, Audubon included a number of birds from the western part of the country. These were his least successful efforts, probably because he had not seen these species in life.

## Audubon as an Artist

AUDUBON IMPLIED THAT as a youth he had studied under the French master Jacques Louis David, and in doing so laid the foundation of his ability to draw. However, recent research has disputed this. Perhaps it was a good thing that his art was truly his own; like many another innovative genius he was not a clone of his professor. Nor were his paintings like the dull, documentary drawings of Alexander Wilson and his other contemporaries.

The thing that separated Audubon from his predecessors was that he was the first to give his birds the simulation of life. The others portrayed them stiffly and archaically as though they were on museum pedestals. To invest his birds with vitality and movement, Audubon worked from freshly killed specimens, wiring them into lifelike positions. In his youth he had tried hundreds of outline sketches but found it difficult to finish them. He fashioned a wooden model, "a tolerable-looking Dodo. . . . I gave it a kick, broke it to atoms, walked off, and thought again." It was then that he conceived the procedure he was to follow for many years. He wrote: "One morning I leapt out of bed . . . went to the river, took a bath and returning to town inquired for wire of different sizes, bought some and was soon again at Mill Grove. I shot the first Kingfisher I met, pierced the body with wire, fixed it to the board, another wire held the head, smaller ones fixed the feet. . . . There stood before me the real Kingfisher. I outlined the bird, colored it. This was my first drawing actually from nature."

It has been remarked that a Fuertes bird in repose has more the essence of the living bird than an Audubon bird vividly animated. This is understandable when one keeps in mind that Audubon wired up his specimens, and they sometimes looked it. In most cases this method worked fairly well, but the wild turkey cock, wired with its head looking over its back so as to fit the sheet, is almost a caricature. So are Audubon's barred owl with the grinning squirrel and his two red-tailed hawks quarreling in mid-air for possession of a rabbit. His golden eagle frozen in flight with a hare, his two barn owls at night, and his squabbling caracaras are all too contrived. His two blue-winged teals look as though they were thrown through the air like footballs. Inasmuch as Audubon did not know some of the pelagic birds—the fulmar, greater shearwater, and tropic-bird—on their nesting ground, he showed them standing on their toes rather than resting on their bellies with their tarsi flat on the ground.

We can, if we choose, be critical of these errors, but the wildlife artist of today is able to step on the shoulders of those who have gone before. Audubon made the great leap forward at a time when most birds were drawn as though "stuffed" and fastened to wooden perches in museum cases. He took birds out of the glass case and gave them a semblance of life. His paintings have a dramatic impact seldom equaled by those of his successors.

Louis Agassiz Fuertes, in a remarkable letter to his young protégé George Miksch Sutton, extolled Audubon's strengths and defended his shortcomings, unaware that his "training under David" was apparently a myth:

> Say what you will of Audubon, he was the first and only man whose bird drawings showed the faintest hint of anatomical study, or that the fresh bird was in hand when the work was done, and is so immeasurably ahead of anything, up to his time or since, until the modern idea of drawing endlessly from life began to bear fruit, that its strength deserves all praise and honor, and its many weaknesses condonement, as they were the fruit of his training; stilted, tight, and unimaginative old [Jacques Louis] David sticks out in the stiff landscape, the hard outline, and the dull, lifeless shading, while the overpowering virility of Audubon is shown in the snappy, instantaneous attitudes, and dashing motion of his subjects. While there's much to criticize there is also much to learn, and much to admire, in studying the monumental classic that he left behind him. He made many errors, but he also left a living record that has been of inestimable value and stimulus to students, and made an everlasting mark in American ornithology. It is indeed hard to imagine what the science would be like in this country— and what the state of our bird world—had he not lived and wrought, and become a demigod to the ardent youth of the land. (From *Bird Study, an Autobiography*, by George Miksch Sutton, Austin: University of Texas Press, 1980.)

Sutton, who himself later became a distinguished bird artist, wrote: "It was Audubon's instinctive urge to dramatize which led him to represent so many of his birds in violent action. As several admirers of the great artist have pointed out, he was so surfeited with the conventional and lifeless poses used by the bird artists before him that he swung away from the traditional in a sort of furious huff. . . . This was Audubon, lover of beauty, lover of the dramatic, avowed opponent of the prosy." If his art had been less startling and dramatic, it probably would not have survived and we would have heard little about Audubon, for relatively few people read his extensive writings.

In the beginning, Audubon vowed he would paint only from fresh specimens of birds he had collected after observing them in life. Halfway through his project, this resolve broke down. While he was involved in reproducing his paintings in London, many new species were being discovered in the American West. Since he had no immediate hope of reaching the Rockies or the Pacific himself, he was forced to draw them from specimens furnished by Dr. Thomas Nuttall, a New England botanist, and Dr. John Kirk Townsend, an experienced ornithologist, who set out together in 1834 on an exploratory journey to the mouth of the Columbia River. Captain Ross of the Royal Navy furnished additional seabirds that had been taken during his explorations in the Arctic. Other specimens were borrowed from the British Museum. Few of Audubon's later drawings were as inspired as his earlier efforts, because he had never seen these species in life. Many single drawings showed three, four, or five species.

## Apprentices

MUCH HAS BEEN SAID of the fine sense of pattern and composition in some of Audubon's plates. However, it should be pointed out that, like many another artist of an earlier day, he had apprentices. Many of the backgrounds, leaves, flowers, and other botanical accessories were painted by others, but the birds in almost every instance were the work of the master himself. Some compositions remind us of Chinese prints, but we are quite sure Audubon's work was in no way imitative.

The elaborate composition of black-billed cuckoos (plate 233) was probably a cooperative effort. Although Audubon did not give him credit, it is quite certain that Joseph Mason painted the magnolia blossoms and leaves. Audubon wrote to Lucy, "He now draws flowers better than any man probably in America."

Joseph Mason, who as a remarkable boy of thirteen had been one of Audubon's pupils in Cincinnati when he was giving art lessons to raise funds, showed such promise as a botanical artist that Audubon took him on his 1820 trip down the Mississippi. Mason was his assistant for about two years, and most of the leaves and flowers in those plates painted in Louisiana during 1821 and 1822 are his work. At least 57 backgrounds are credited to this young genius. He seems to have disappeared into limbo after leaving Audubon's employ, but he is immortalized in Audubon's bird prints.

During the next several years Audubon may have painted his own backgrounds, but in 1829 he met George Lehman, who was to assist him for the next four years, accompanying him on his trips to the shore and to Florida. Although Lehman was an experienced landscape painter, his leaves and other accessories are a bit more labored and cluttered than those of Mason, who had an innate sense of abstraction and pattern. Lehman's landscapes give a different look to many of the paintings that were made during that productive period; they were more environmental, but less decorative. Lehman is known to have painted the backgrounds for about forty plates, but he probably did more. He even painted an occasional bird; the lesser yellow legs in plate 163 is credited to him.

Time was important once the great work was fully under way. Flowers and leaves took as long to paint as the birds, so Audubon was pleased to enlist a third helper, whom he met in Charleston, a maiden lady by the name of Maria Martin, who later became Reverend John Bachman's second wife. She had a well-tended garden, painted flowers and butterflies quite well, and is credited with drawing the flowers and leaves in about twenty of the paintings. They are not the equal of Joseph Mason's work; her twigs and stems lack his structural strength. The butterflies and moths that appear in six of the plates are presumably hers.

Audubon's two sons were also drawn into the project. His younger son, John Woodhouse Audubon, who became an accomplished artist, helped with the work while in London and actually drew a few of the birds, notably the American bitterns in plate 40. The elder son, Victor Gifford Audubon, painted some of the backgrounds in the later western subjects, but they are more stilted than those of Lehman. It is believed that even Lucy Audubon may have painted at least one bird, the swamp sparrow (plate 426). Add to these efforts the skill and innovation of Robert Havell Jr., the engraver, who improvised branches and twigs where needed, or even full backgrounds where none existed, and we have, in effect, paintings by committee.

Twelve years after Audubon's death in 1851, his widow Lucy sold the original paintings to the New-York Historical Society, where they can be seen today. Reproductions of Audubon's work invariably were made from the Havell prints until 1966, when the American Heritage Publishing Company of New York and the Houghton Mifflin Company of Boston went directly to the original watercolors. It is instructive to compare the originals with the prints, because Havell was in a sense no less a genius than Audubon and left his own artistic stamp on the plates, sometimes even improving them. Some are literally scissors-and-paste jobs. A pastel made in 1820 might be copied in watercolor ten or twelve years later or simply cut out and pasted onto another drawing. Audubon did not hesitate to mix mediums. Pencil, ink, pastel, watercolor, and even oil were combined in some compositions.

America was reawakened to the splendor of Audubon's work in 1937, when the Macmillan Company of New York reproduced, in smaller size, 435 prints from the Elephant Folio and an additional 65 prints from the octavo edition. Although the reproductions left much to be desired, they were a breakthrough. Audubon's prints have been reproduced a number of times since in various forms, and they reached their greatest audience when they graced the calendars of the Northwestern Mutual Life Insurance Company of Milwaukee. Over a period of twenty years more than ten million well-reproduced and framable Audubon prints were distributed in these calendars.

## The Double Elephant Folio

AUDUBON'S REPUTATION SKYROCKETED upon publication of his great work. Baron Cuvier, the French naturalist, rated it the "most magnificent monument which has ever been raised to ornithology." But every genius has his or her critics. One subscriber discontinued her subscription after she received the first lot of prints, numbers 1 to 9. She pronounced them so very bad that she could not think of giving "house room" to any more such "trash."

Not counting his own living costs and those of his family, Audubon spent $115,640 to complete his project. Approximately 200 sets of the Double Elephant Folio were bound and distributed. They were priced at $1,000 each. It was thought that more than half these sets had been broken up by 1970 and sold by dealers as individual prints. However, through the extraordinary investigation of Waldeman H. Fries, we find this was far from true. When he documented the sets in his scholarly work *The Double Elephant Folio: The Story of Audubon's Birds of America* (Chicago: American Library Association, 1973), about 134 complete sets survived. Of these, 94 were in the United States, 17 in England, and the remainder in twelve other countries. It attests to the fortitude of Fries (and his wife) that he was able to examine all but six of these sets. In addition, 14 incomplete sets survived, 28 sets were broken up, 11 were destroyed by fire or war, and 14 had disappeared. It was rumored that one unanticipated spinoff of the Fries book was that thieves, finding the locations of existing sets pinpointed, made off with three of them. All three were eventually recovered.

Nearly a century elapsed before the original investment of $1,000 per set really began to pay off in the collector's market, in direct proportion to the vastly increased interest in birds that had begun to accelerate with the publication of modern field guides. In the 1920s, a collector or speculator could have acquired a set of Audubon at auction for about $2,500. By the mid- or late thirties it would have been closer to $12,000 or $14,000; by the mid-forties, $18,000; in 1960, $60,000 was paid for a set; and in 1969, $216,000. In 1977 a set was sold at auction for $400,000, and the price continued to climb. On June 23, 1989, at an auction at Sotheby's, the total realized from a set that had been broken up was $3,960,000!

# I

## DIVERS OF LAKES AND BAYS,

## WANDERERS

## OF SEAS AND COASTS

Loons, Grebes, Albatrosses, Fulmars, Shearwaters,

Storm Petrels, Tropicbirds, Pelicans, Boobies,

Gannets, Cormorants, Darters, Frigatebirds, Herons,

Bitterns, Storks, Ibises, Spoonbills, and Flamingos

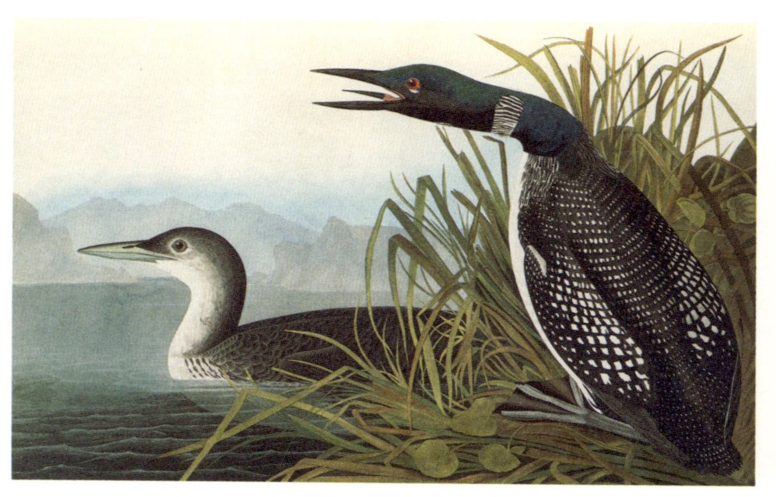

1 Common Loon [Great Northern Diver]
*Gavia immer*

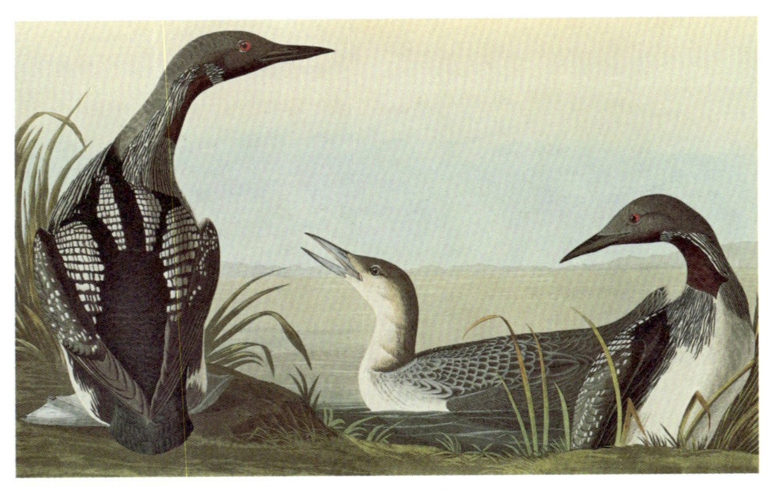

2    Arctic Loon [Black-throated Diver]
*Gavia arctica*

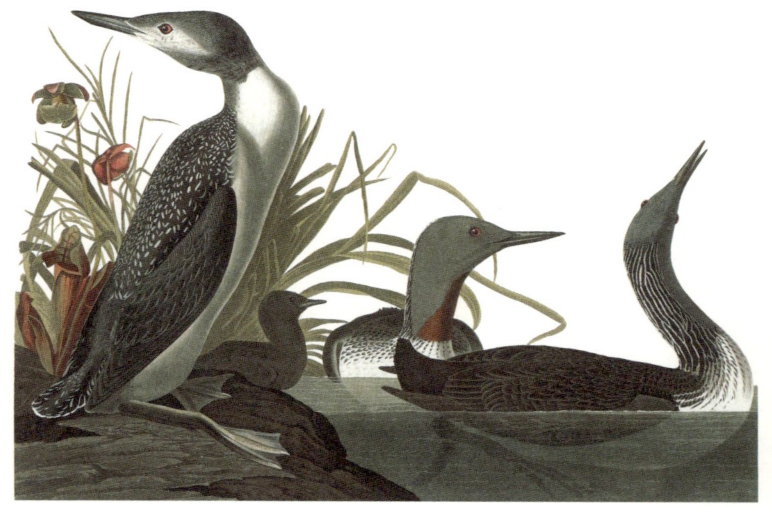

3   Red-throated Loon [Red-throated Diver]
*Gavia stellata*

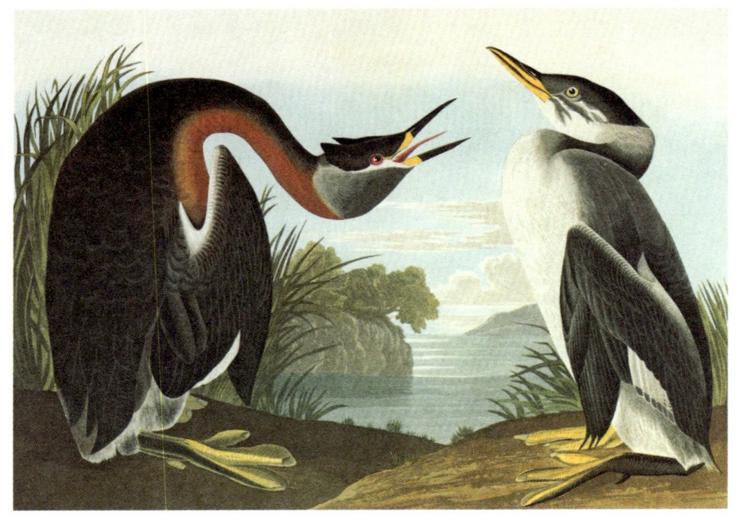

4    Red-necked Grebe

*Podiceps grisegena*

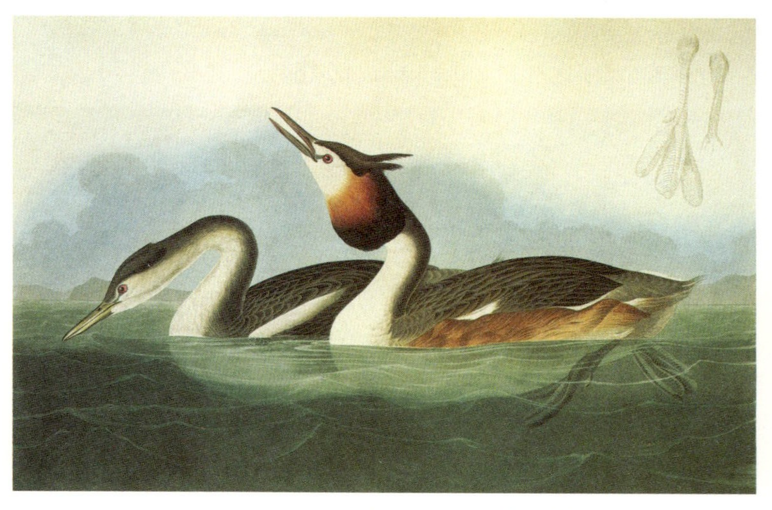

5    Great Crested Grebe [Crested Grebe]
*Podiceps cristatus*

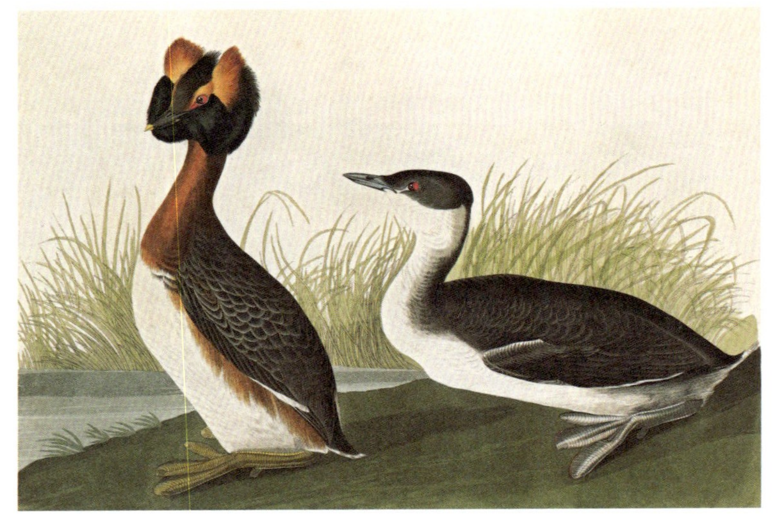

6    Horned Grebe
*Podiceps auritus*

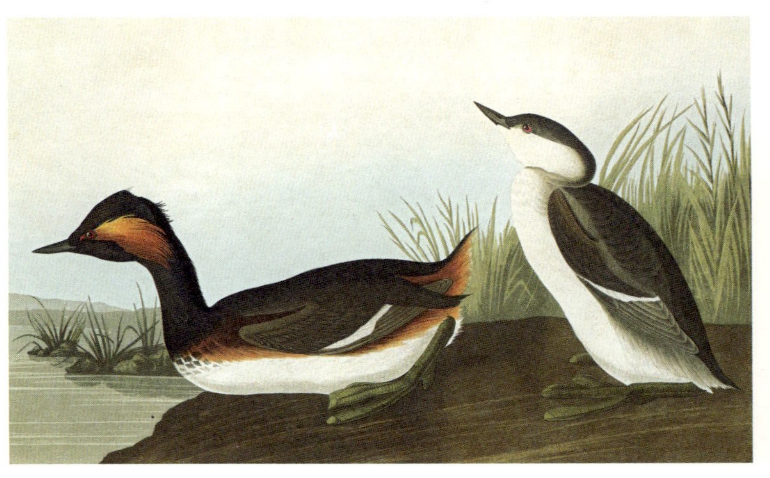

7　Eared Grebe
*Podiceps nigricollis*

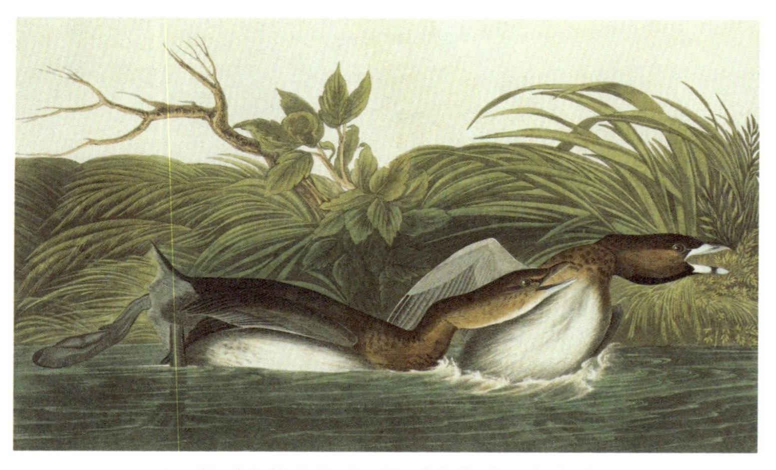

8    Pied-billed Grebe [Pied-billed Dobchick]

*Podilymbus podiceps*

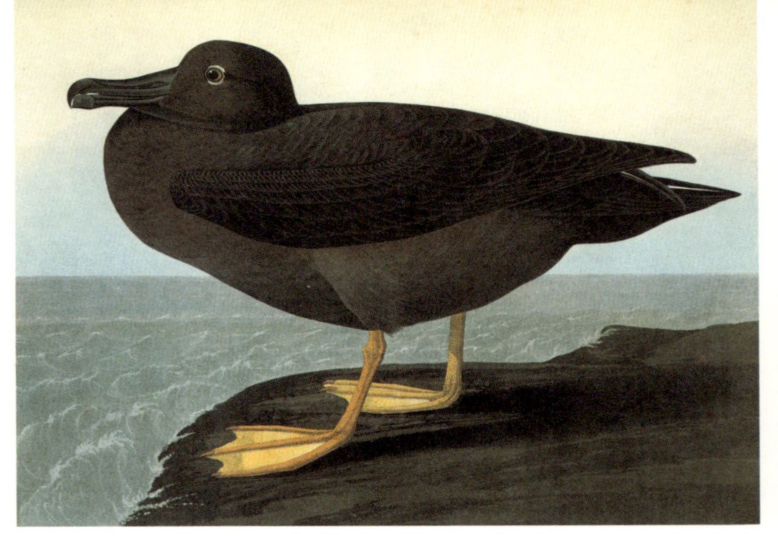

9　Sooty Albatross [Dusky Albatross]
*Phoebetria palpebrata*

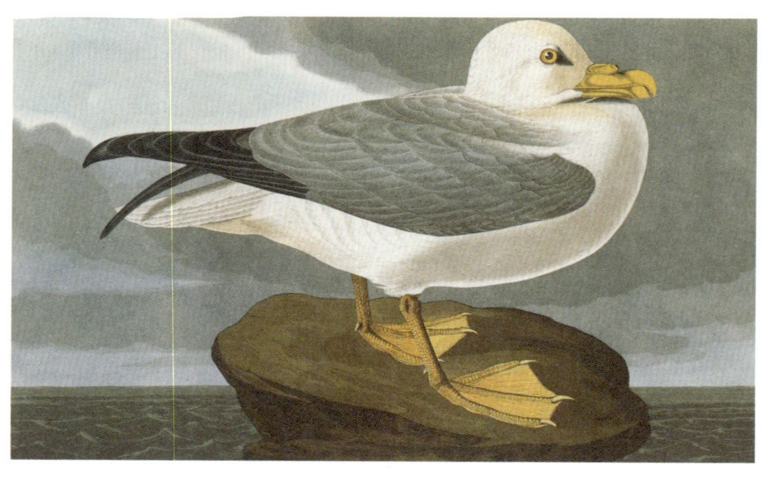

10   Northern Fulmar [Fulmar Petrel]
*Fulmarus glacialis*

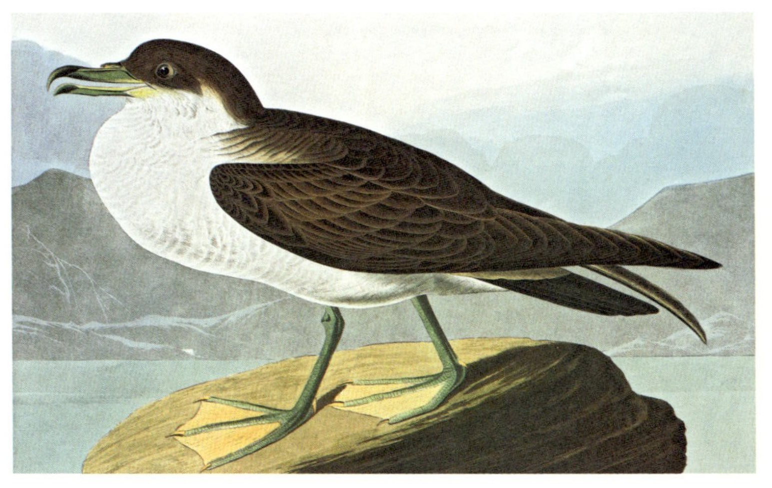

II   Greater Shearwater [Wandering Shearwater]
*Ardenna gravis*

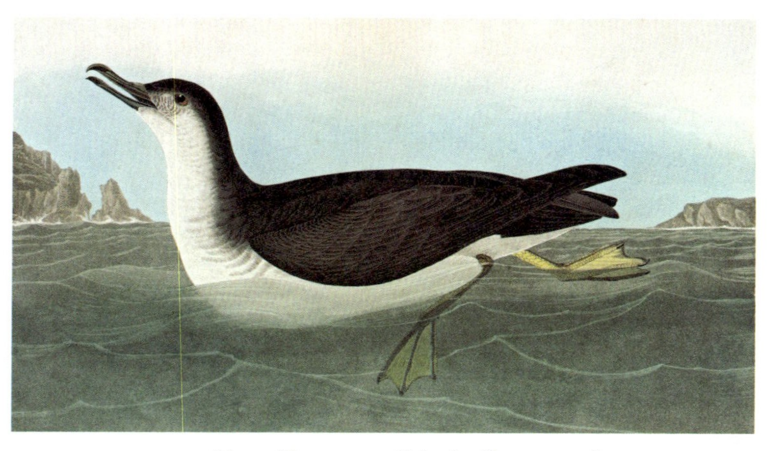

12  Manx Shearwater [Manks Shearwater]
*Puffinus puffinus*

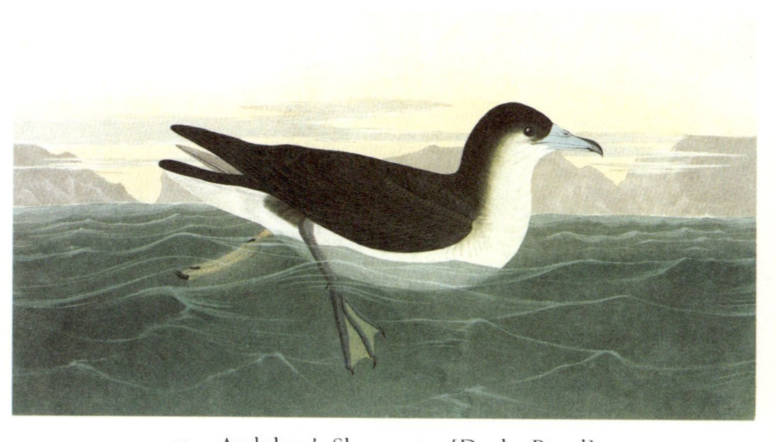

13　Audubon's Shearwater [Dusky Petrel]
*Puffinus lherminieri*

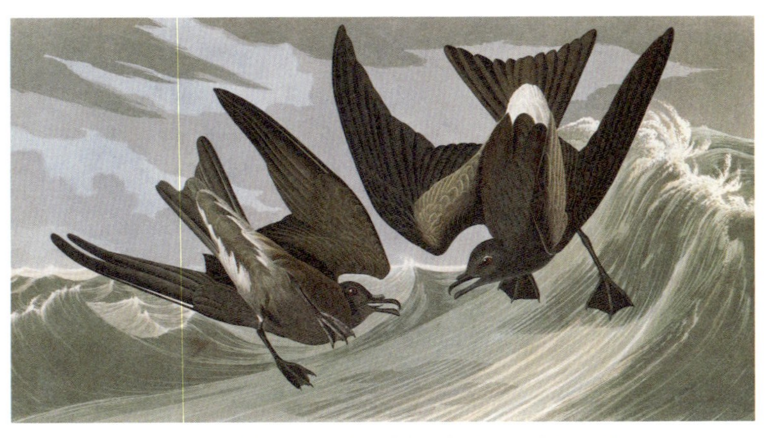

14 Leach's Storm-Petrel [Forked-tailed Petrel]
*Oceanodroma leucorhoa*

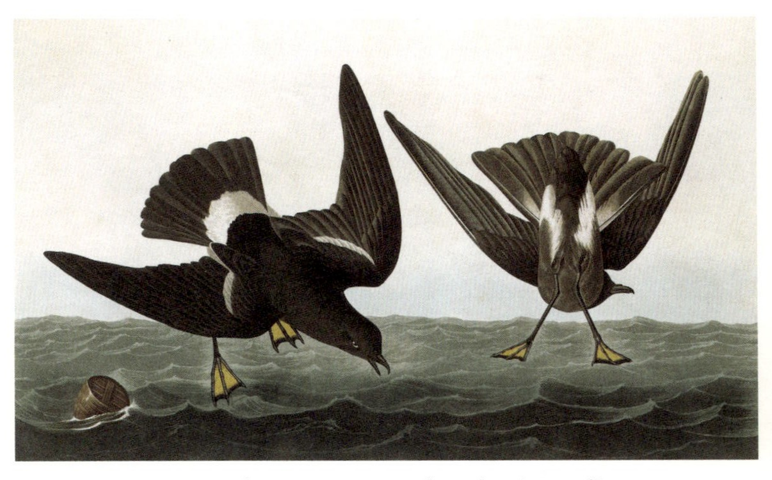

15   Wilson's Storm-Petrel [Wilson's Petrel]
*Oceanites oceanicus*

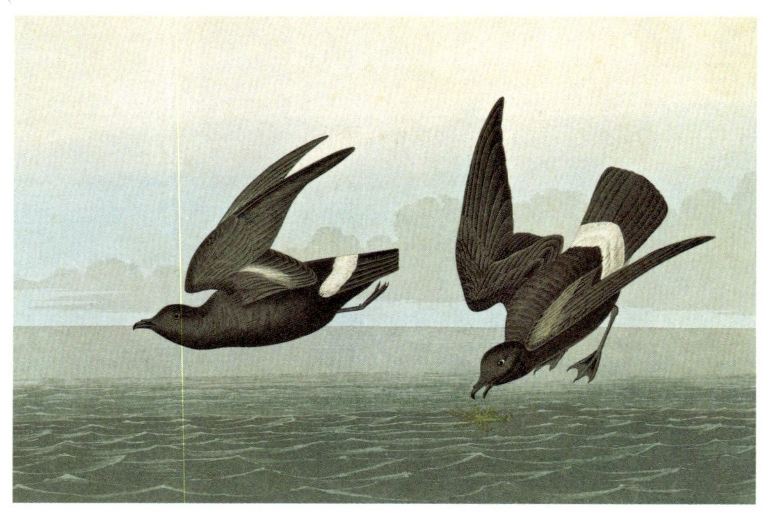

16 European Storm-Petrel [Least Petrel]
*Hydrobates pelagicus*

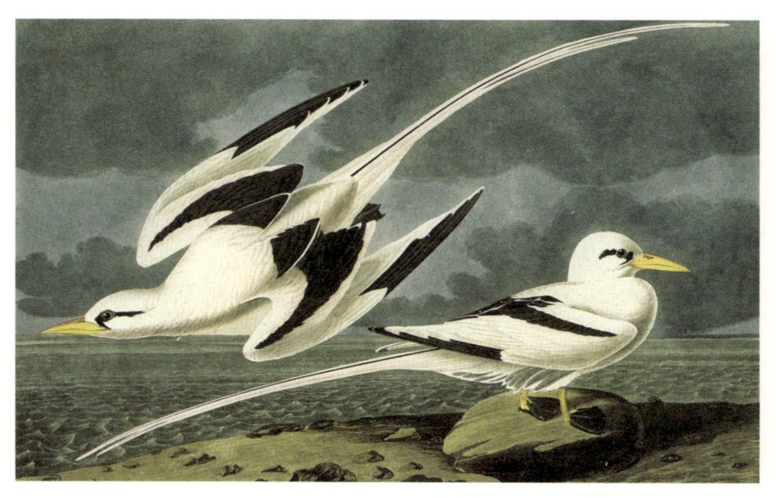

17   White-tailed Tropicbird [Tropic Bird]
*Phaethon lepturus*

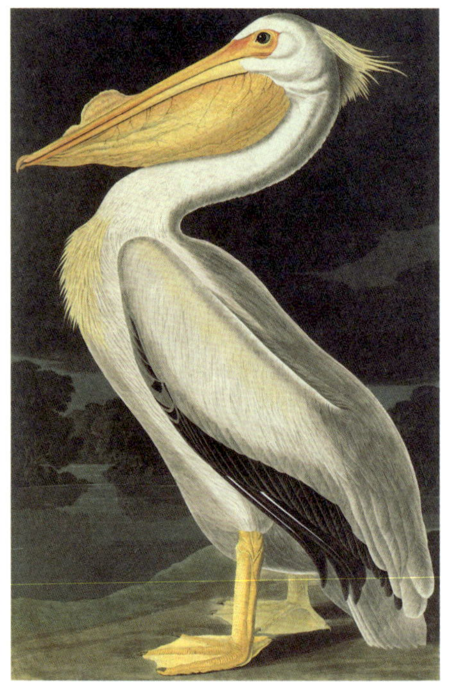

18  American White Pelican
*Pelecanus erythrorhynchos*

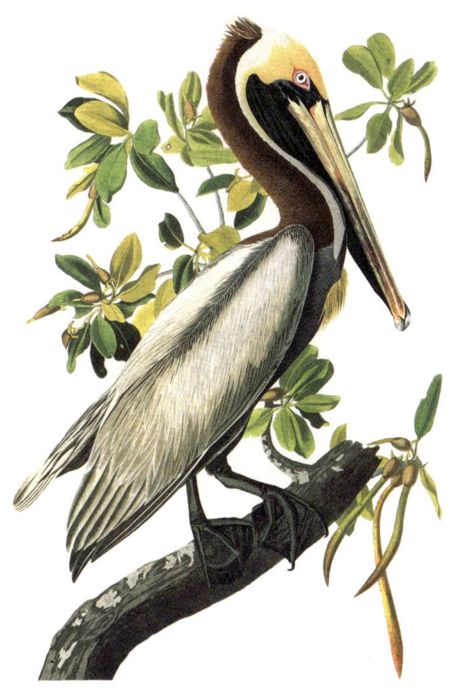

19   Brown Pelican
*Pelecanus occidentalis*

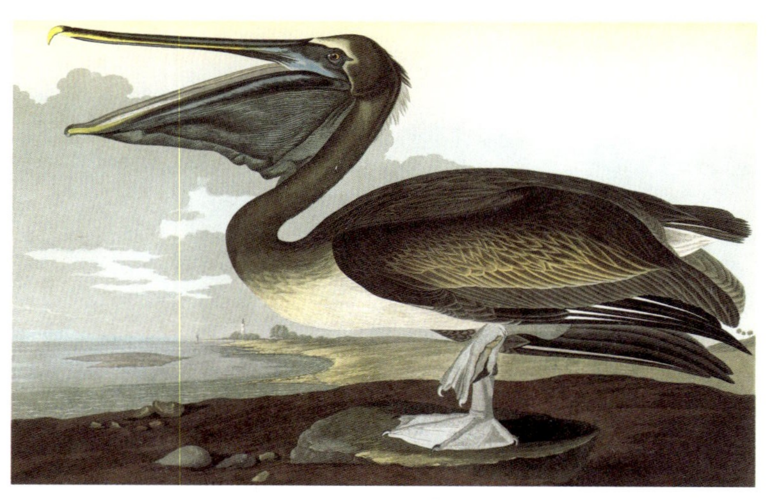

20    Brown Pelican
*Pelecanus occidentalis*

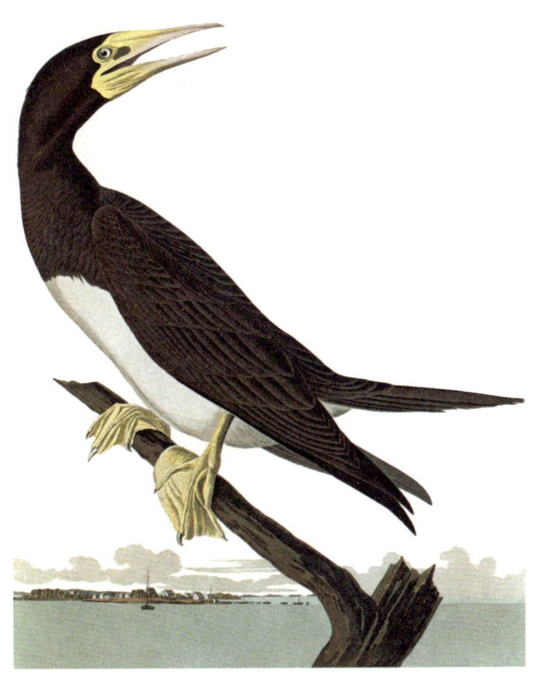

21  Brown Booby [Booby Gannet]
*Sula leucogaster*

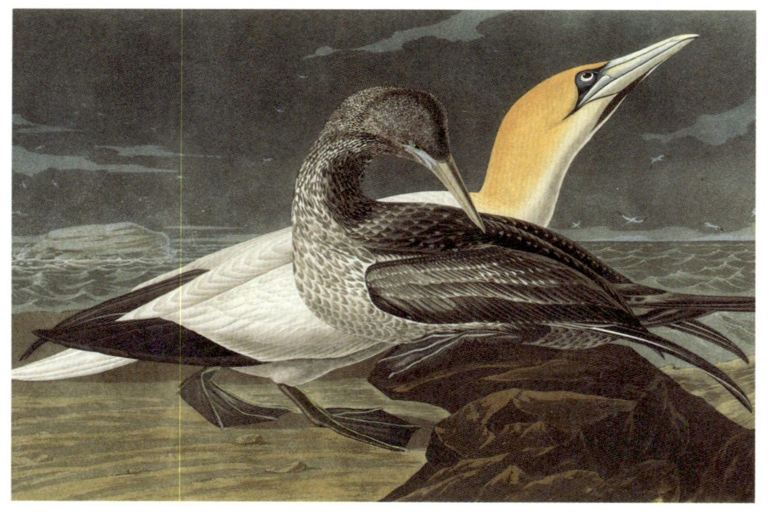

22    Northern Gannet [Common Gannet]
*Sula bassanus*

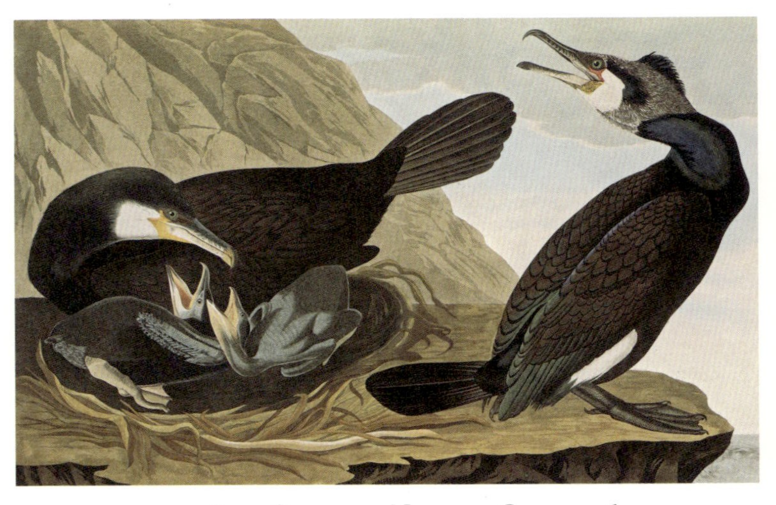

23    Great Cormorant [Common Cormorant]
*Phalacrocorax carbo*

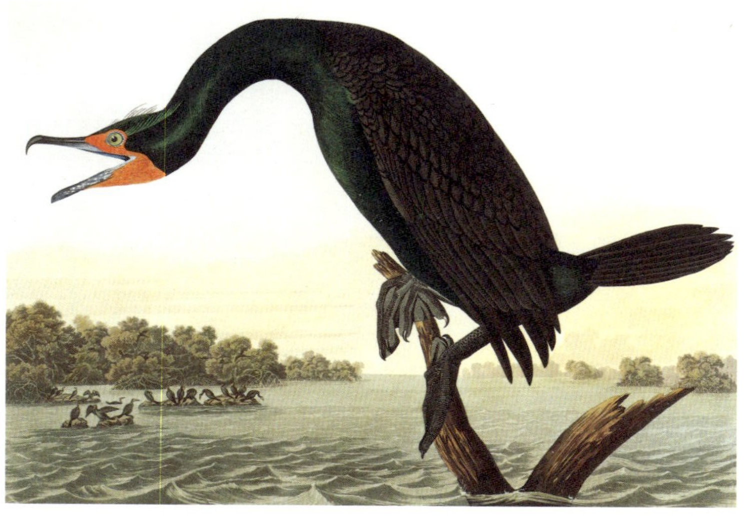

24 Double-crested Cormorant [Florida Cormorant]
*Phalacrocorax auritus*

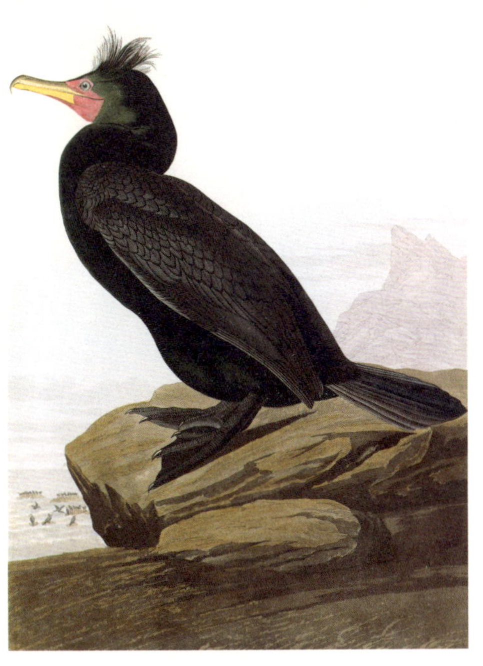

25    Double-crested Cormorant
*Phalacrocorax auritus*

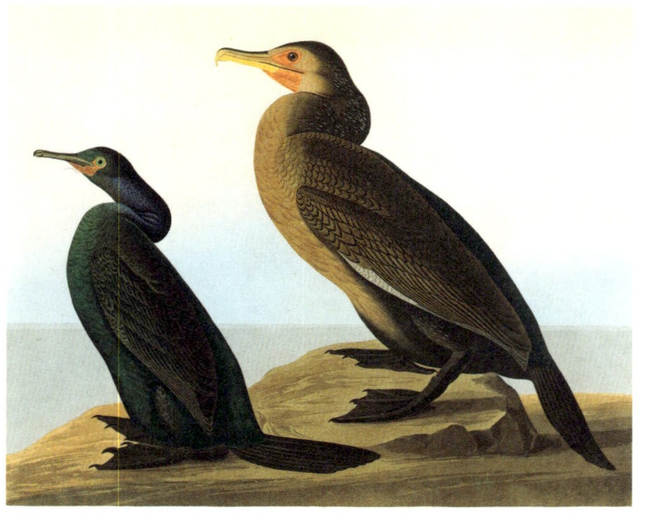

26    Pelagic Cormorant
[Violet-green Cormorant]
*Urile pelagicus*

Brandt's Cormorant
[Townsend's Cormorant]
*Urile penicillatus*

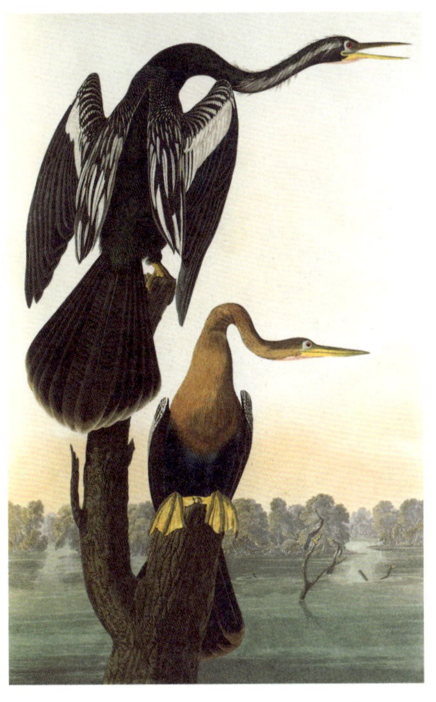

27    American Anhinga [Black-bellied Darter]
*Anhinga anhinga*

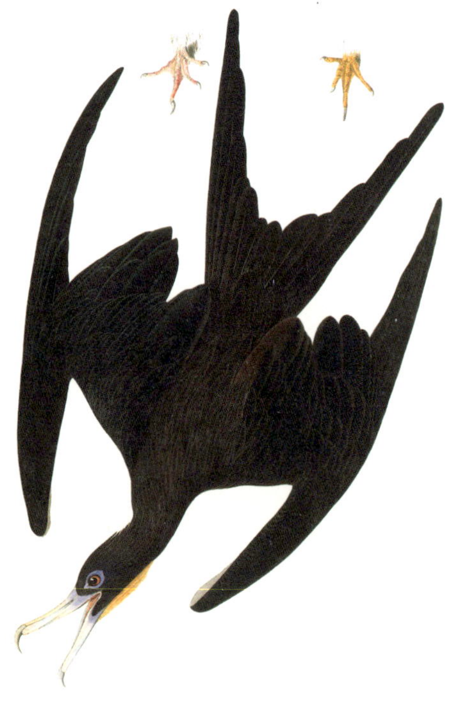

28　Magnificent Frigatebird [Frigate Pelican]
*Fregata magnificens*

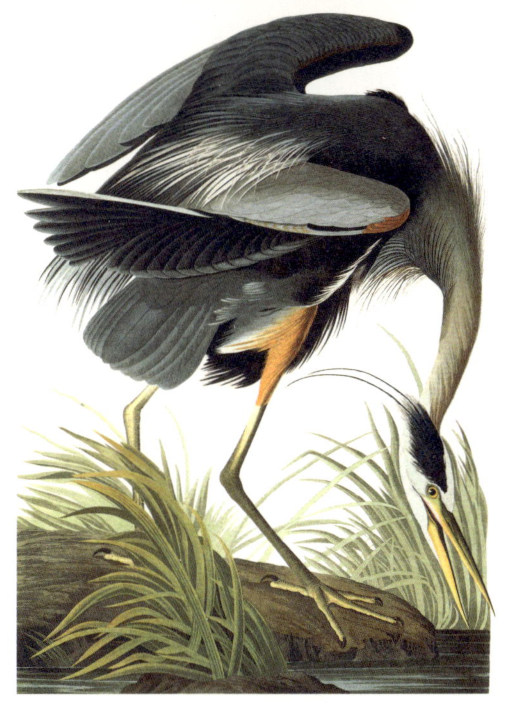

29   Great Blue Heron
*Ardea herodias*

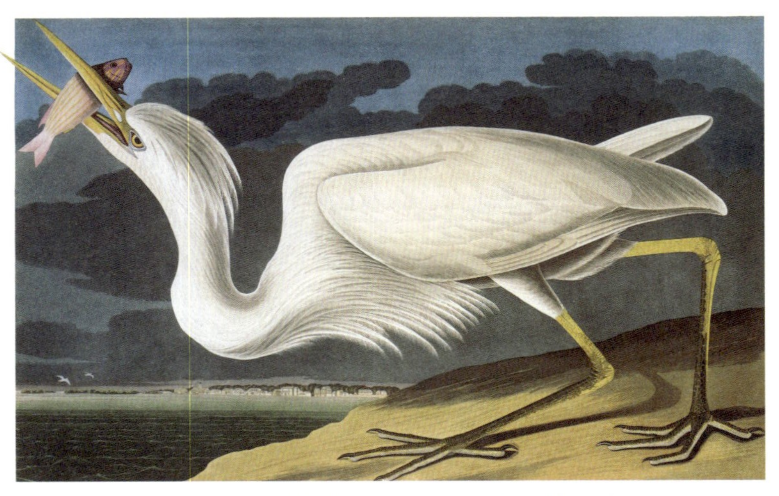

30 Great Blue Heron [Great White Heron]
*Ardea herodias*

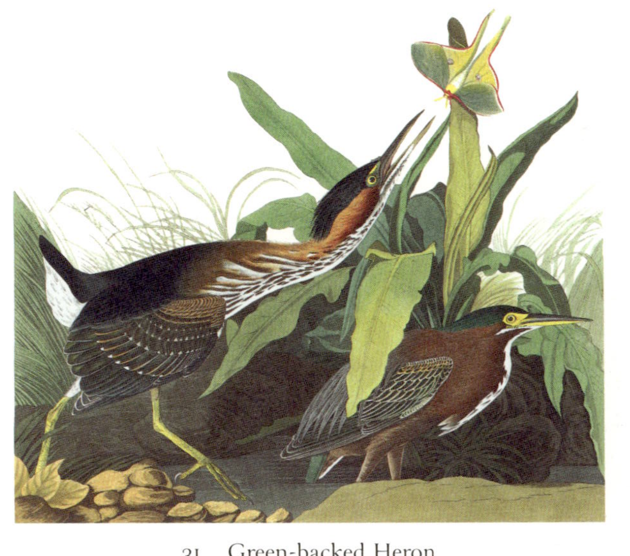

31   Green-backed Heron
*Butorides virescens*

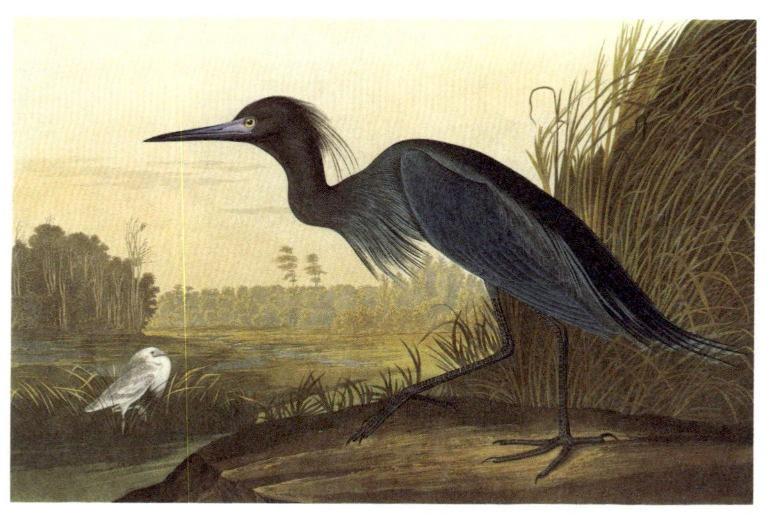

32   Little Blue Heron [Blue Crane or Heron]
*Egretta caerulea*

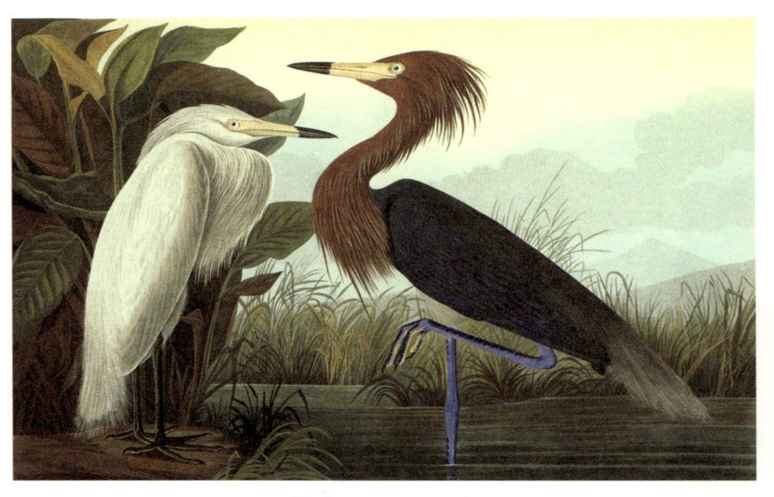

33    Reddish Egret [Purple Heron]
*Egretta rufescens*

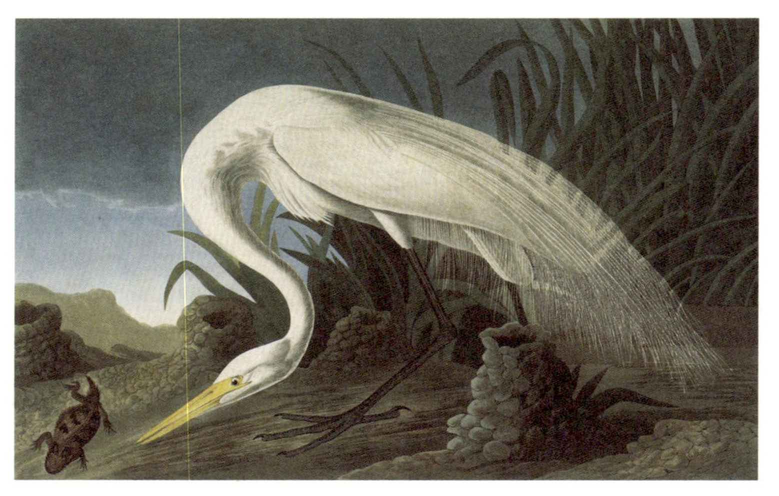

34   Great Egret [White Heron]
*Ardea alba*

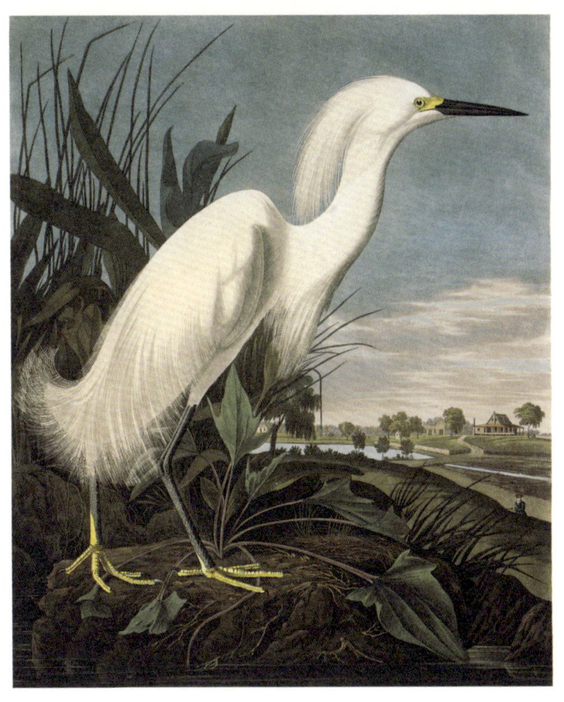

35    Snowy Egret [Snowy Heron]
*Egretta thula*

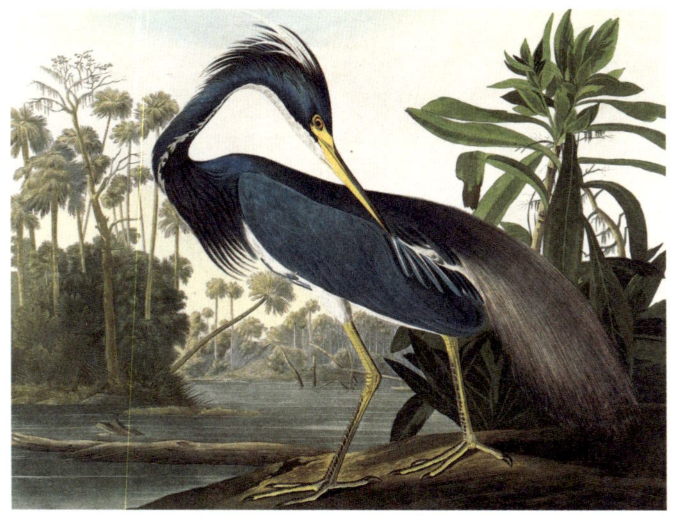

36   Tricolored Heron [Louisiana Heron]
*Egretta tricolor*

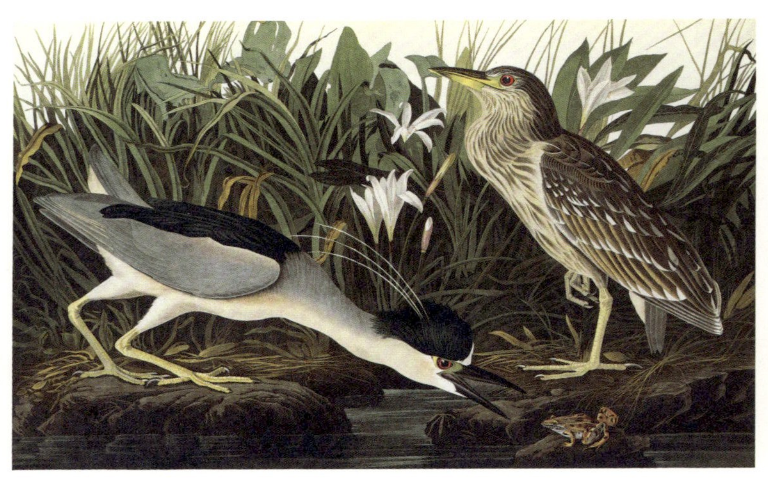

37  Black-crowned Night Heron [Night Heron or Qua Bird]
*Nycticorax nycticorax*

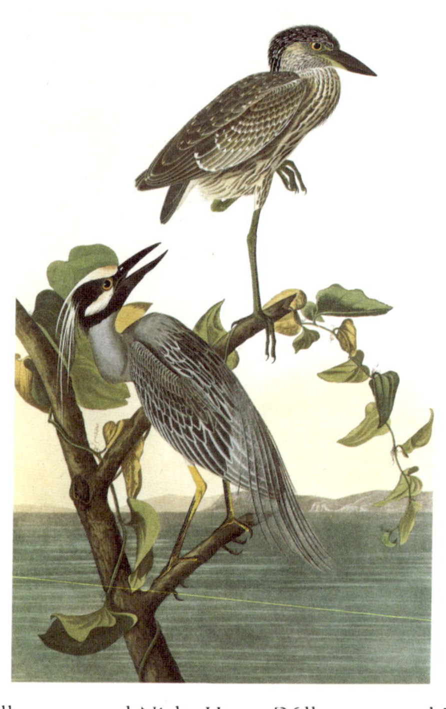

38  Yellow-crowned Night-Heron [Yellow-crowned Heron]
*Nyctanassa violacea*

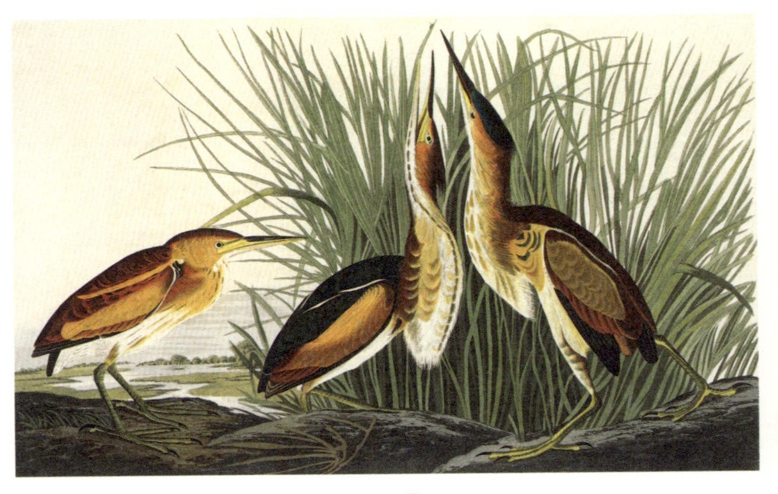

39   Least Bittern

*Ixobrychus exilis*

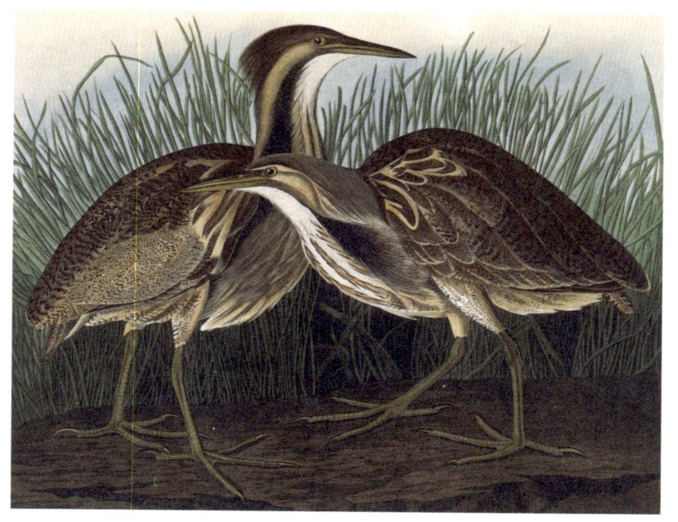

40   American Bittern
*Botaurus lentiginosus*

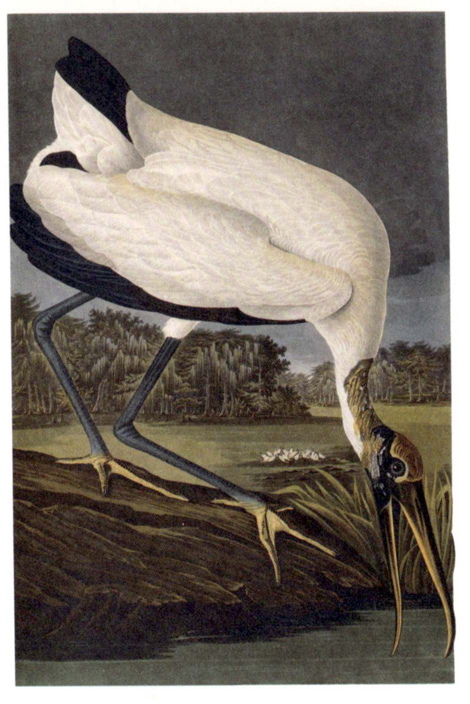

41  Wood Stork [Wood Ibis]
*Mycteria americana*

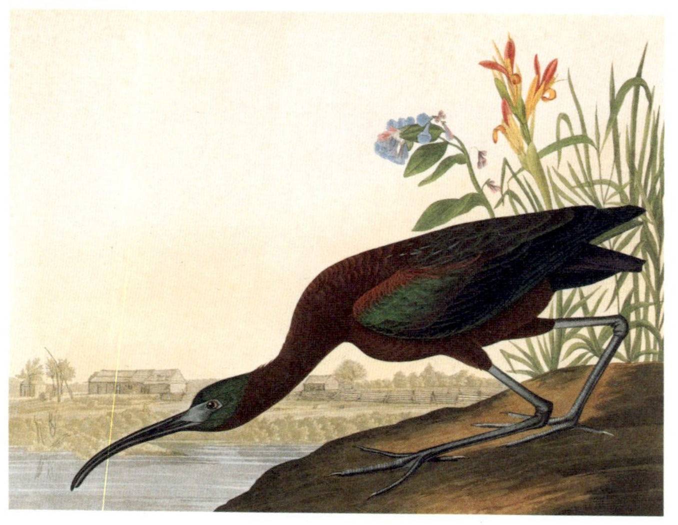

**42    Glossy Ibis**

*Plegadis falcinellus*

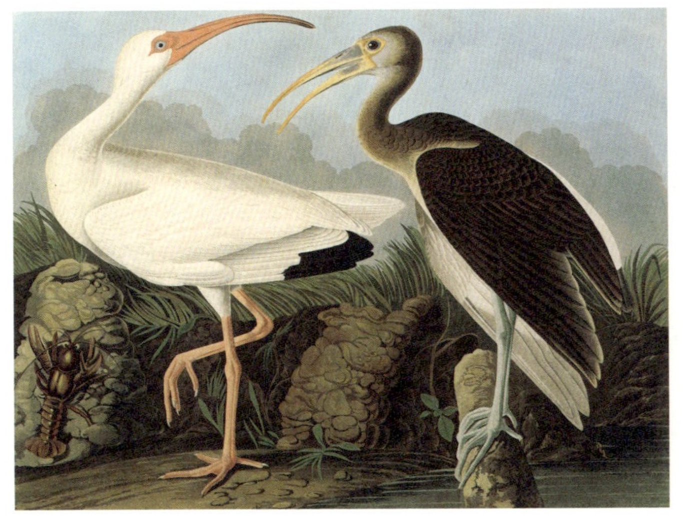

**43   White Ibis**

*Eudocimus albus*

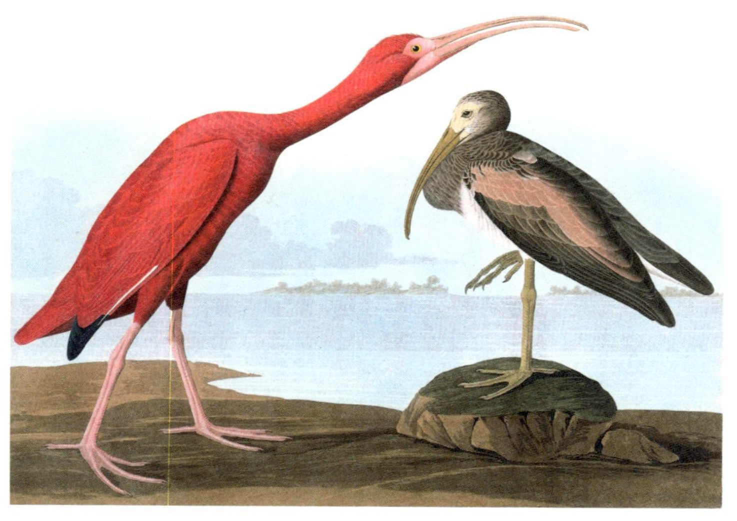

**44**   Scarlet Ibis

*Eudocimus ruber*

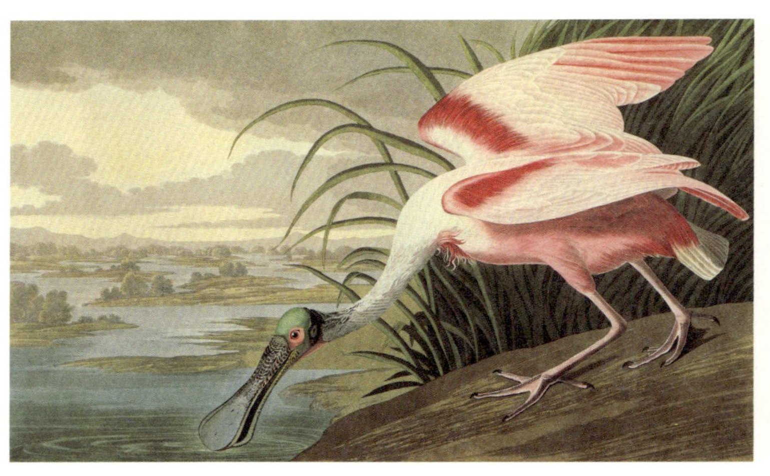

45　Roseate Spoonbill

*Platalea ajaja*

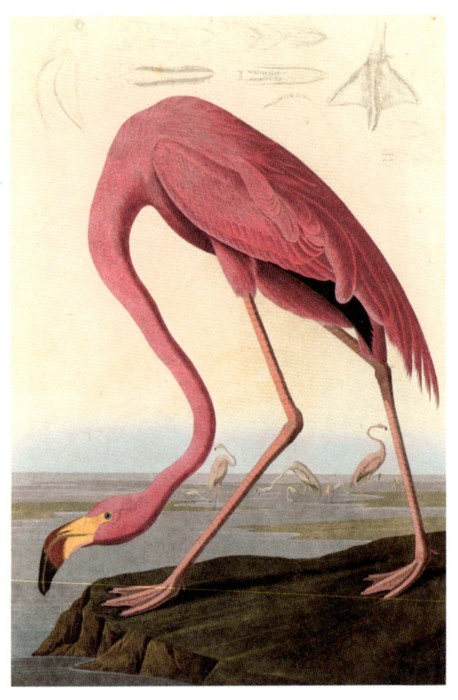

46 American Flamingo

*Phoenicopterus ruber*

# II

# WATERFOWL

Swans, Geese, and Ducks

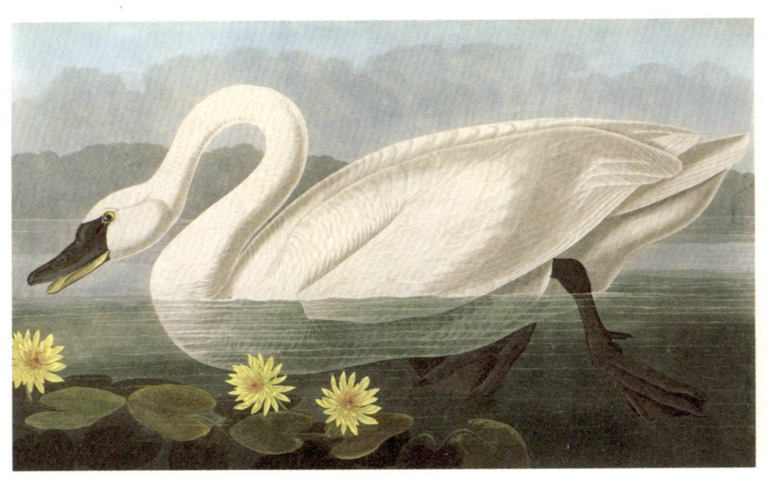

47   Tundra Swan [Common American Swan]
*Cygnus columbianus*

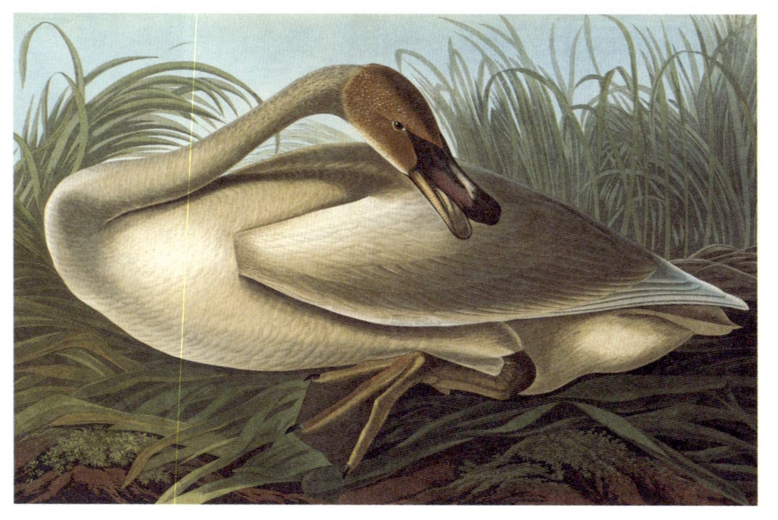

48　Trumpeter Swan
*Cygnus buccinator*

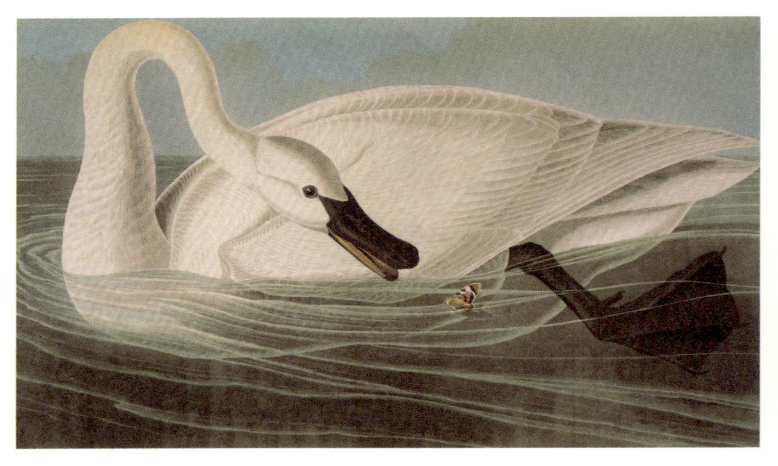

49   Trumpeter Swan
*Cygnus buccinator*

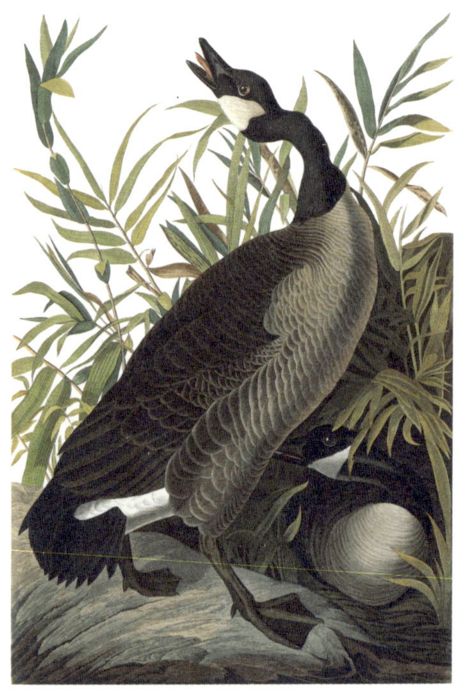

50   Canada Goose
*Branta canadensis*

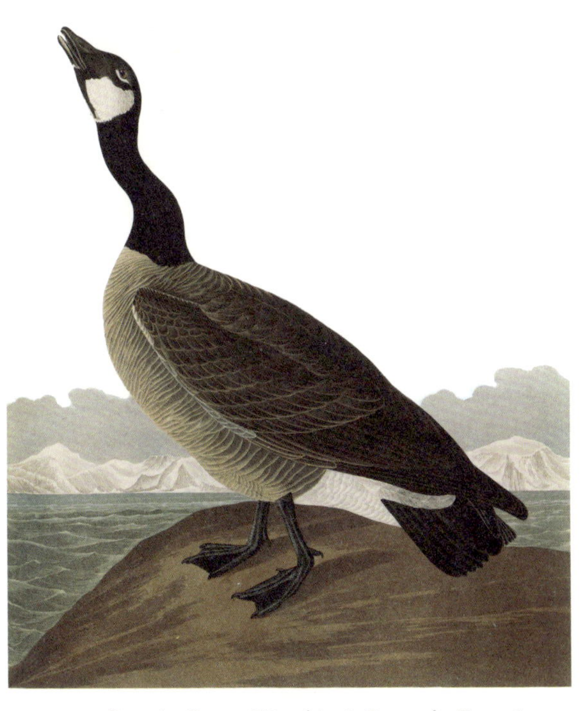

51   Canada Goose [Hutchins's Barnacle Goose]
*Branta canadensis*

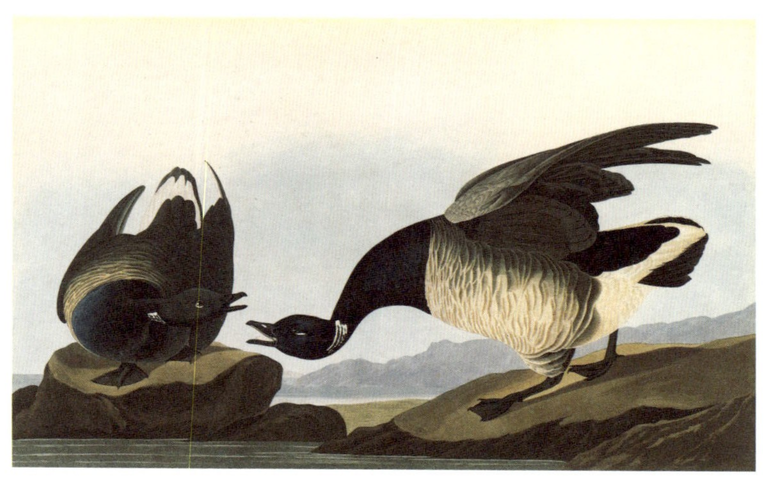

52  Brant [Brent Goose]
*Branta bernicla*

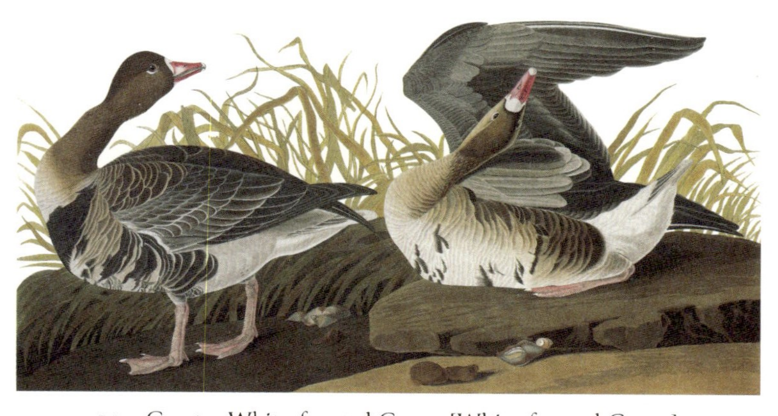

54 **Greater White-fronted Goose [White-fronted Goose]**
*Anser albifrons*

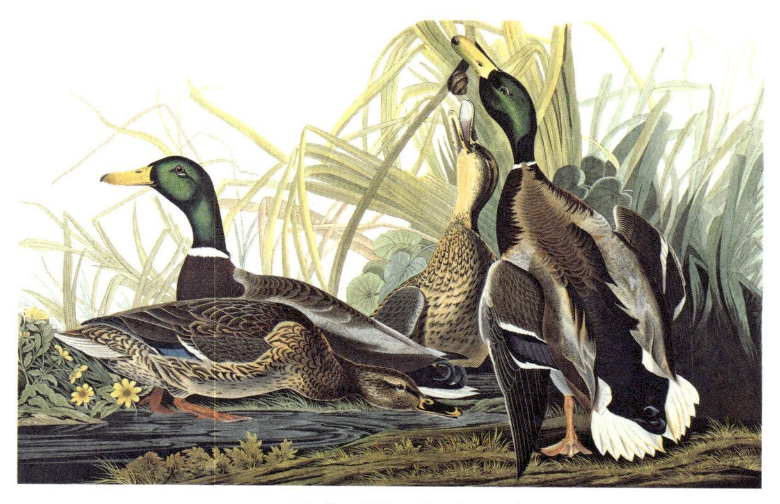

56　Mallard [Mallard Duck]
*Anas platyrhynchos*

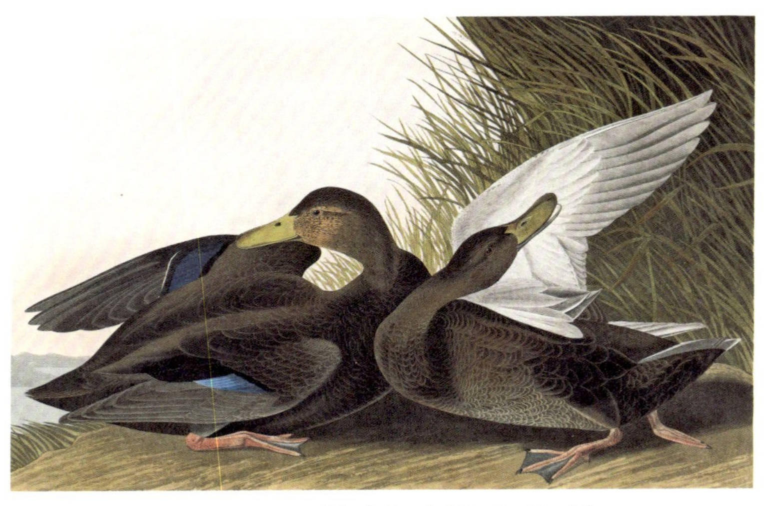

58   American Black Duck [Dusky Duck]
*Anas rubripes*

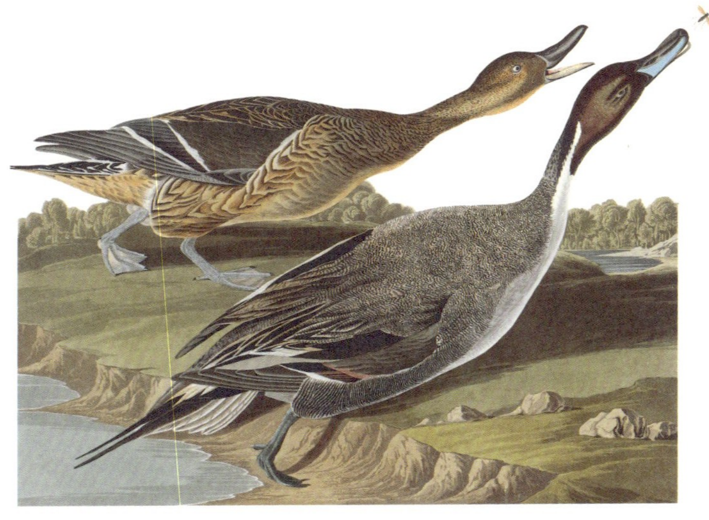

60 Common Pintail [Pintail Duck]
*Anas acuta*

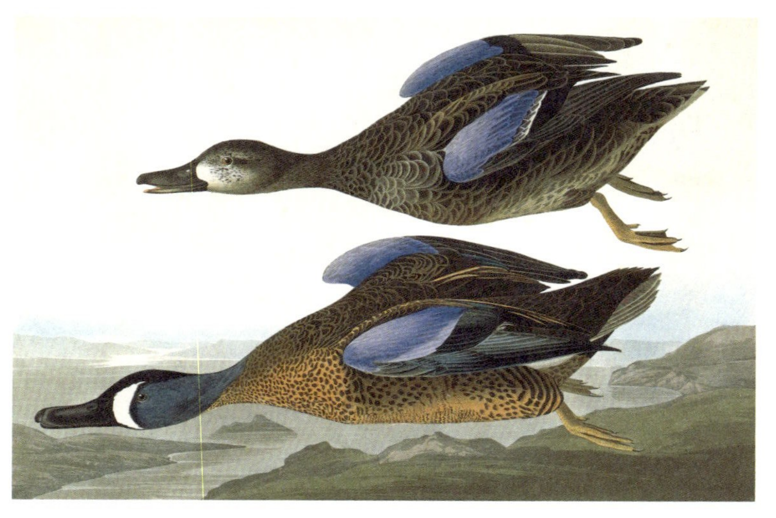

62    Blue-winged Teal
*Spatula discors*

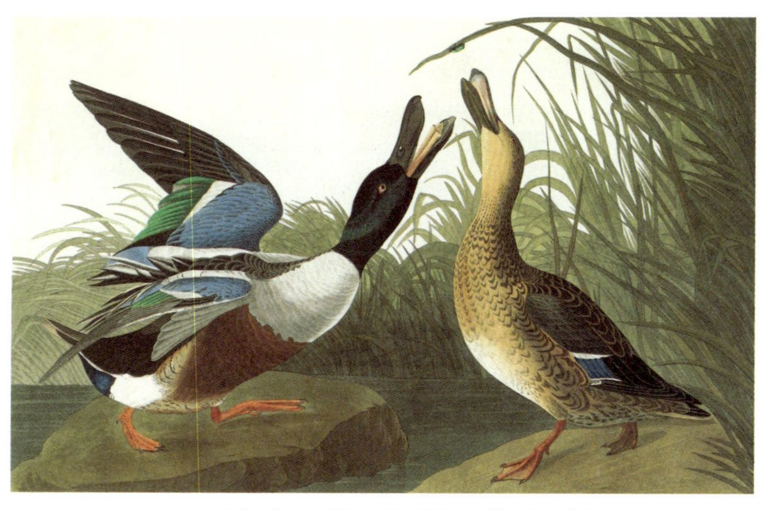

64   Northern Shoveler [Shoveller Duck]
*Spatula clypeata*

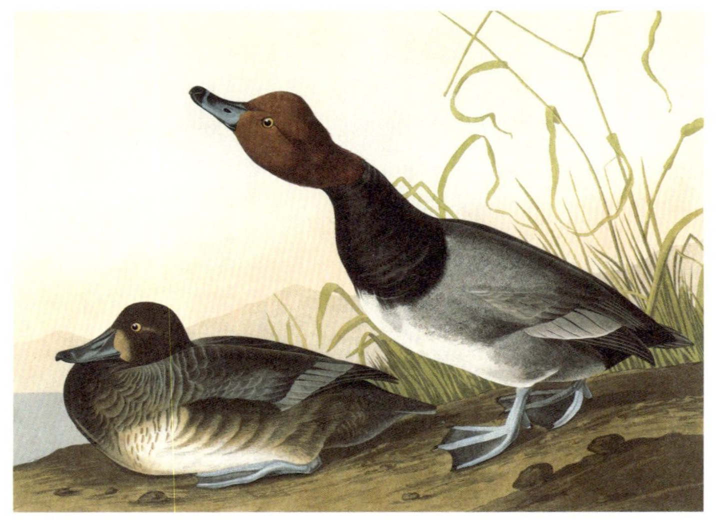

66    Redhead [Red-headed Duck]
*Aythya americana*

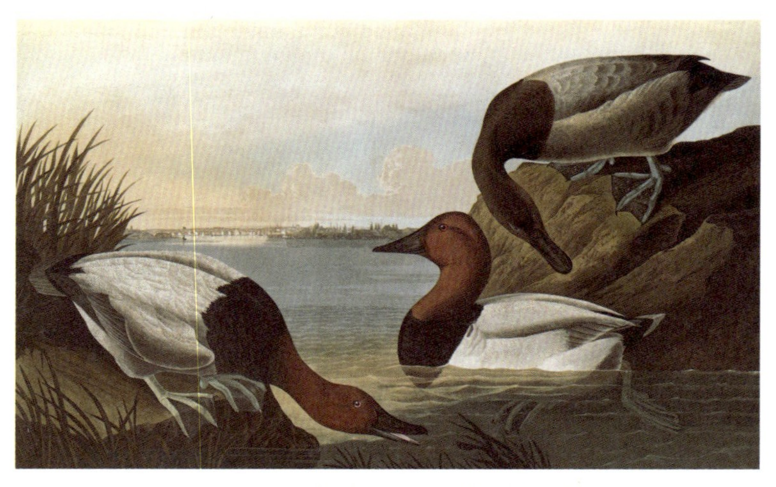

68    Canvasback [Canvass-back Duck]
*Aythya valisineria*

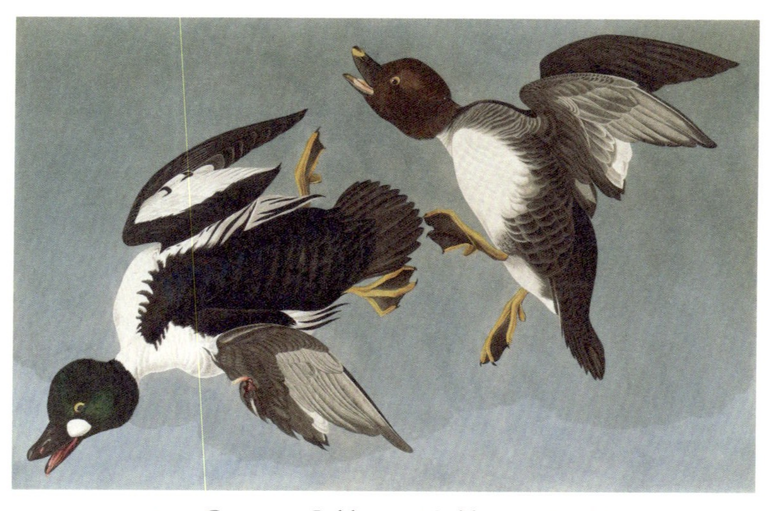

70   Common Goldeneye [Golden-eye Duck]
*Bucephala clangula*

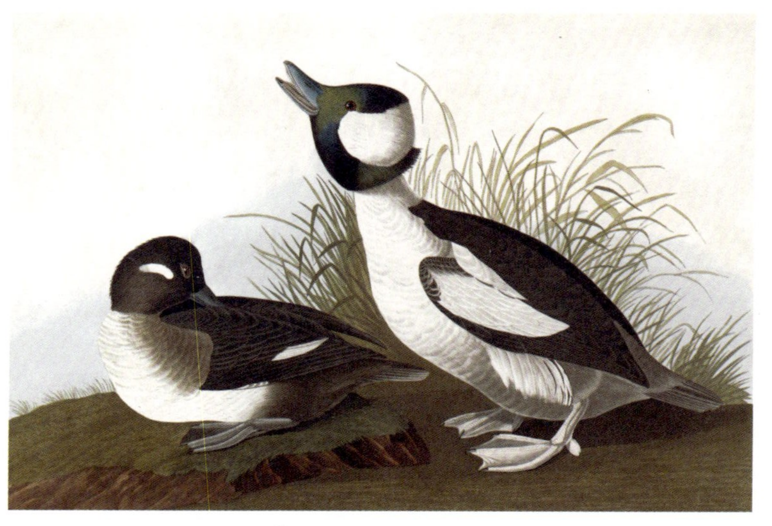

72 Bufflehead [Buffel-headed Duck]
*Bucephala albeola*

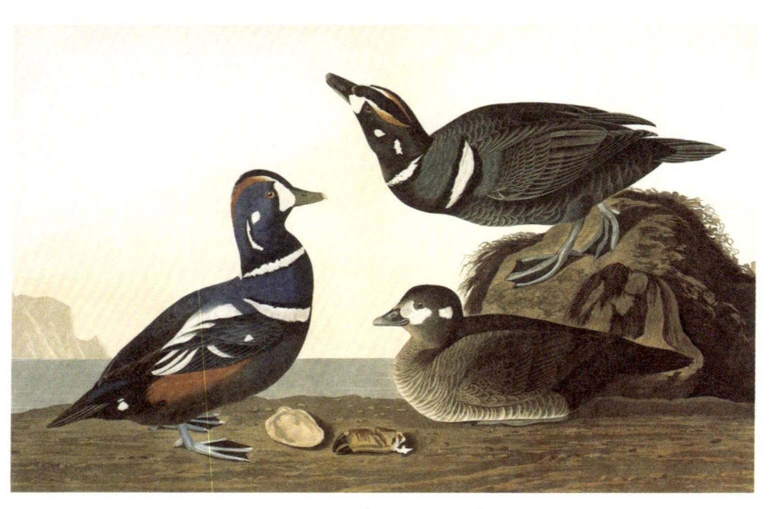

74   Harlequin Duck
*Histrionicus histrionicus*

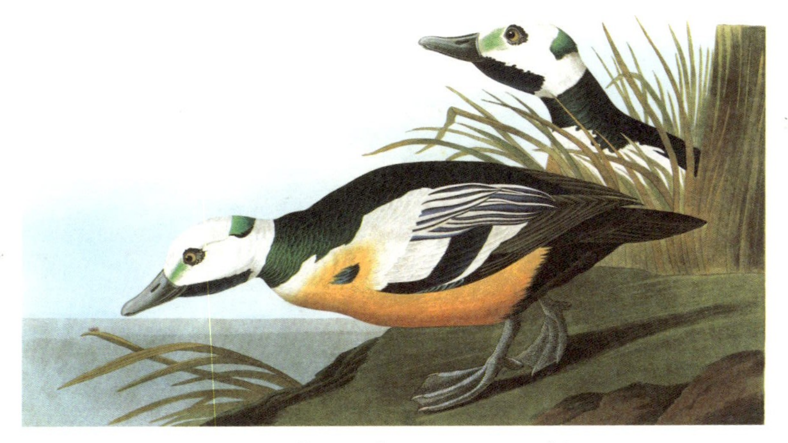

76  Steller's Eider [Western Duck]
*Polysticta stelleri*

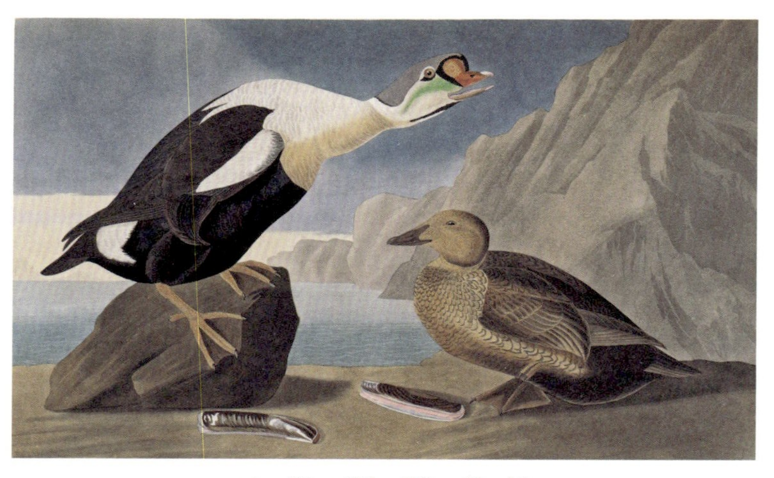

78   King Eider [King Duck]
*Somateria spectabilis*

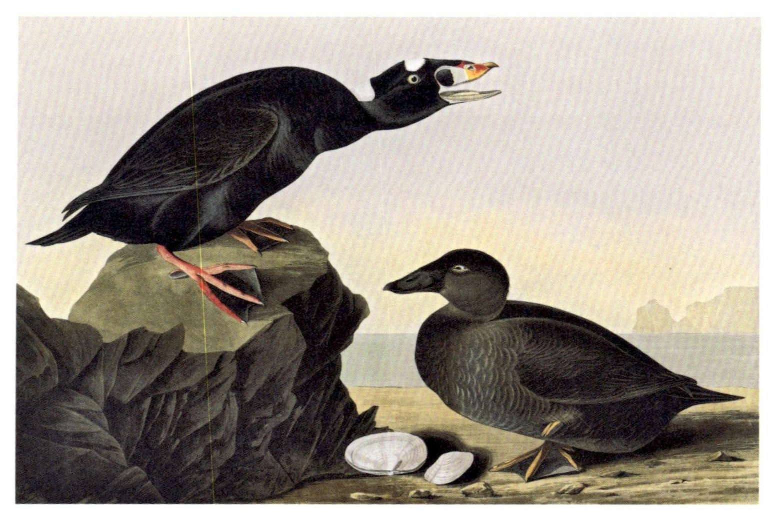

80   Surf Scoter [Surf Duck]
*Melanitta perspicillata*

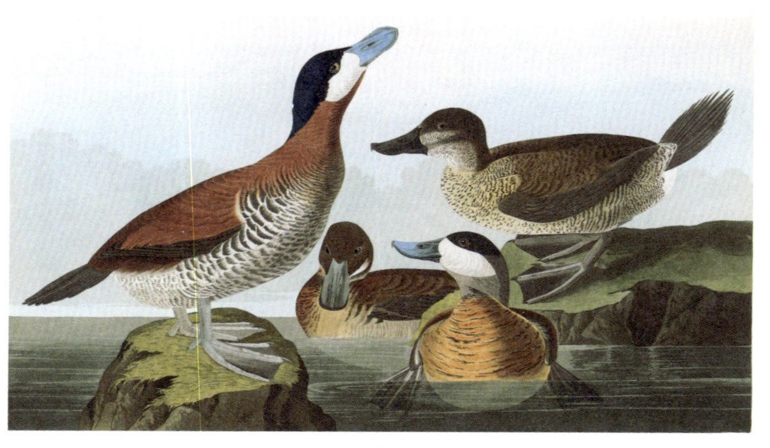

82   Ruddy Duck

*Oxyura jamaicensis*

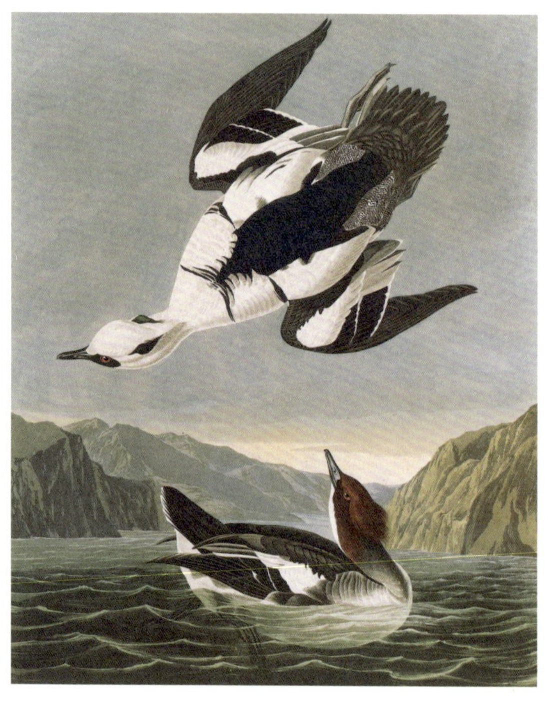

84   Smew [Smew or White Nun]
*Mergellus albellus*

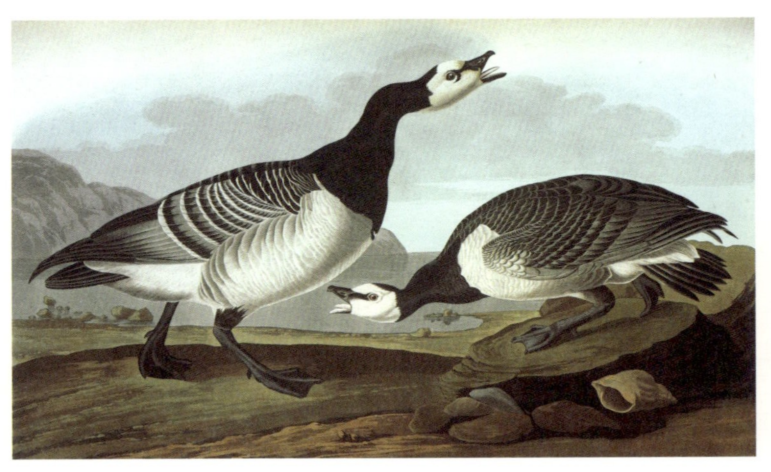

53    Barnacle Goose
*Branta leucopsis*

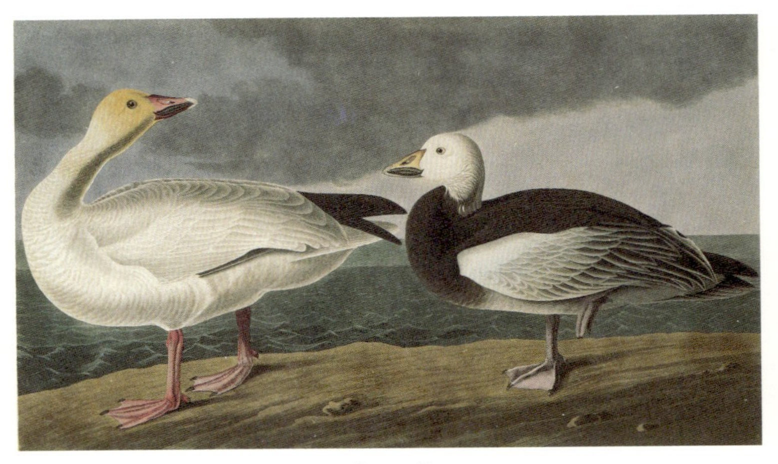

55   Snow Goose
*Anser caerulescens*

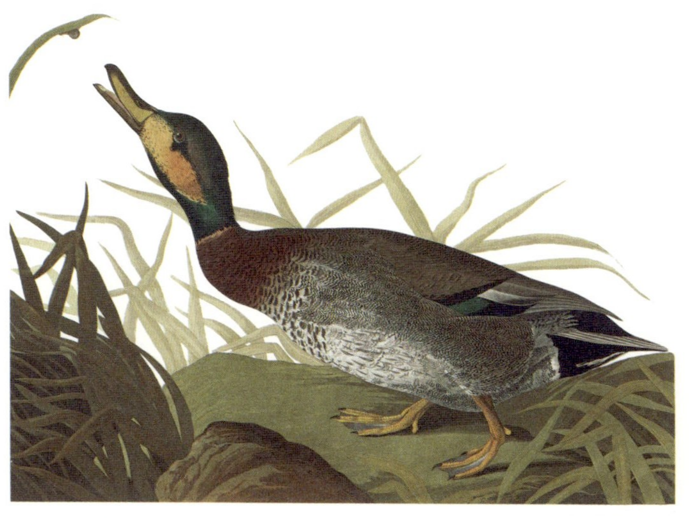

57  Mallard X Gadwall hybrid [Brewer's or Bemaculated Duck]
*Anas platyrhynchos X strepera*

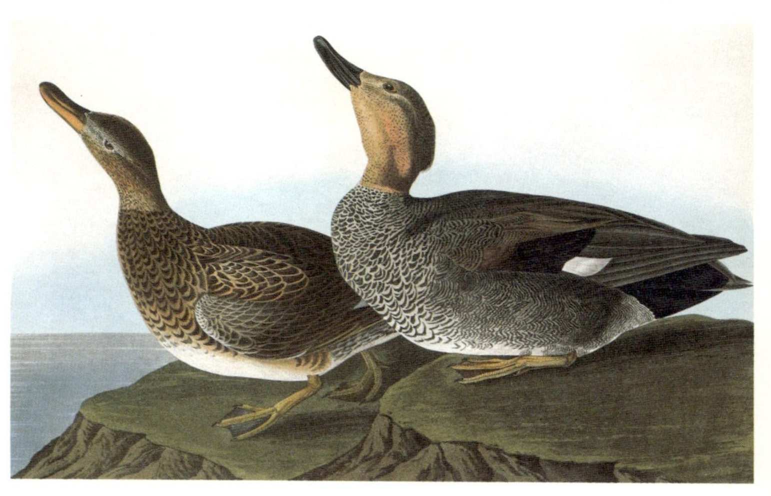

59 Gadwall [Gadwall Duck]

*Mareca strepera*

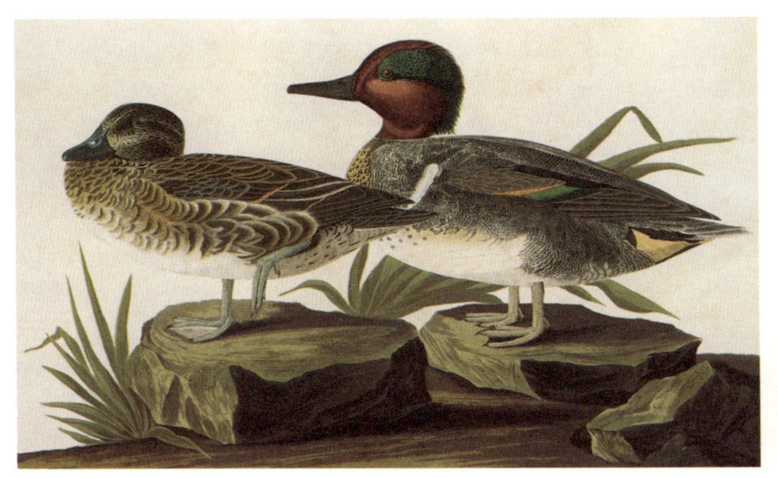

**6I    Green-winged Teal**

*Anas crecca*

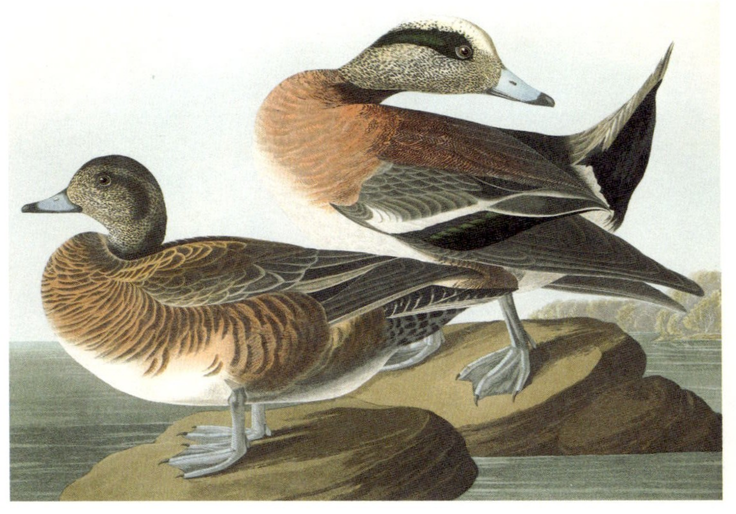

63   American Wigeon [American Widgeon]
*Mareca americana*

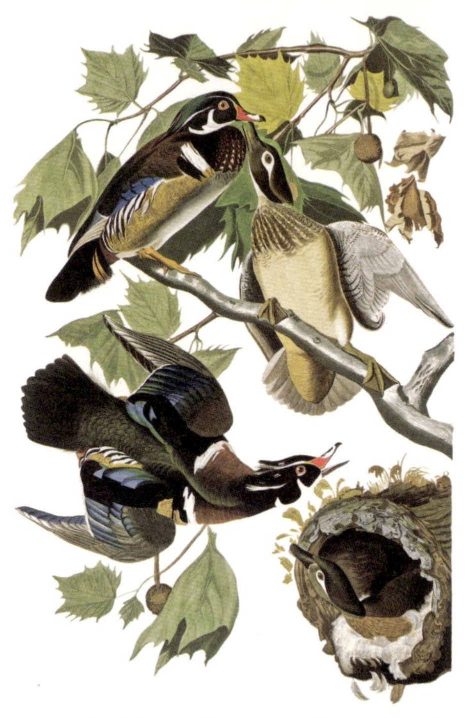

65   Wood Duck [Summer or Wood Duck]
*Aix sponsa*

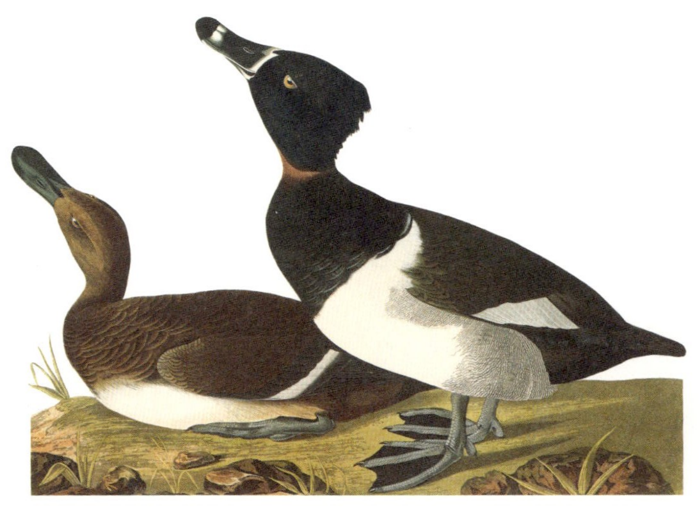

67 Ring-necked Duck
*Aythya collaris*

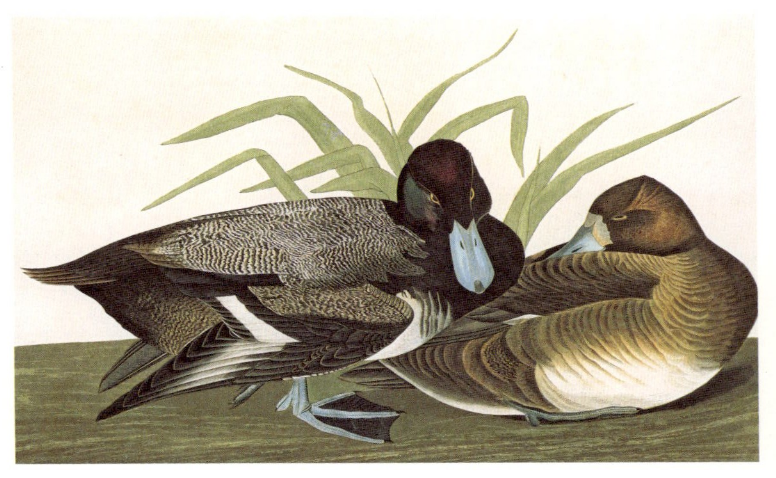

69    Greater Scaup [Scaup Duck]
*Aythya marila*

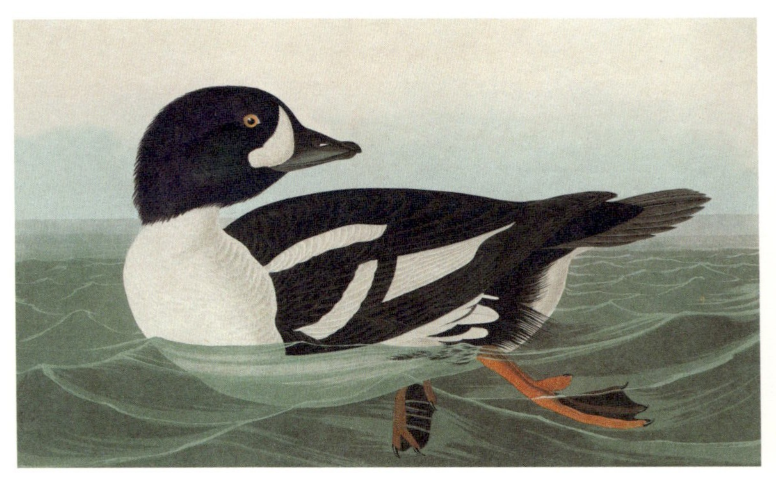

71   Barrow's Goldeneye [Golden-eye Duck]
*Bucephala islandica*

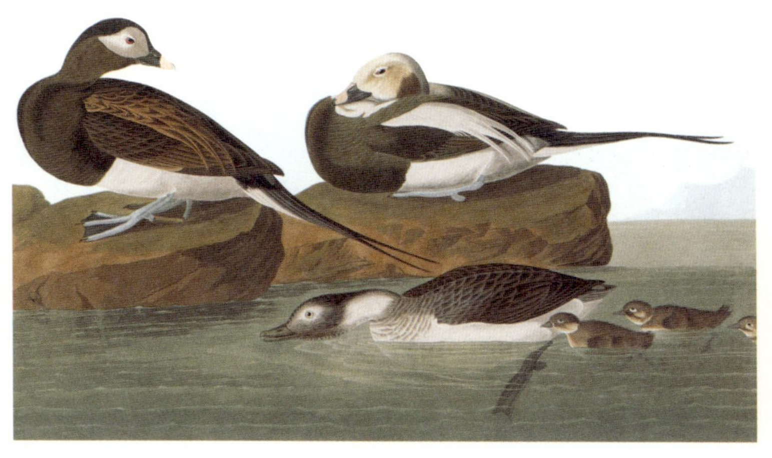

73  Long-tailed duck
*Clangula hyemalis*

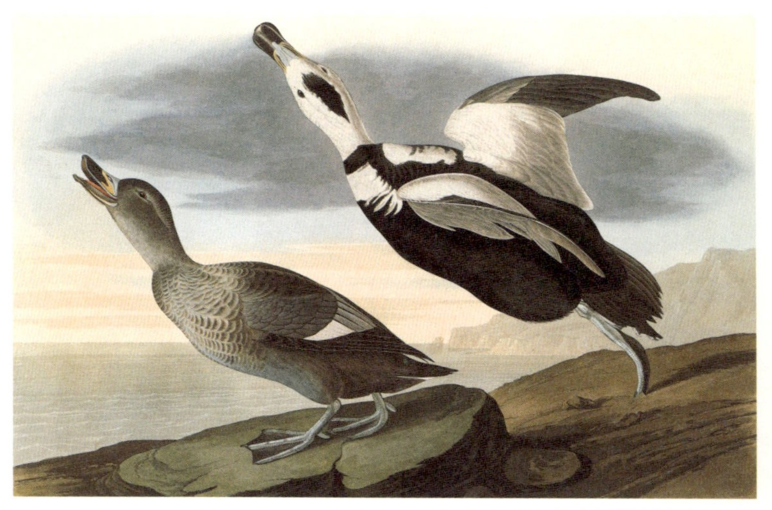

75   Labrador Duck [Pied Duck]

*Camptorhynchus labradorius*

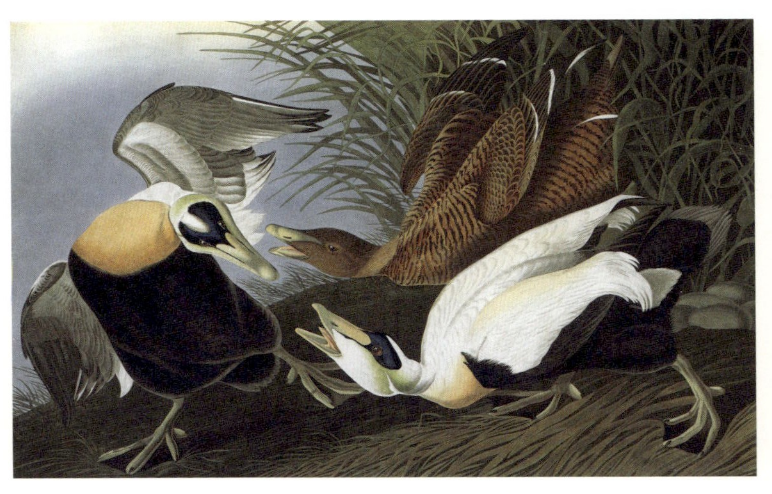

77   Common Eider [Eider Duck]
*Somateria mollissima*

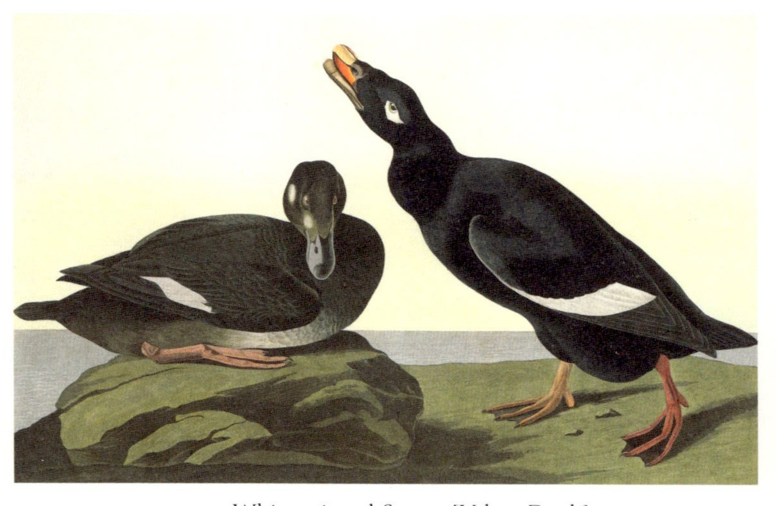

79 White-winged Scoter [Velvet Duck]
*Melanitta deglandi*

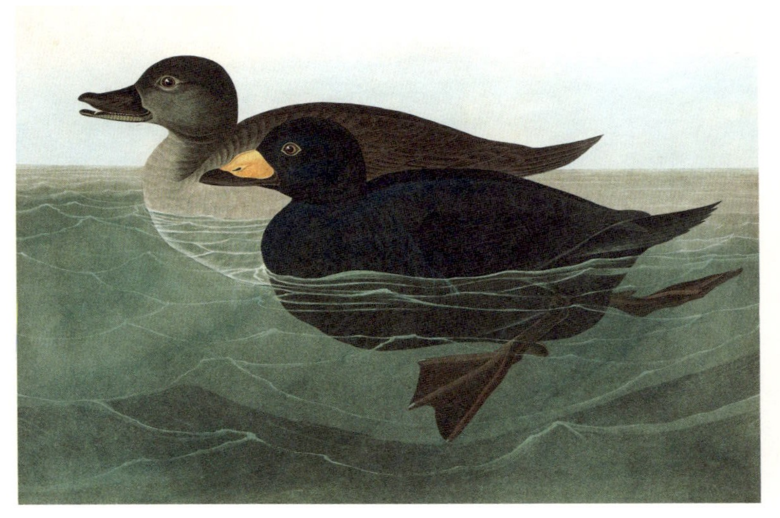

81   Black Scoter [American Scoter Duck]
*Melanitta americana*

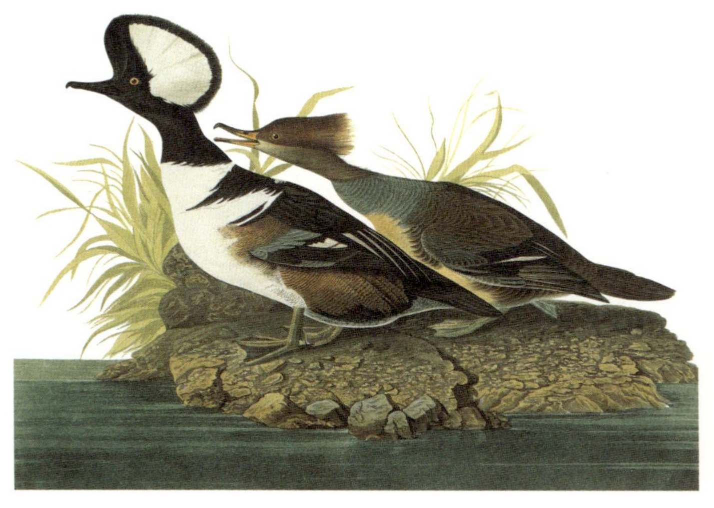

83   Hooded Merganser
*Lophodytes cucullatus*

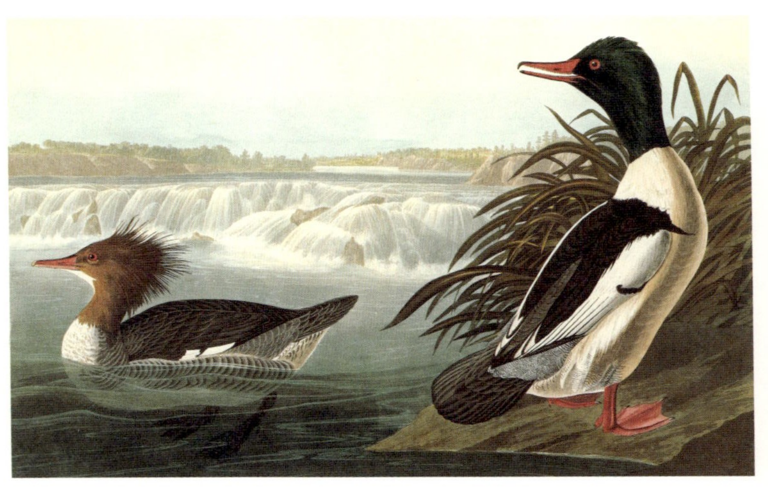

85   Common Merganser [Goosander]

*Mergus merganser*

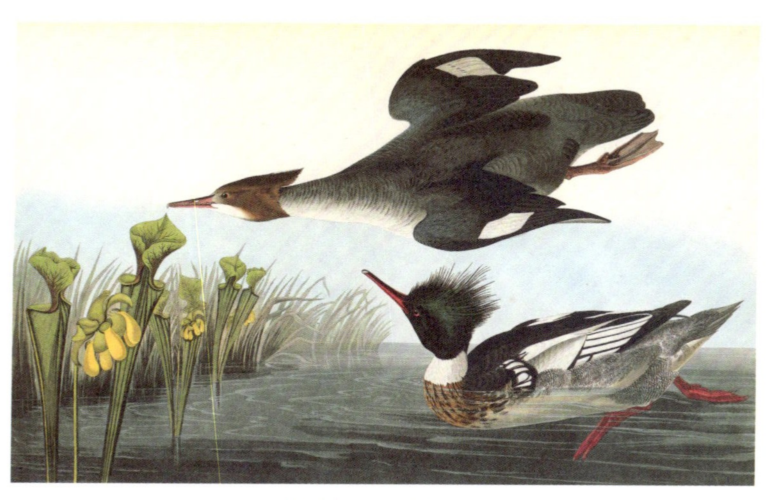

86    Red-breasted Merganser
*Mergus serrator*

# III

## SCAVENGERS AND
## BIRDS OF PREY

Vultures, Kites, Hawks, Eagles,

Harriers, Osprey, Caracaras, and Falcons

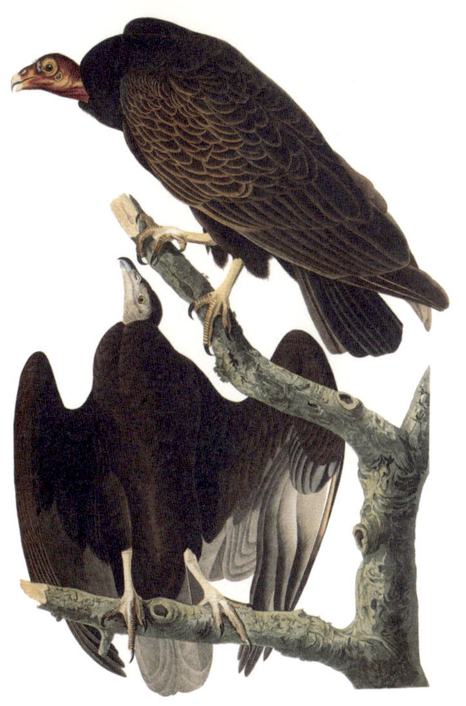

87   Turkey Vulture [Turkey Buzzard]
*Cathartes aura*

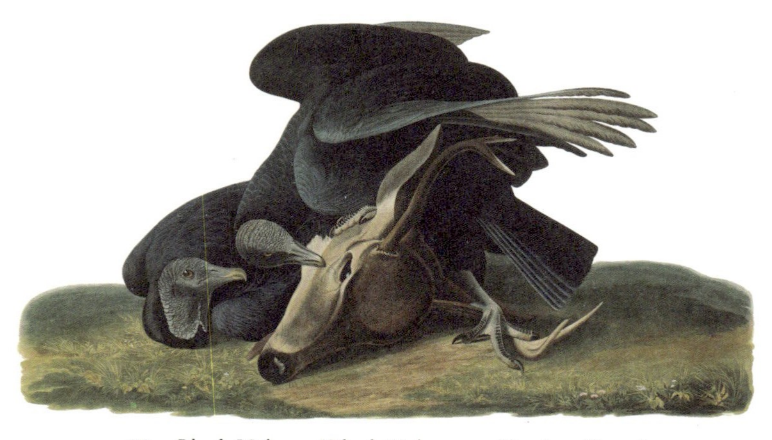

88    Black Vulture [Black Vulture or Carrion Crow]
*Coragyps atratus*

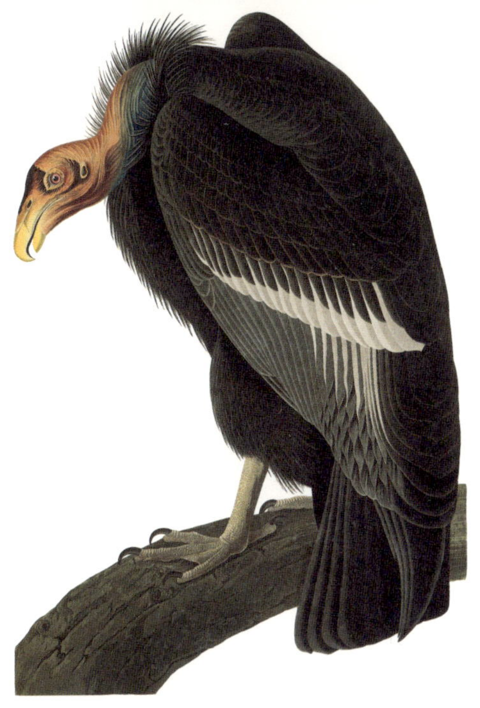

89   California Condor [Californian Vulture]
*Gymnogyps californianus*

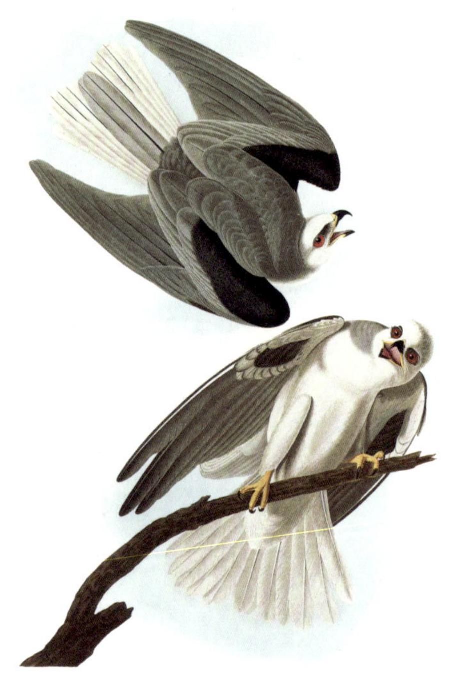

90 Black-shouldered Kite [Black-winged Hawk]
*Elanus caeruleus*

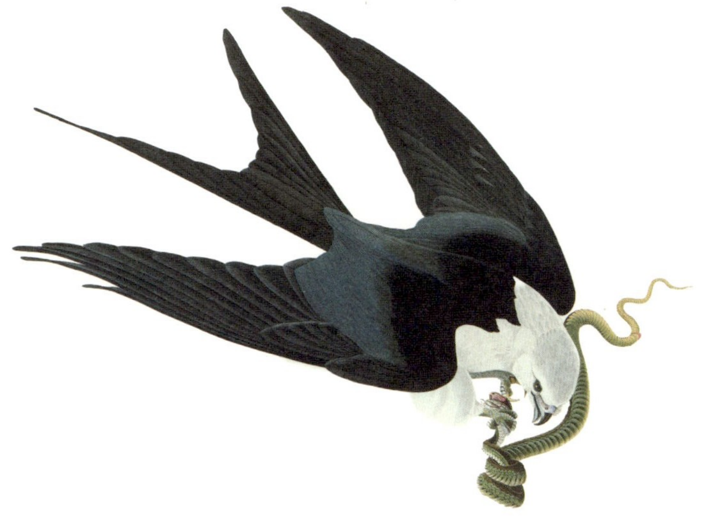

91   American Swallow-tailed Kite [Swallow-tailed Hawk]
*Elanoides forficatus*

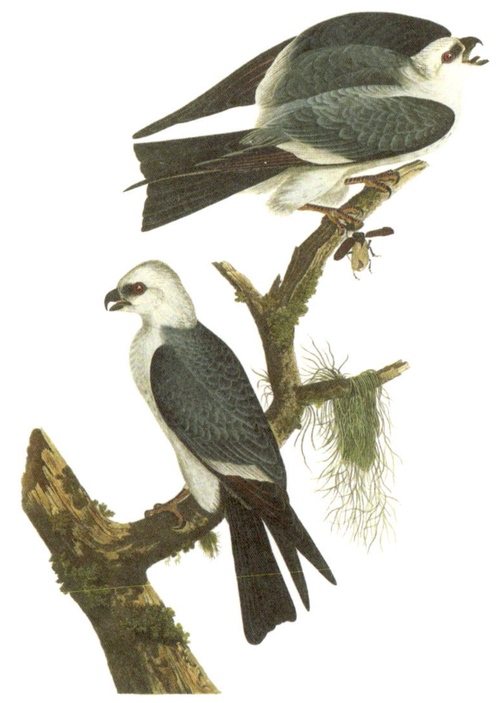

92  Mississippi Kite
*Ictinia mississippiensis*

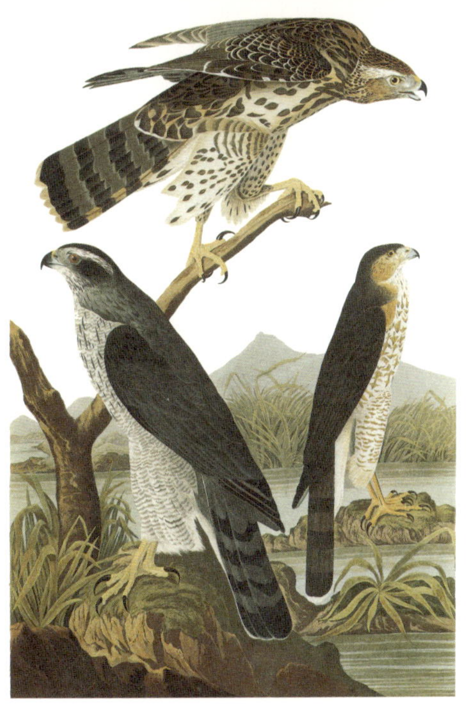

93   Northern Goshawk [Goshawk]
*Accipiter gentilis*

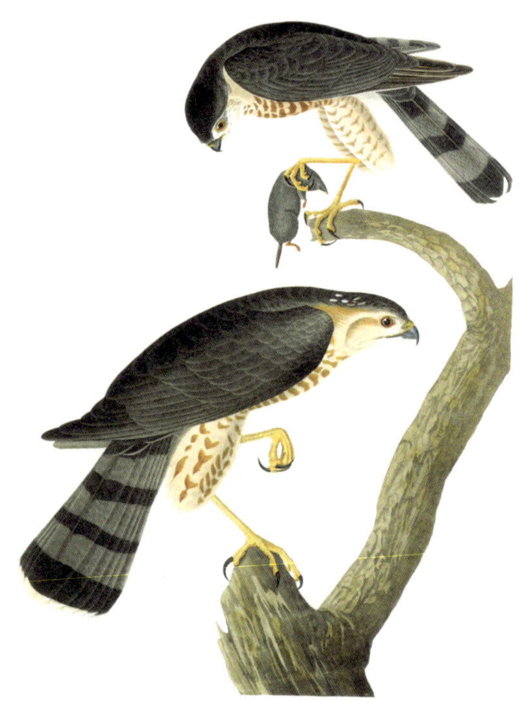

94  Sharp-shinned Hawk
*Accipiter striatus*

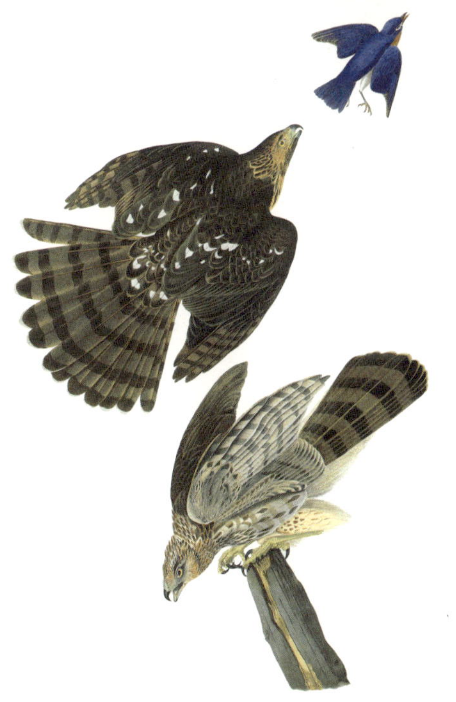

95    Cooper's Hawk [Stanley Hawk]
*Accipiter cooperii*

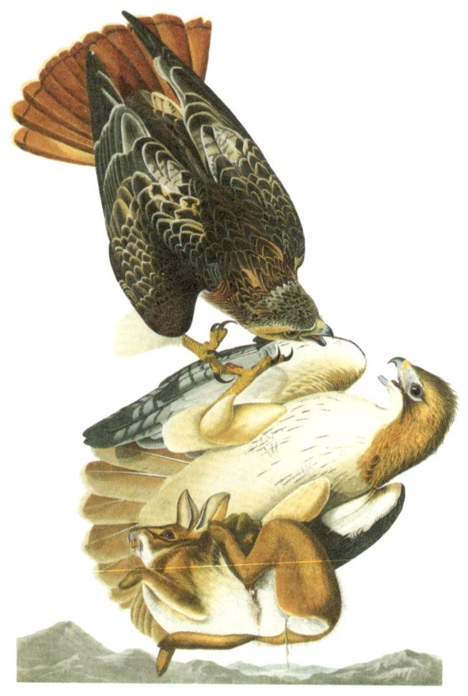

96 Red-tailed Hawk

*Buteo jamaicensis*

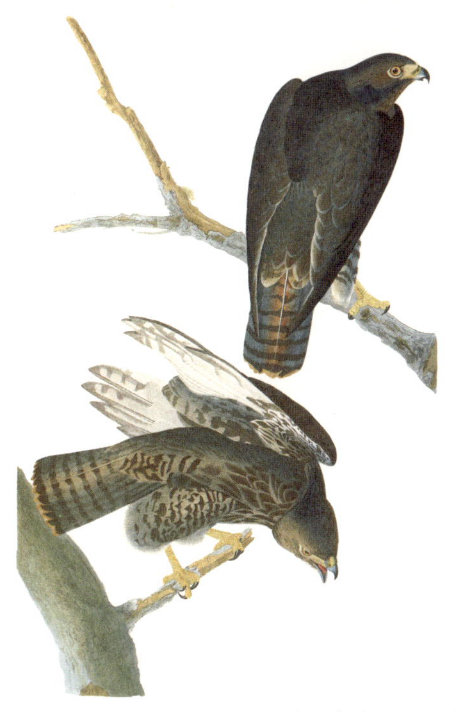

97   "Harlan's" Red-tailed Hawk [Black Warrior]
*Buteo jamaicensis harlani*

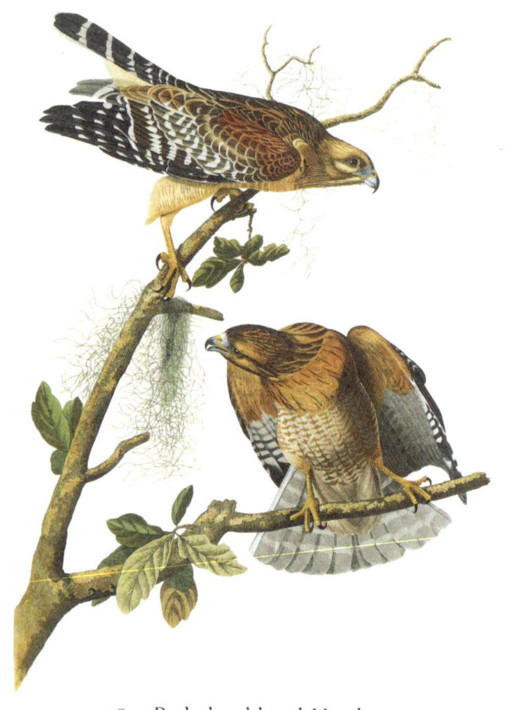

98 Red-shouldered Hawk
*Buteo lineatus*

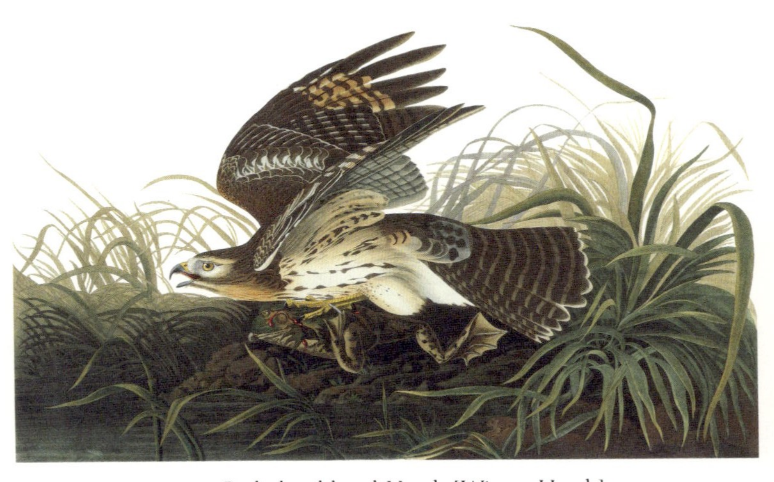

99    Red-shouldered Hawk [Winter Hawk]
*Buteo lineatus*

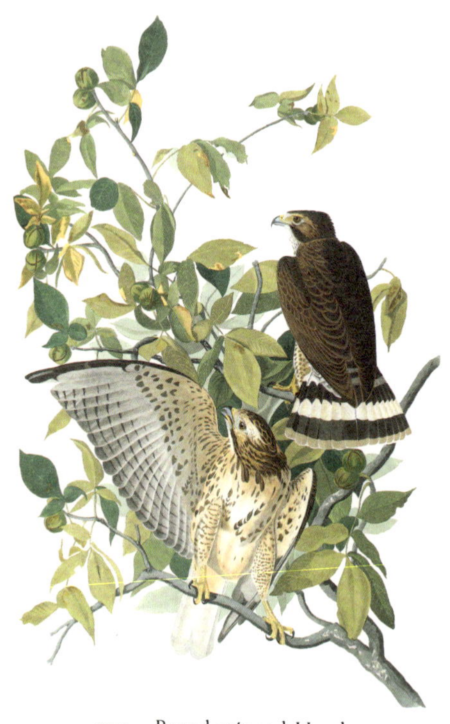

100   Broad-winged Hawk
*Buteo platypterus*

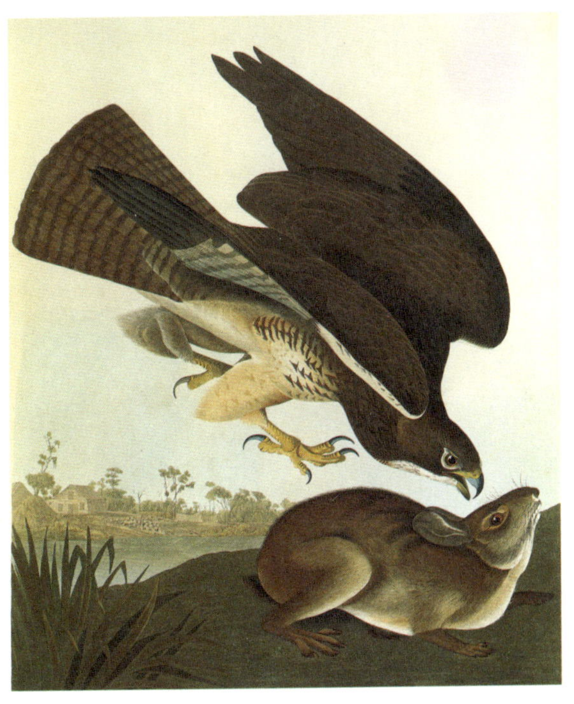

101 Swainson's Hawk [Common Buzzard]
*Buteo swainsoni*

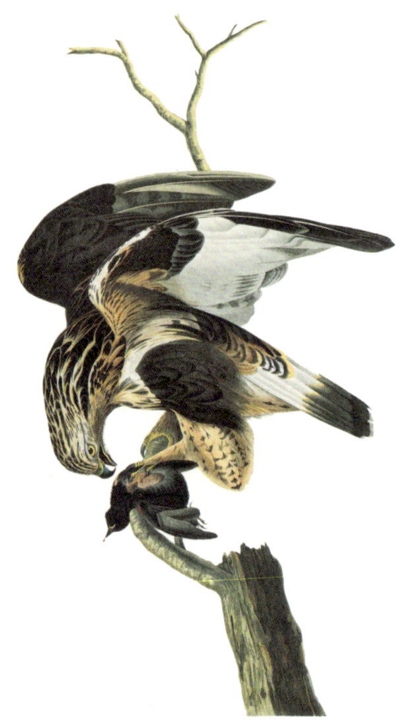

102  Rough-legged Hawk [Rough-legged Falcon]
*Buteo lagopus*

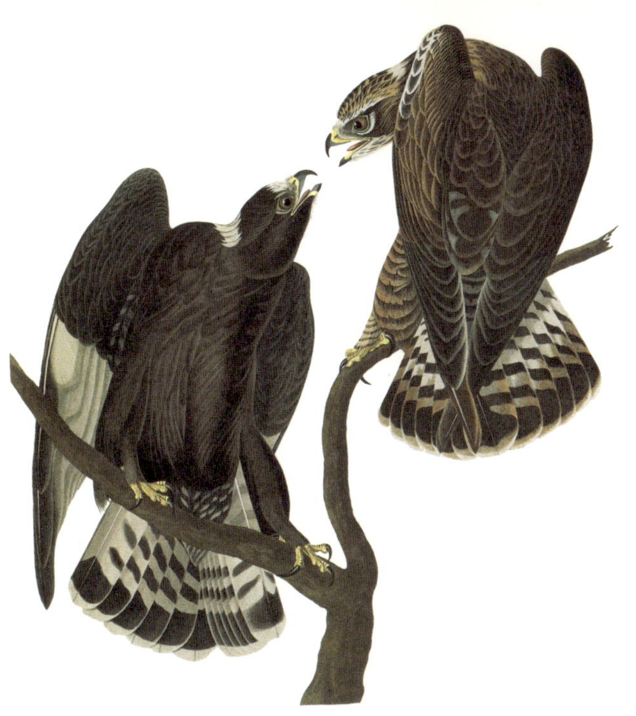

103 Rough-legged Hawk [Rough-legged Falcon]
*Buteo lagopus*

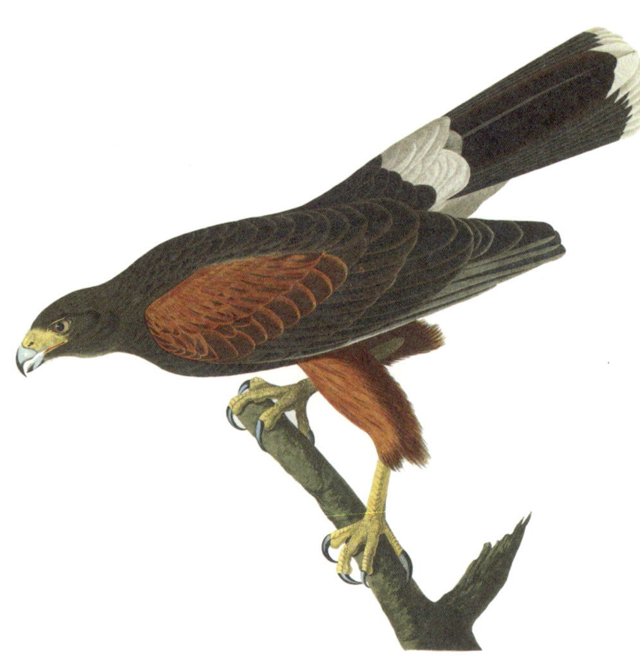

104 Harris' Hawk [Louisiana Hawk]
*Parabuteo unicinctus*

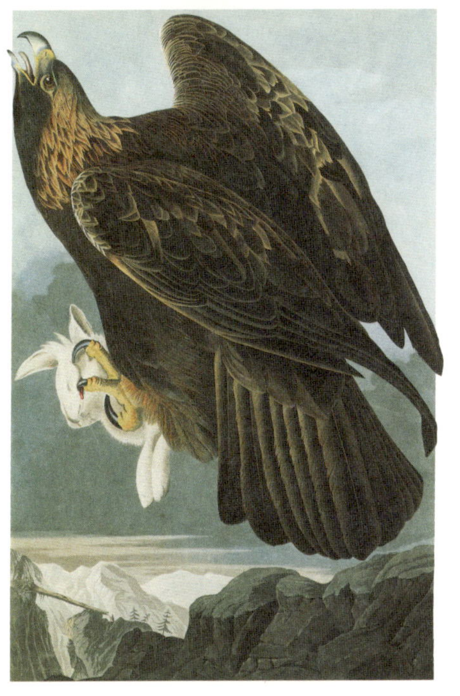

105   Golden Eagle
*Aquila chrysaetos*

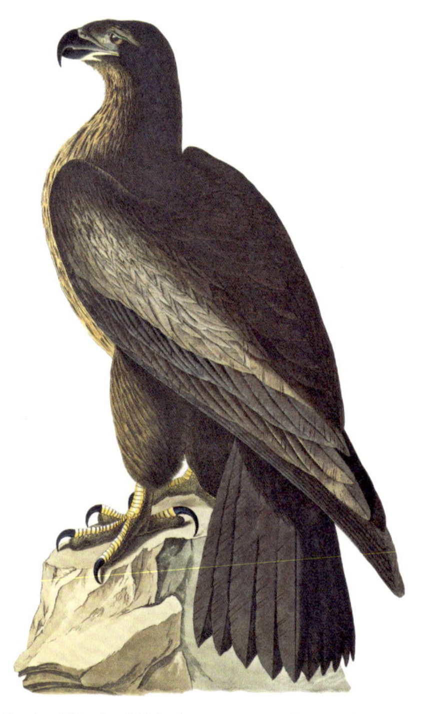

106　Bald Eagle [Bird of Washington or Great American Sea Eagle]
*Haliaeetus leucocephalus*

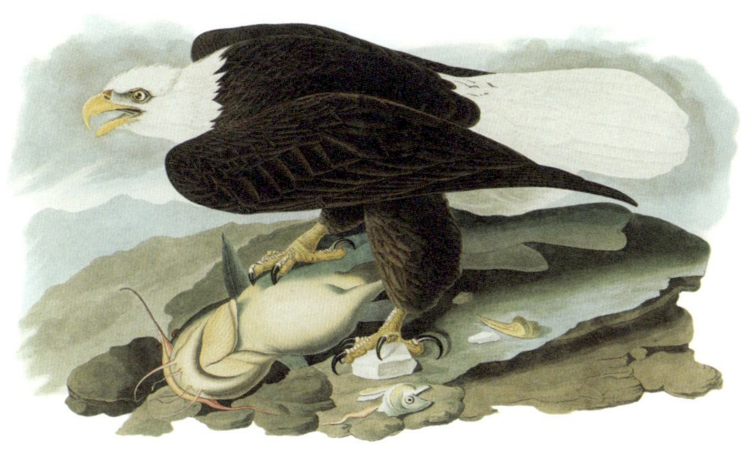

107   Bald Eagle [White-headed Eagle]
*Haliaeetus leucocephalus*

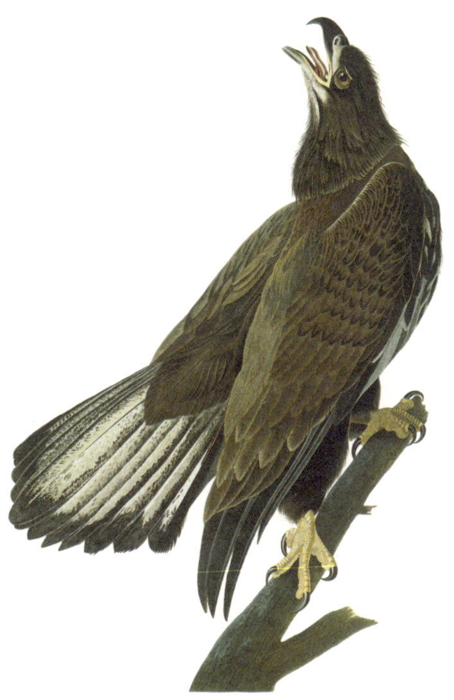

108   Bald Eagle [White-headed Eagle]
*Haliaeetus leucocephalus*

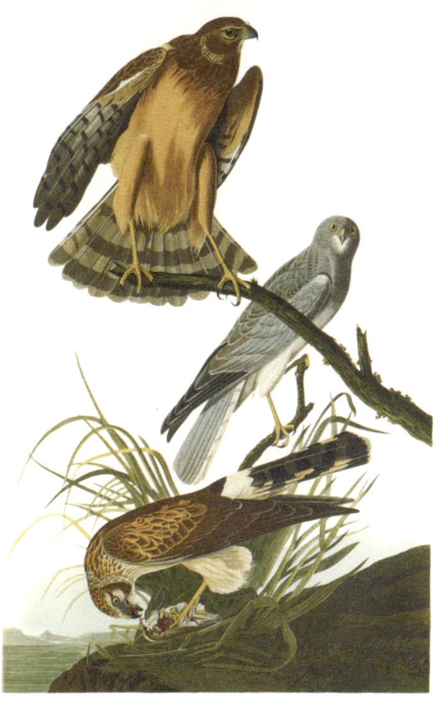

109　Northern Harrier [Marsh Hawk]
*Circus hudsonius*

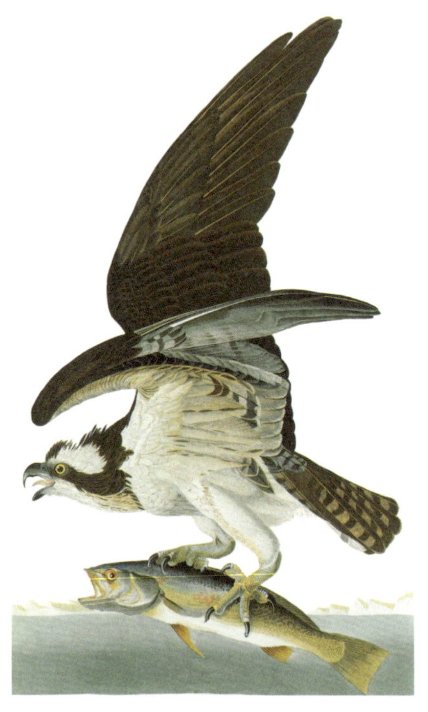

110   Osprey [Fish Hawk]
*Pandion haliaetus*

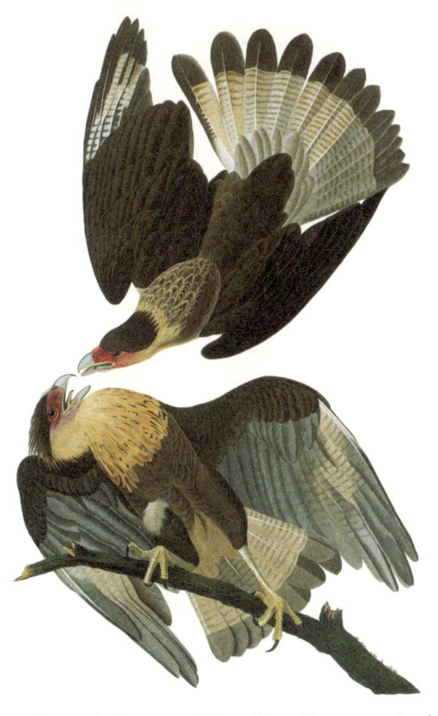

III   Crested Caracara [Brazilian Caracara Eagle]
*Caracara plancus*

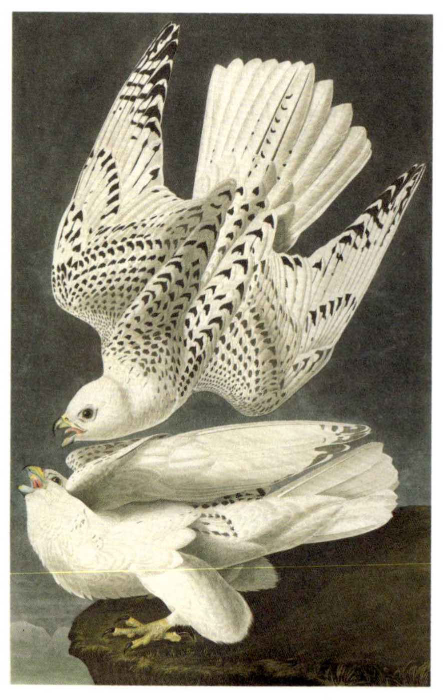

112  Gyrfalcon [Iceland or Jer Falcon]
*Falco rusticolus*

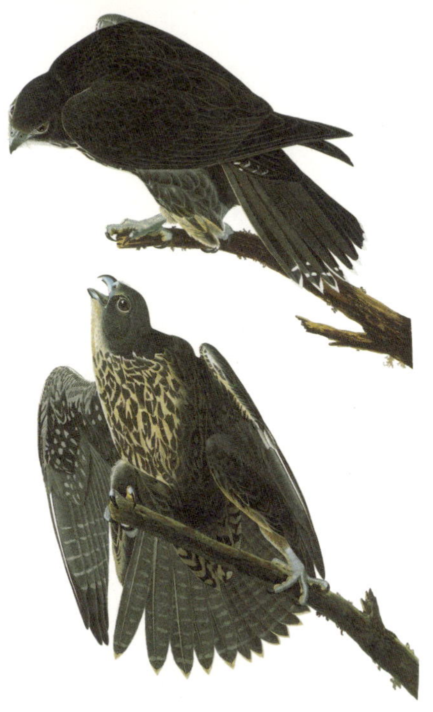

113   Gyrfalcon [Labrador Jer Falcon]
*Falco rusticolus*

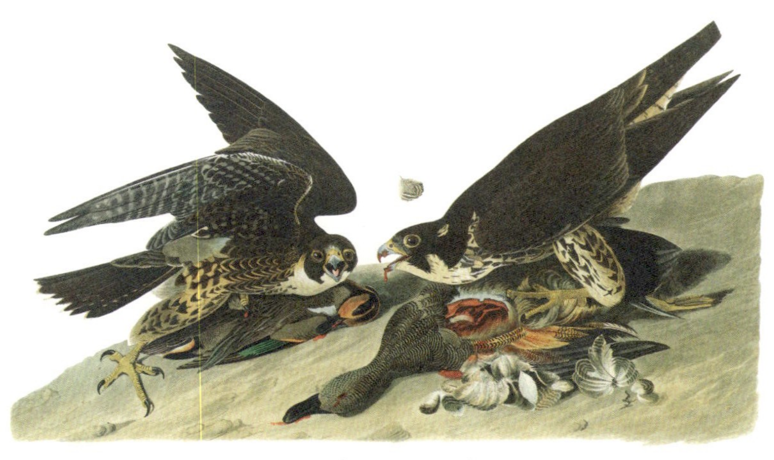

114    Peregrine Falcon [Great-footed Hawk]
*Falco peregrinus*

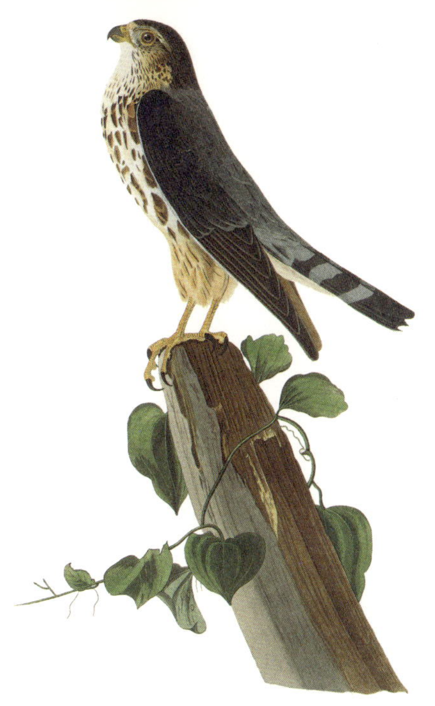

115 Merlin [Le Petit Caporal]
*Falco columbarius*

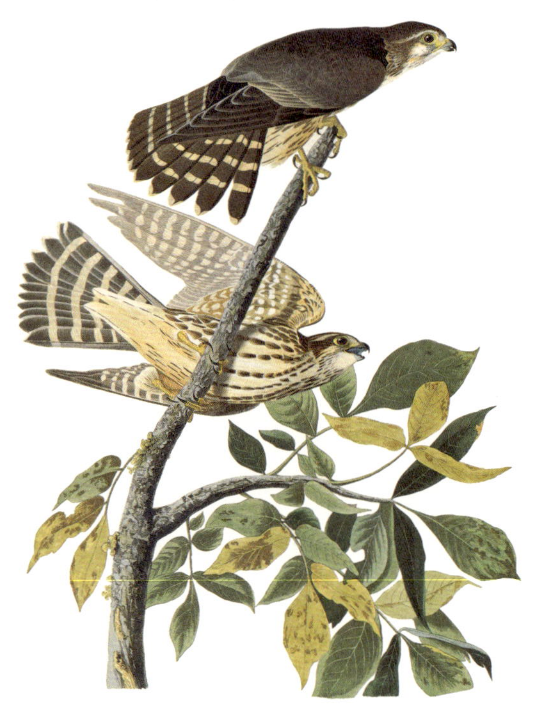

116    Merlin [Pigeon Hawk]
*Falco columbarius*

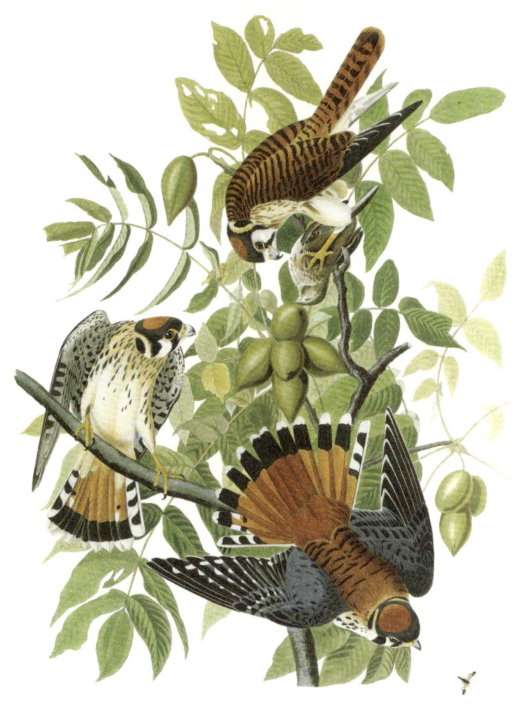

117 American Kestrel [American Sparrow hawk]
*Falco sparverius*

# IV

## UPLAND GAMEBIRDS AND

## MARSH-DWELLERS

Grouse, Ptarmigan, Quails,

Turkeys, Cranes, Limpkins, Rails,

Gallinules, and Coots

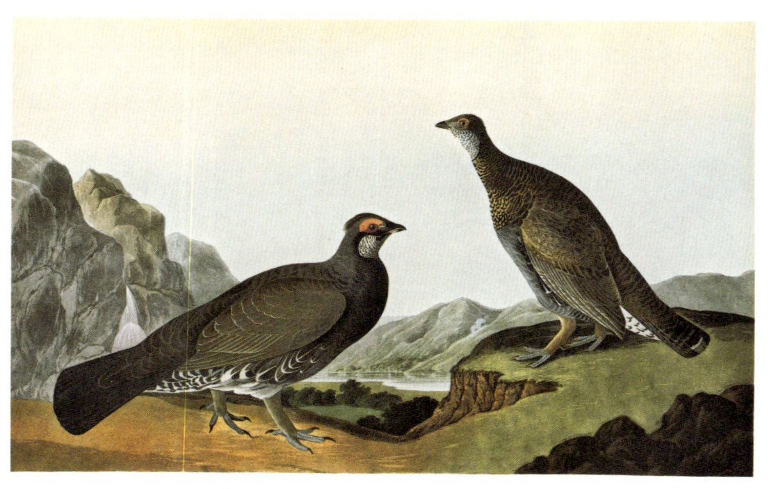

118    Dusky Grouse [Long-tailed or Dusky Grous]
*Dendragapus obscurus*

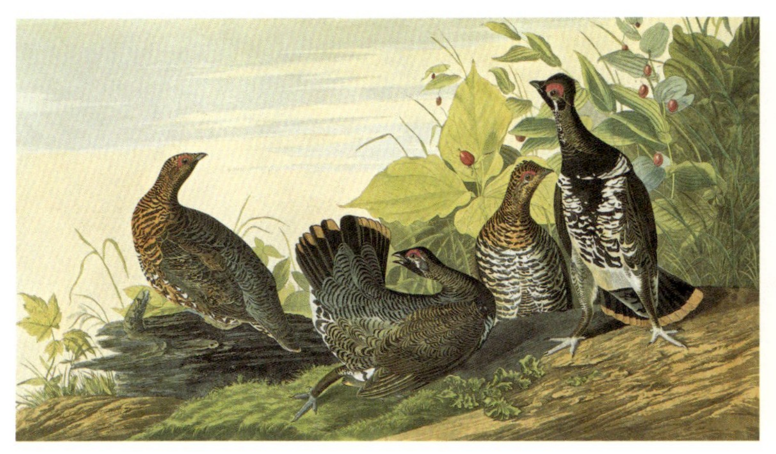

119    Spruce Grouse [Spotted Grous]
*Dendragapus canadensis*

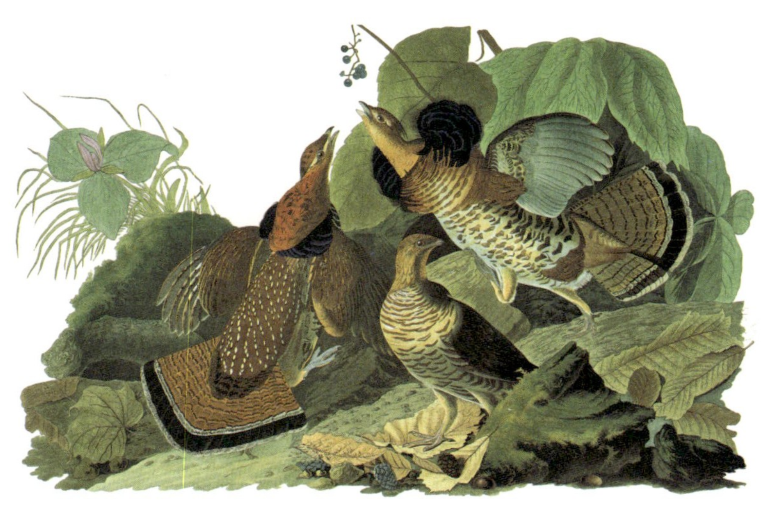

120   Ruffed Grouse [Ruffed Grous]
*Bonasa umbellus*

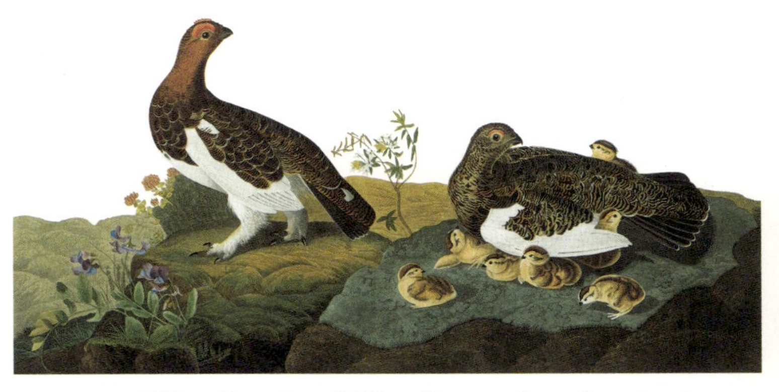

121   Willow Ptarmigan [Willow Grous or Large Ptarmigan]
*Lagopus lagopus*

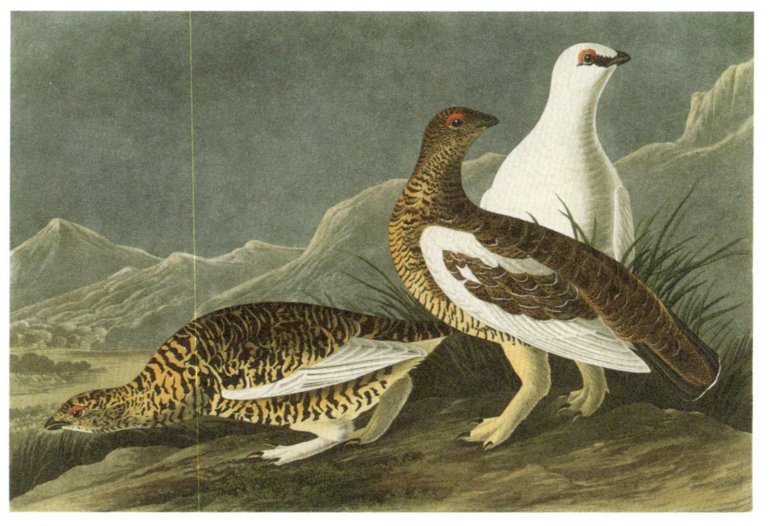

122  Rock Ptarmigan [Rock Grous]
*Lagopus muta*

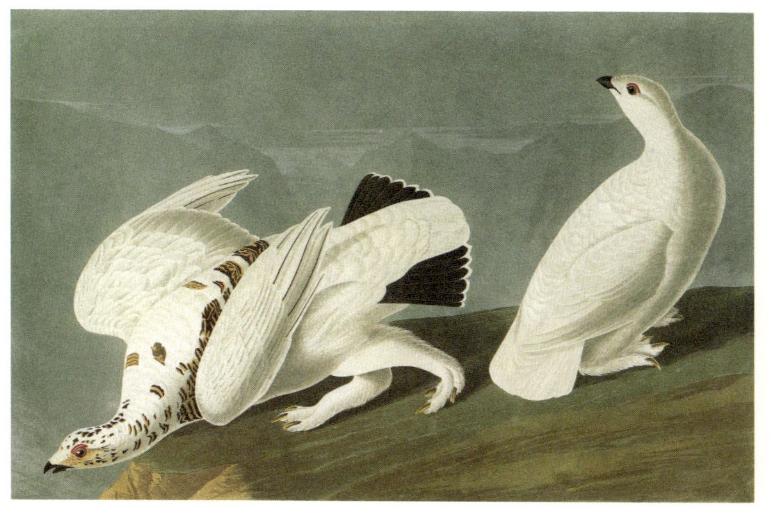

123   Rock Ptarmigan
[American Ptarmigan]
*Lagopus mutus*

White-tailed Ptarmigan
[White-tailed Grous]
*Lagopus leucurus*

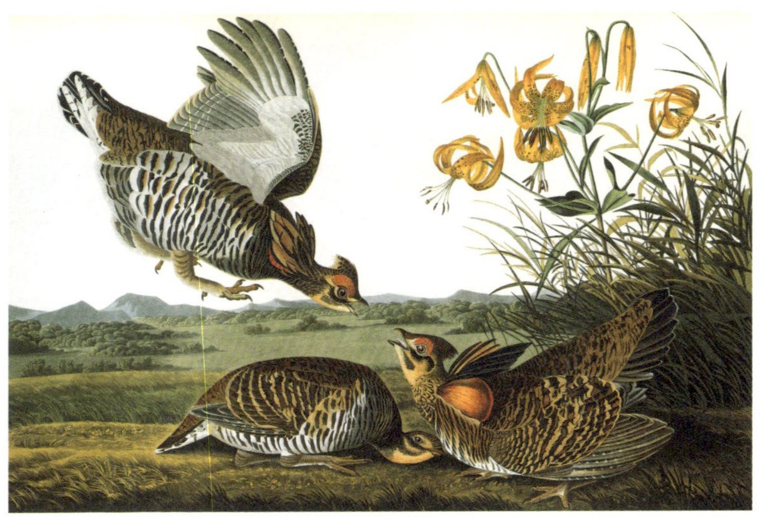

124　Greater Prairie Chicken [Pinnated Grous]
*Tympanuchus cupido*

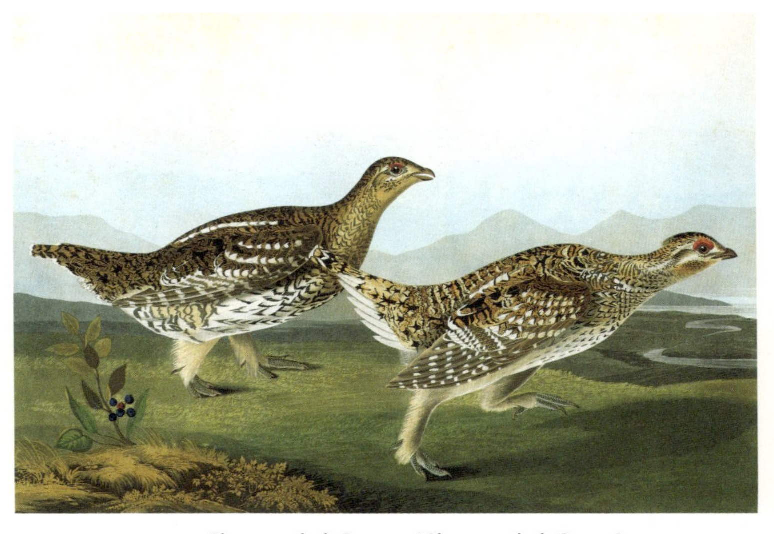

125   Sharp-tailed Grouse [Sharp-tailed Grous]
*Tympanuchus phasianellus*

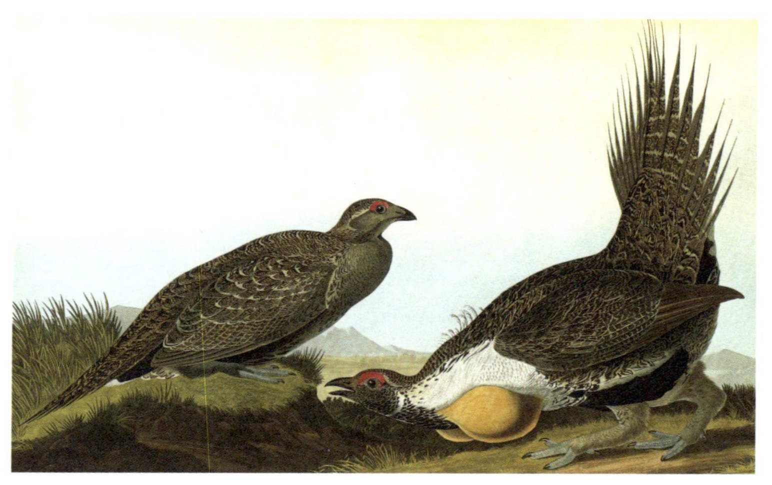

126    Sage Grouse [Cock of the Plains]
*Centrocercus urophasianus*

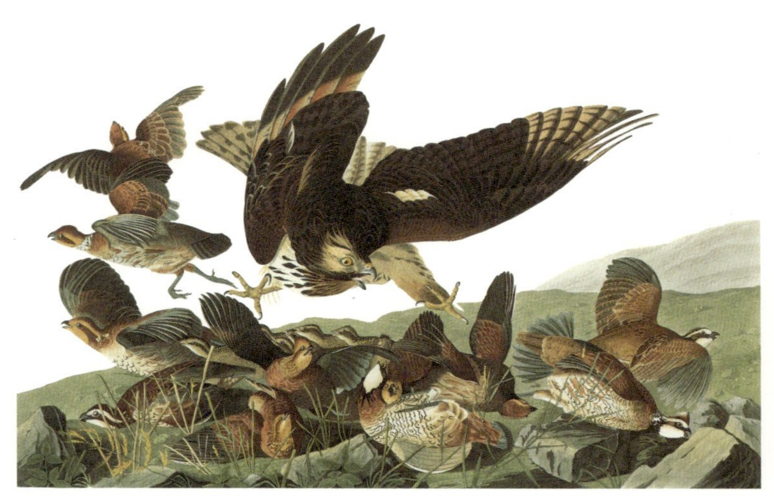

127    Northern Bobwhite [Virginian Partridge]
*Colinus virginianus*
Red-shouldered Hawk [Red-shouldered Buzzard]
*Buteo lineatus*

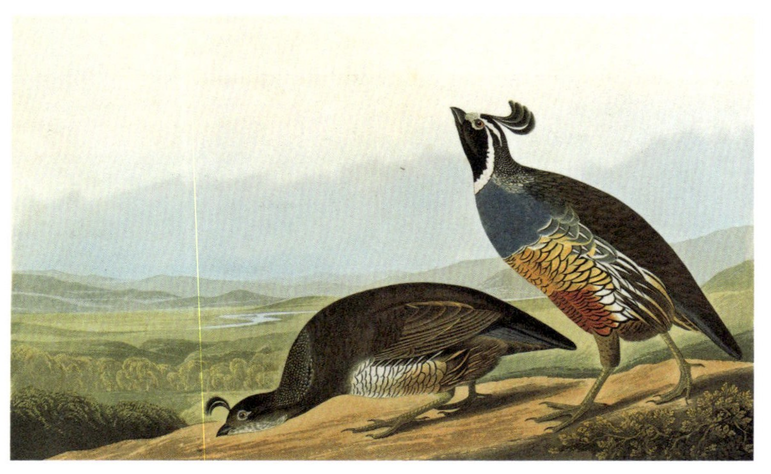

128 California Quail [Californian Partridge]
*Callipepla californica*

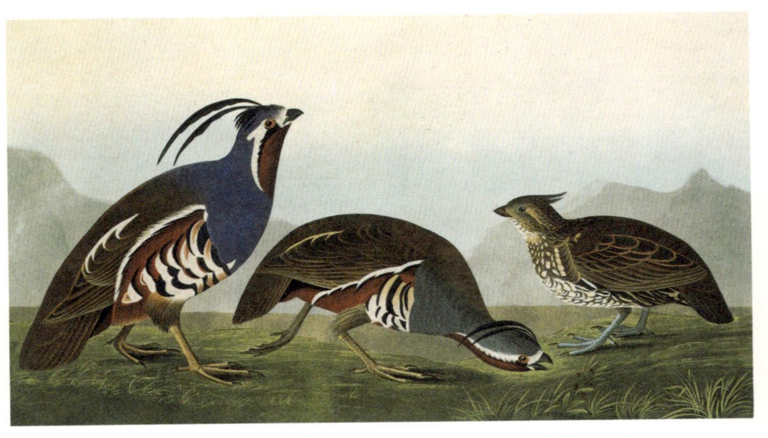

129   **Mountain Quail**
[Plumed Partridge]
*Oreortyx pictus*

**Crested Bobwhite**
[Thick-legged Partridge]
*Colinus cristatus*

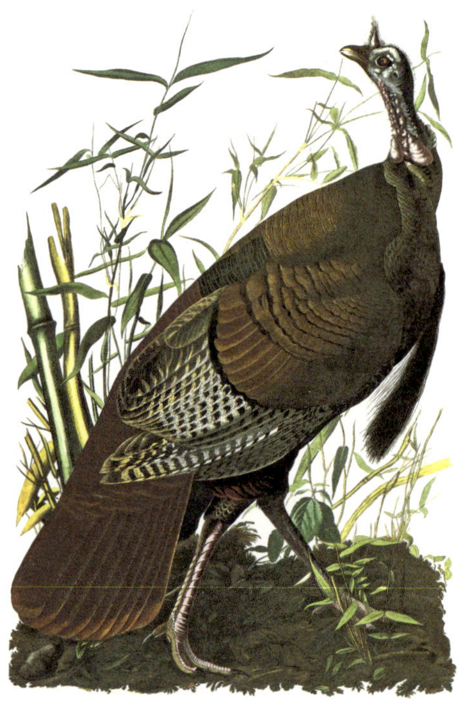

130   Wild Turkey [Great American Cock]
*Meleagris gallopavo*

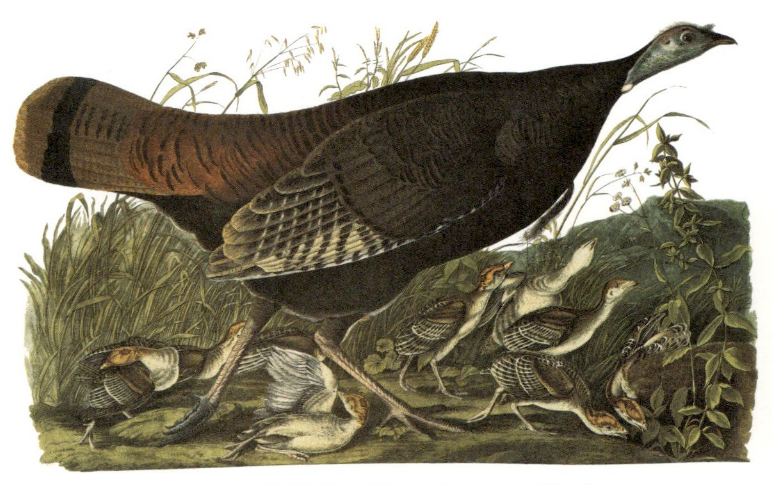

131   Wild Turkey [Great American Hen]
*Meleagris gallopavo*

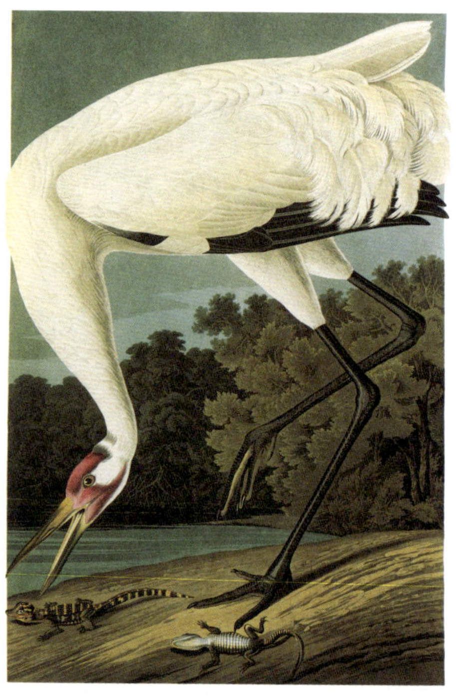

132 Whooping Crane [Hooping Crane]
*Grus americana*

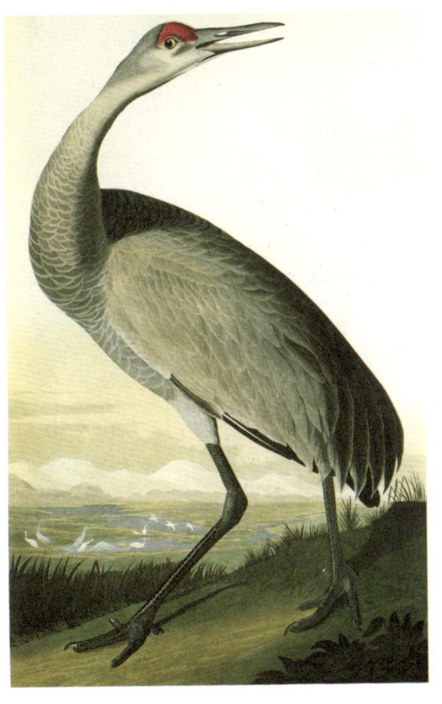

133   Sandhill Crane [Hooping Crane]
*Antigone canadensis*

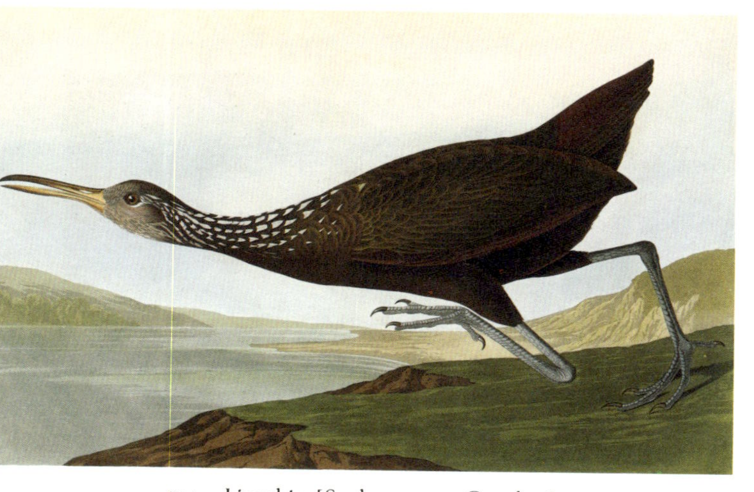

134   Limpkin [Scolopaceous Courlan]
*Aramus guarauna*

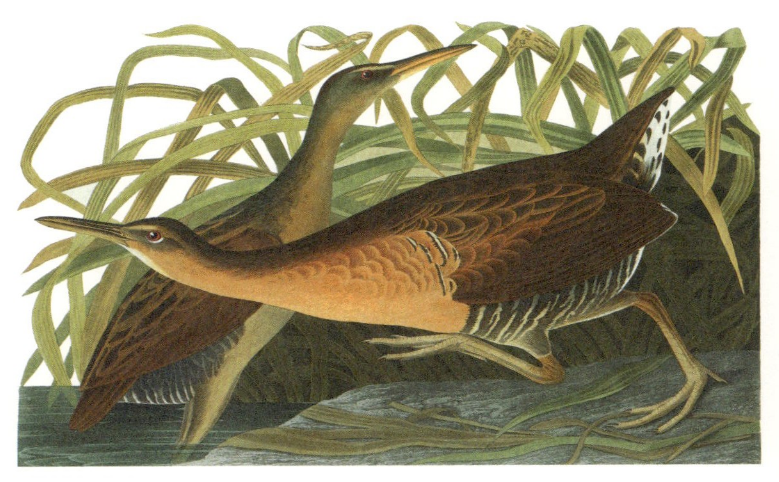

135   King Rail [Fresh-water Marsh Hen]
*Rallus elegans*

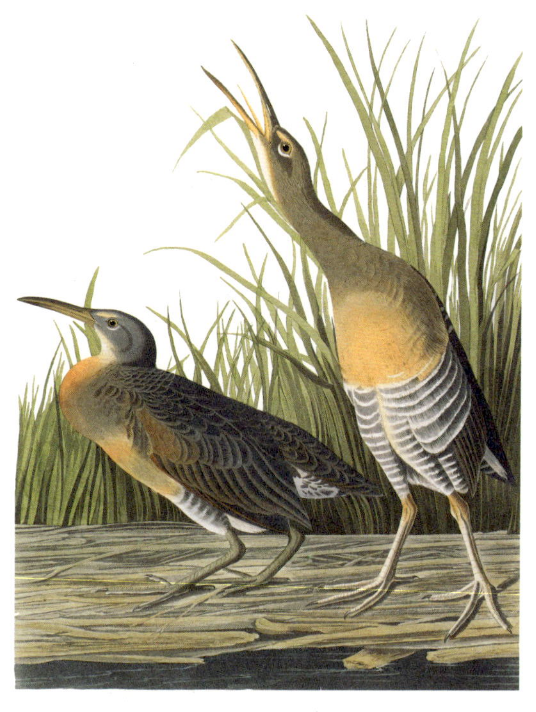

136  Clapper Rail [Salt-water Marsh Hen]
*Rallus crepitans*

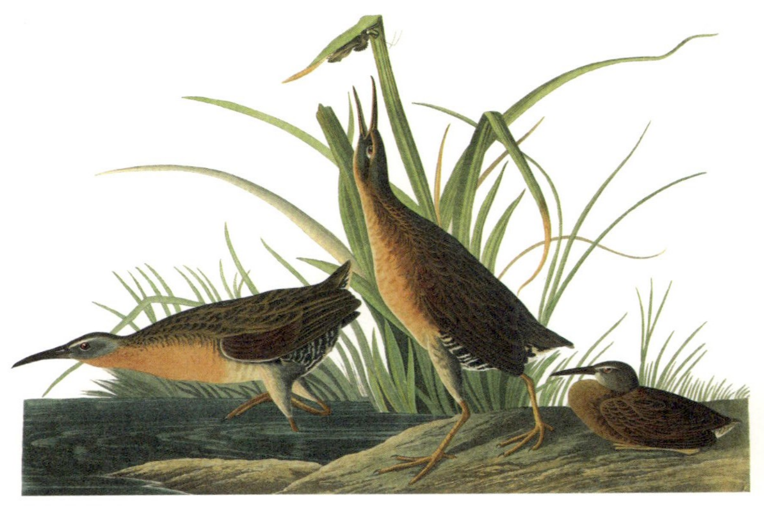

137 Virginia Rail
*Rallus limicola*

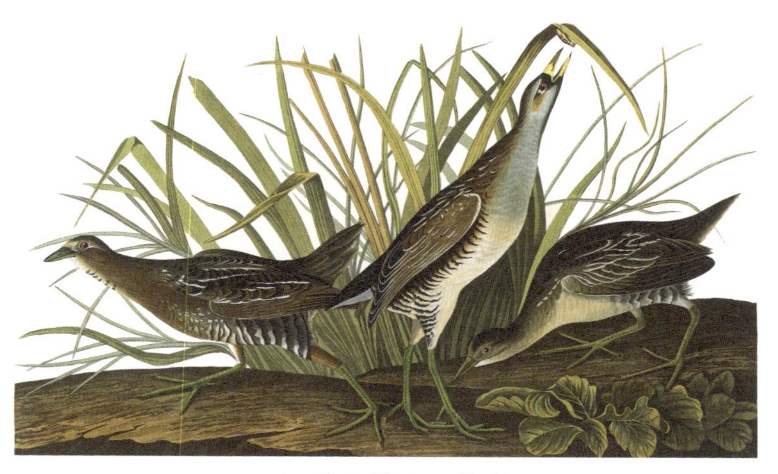

138    Sora [Sora or Rail]
*Porzana carolina*

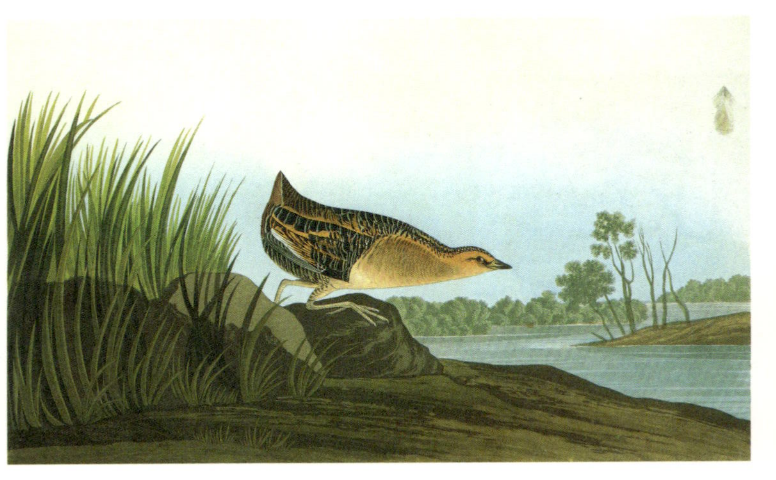

139   Yellow Rail [Yellow-breasted Rail]
*Coturnicops noveboracensis*

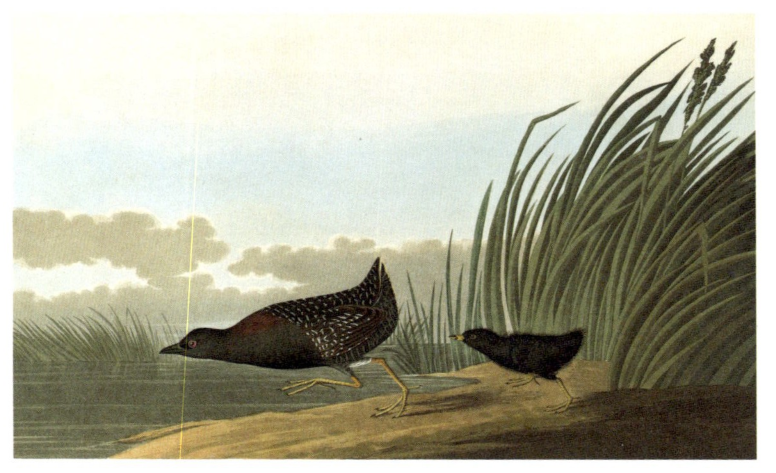

140    Black Rail [Least Water-hen]
*Laterallus jamaicensis*

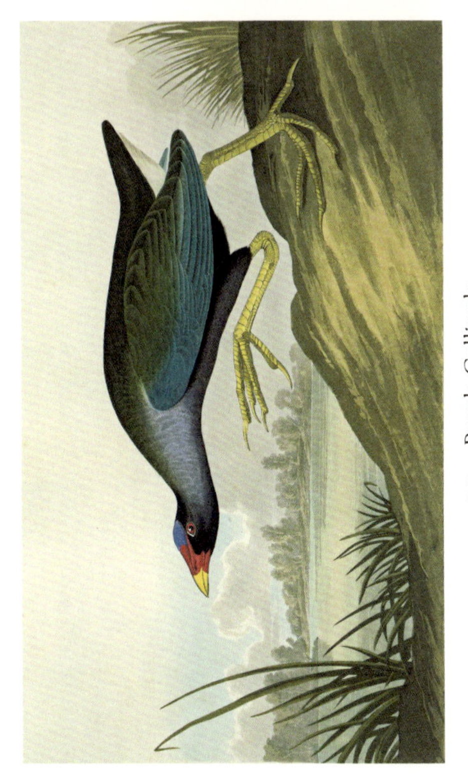

141 Purple Gallinule
*Porphyrula martinicus*

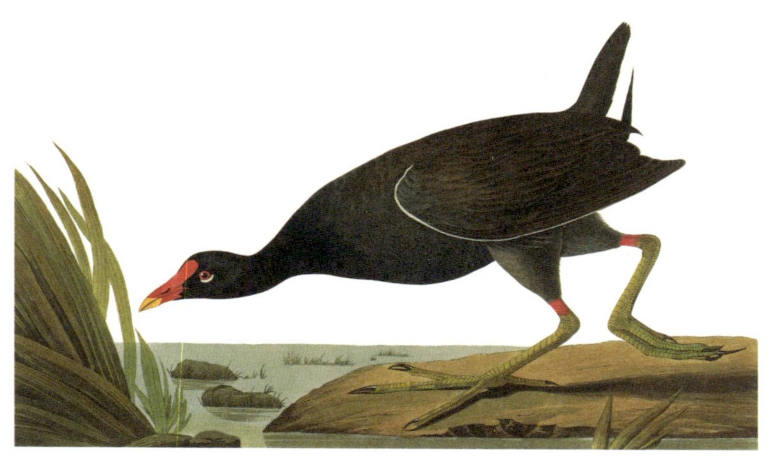

142   Common Moorhen
*Gallinula chloropus*

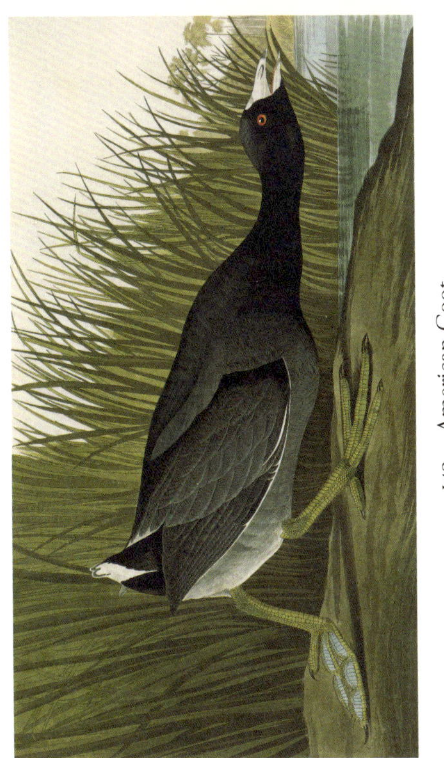

143  American Coot
*Fulica americana*

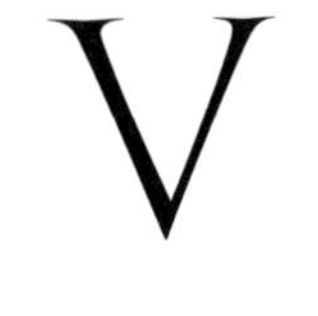

# V

## SHOREBIRDS

Oystercatchers, Stilts, Avocets, Plovers,

Sandpipers, and Phalaropes

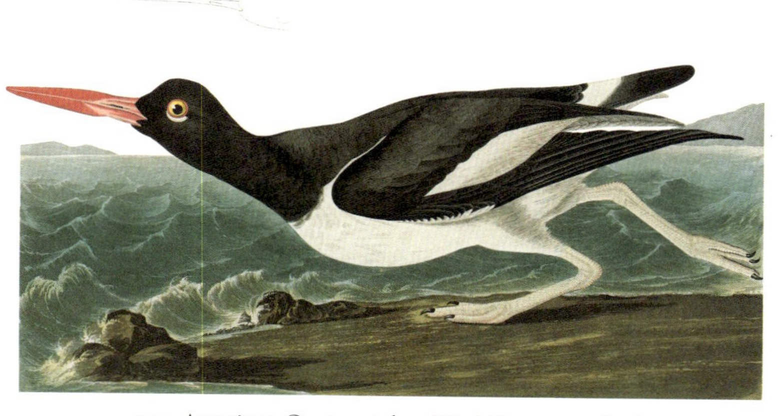

144  American Oystercatcher [Pied Oyster-catcher]
*Haematopus palliatus*

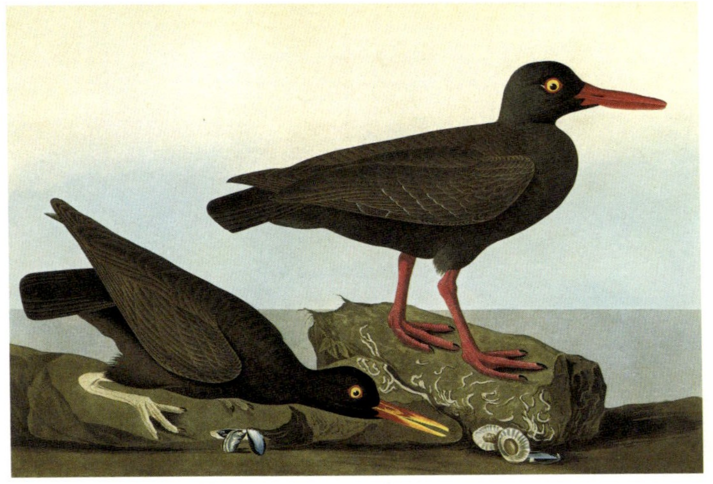

145 Black Oystercatcher [Bachman's or White-legged Oyster-catcher]
*Haematopus bachmani*

Blackish Oystercatcher? [Slender-billed or Townsend's Oyster-catcher]
*Haematopus bachmani?*

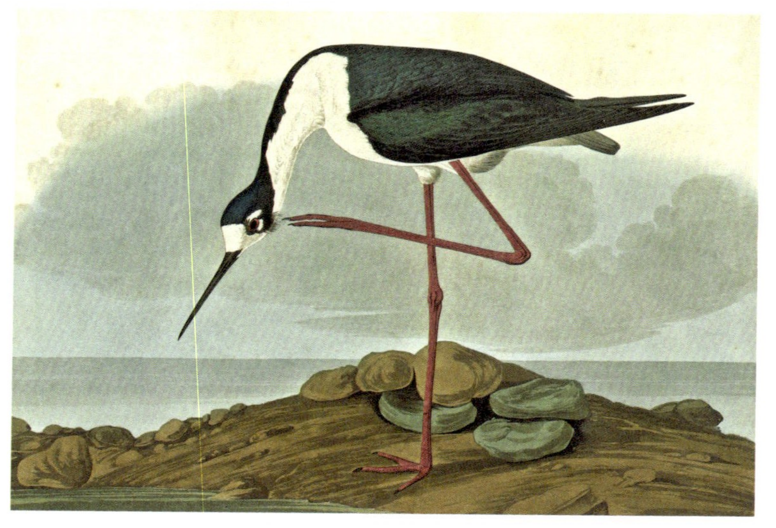

146   Black-necked Stilt [Long-legged Avocet]
*Himantopus mexicanus*

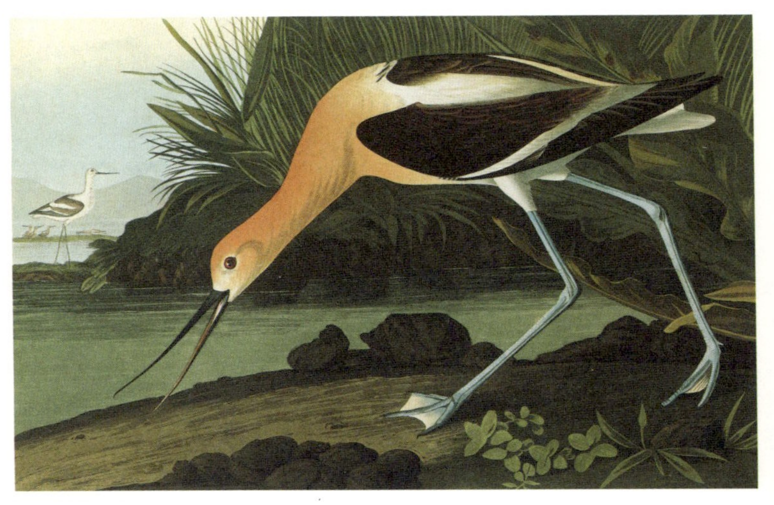

147　American Avocet
*Recurvirostra americana*

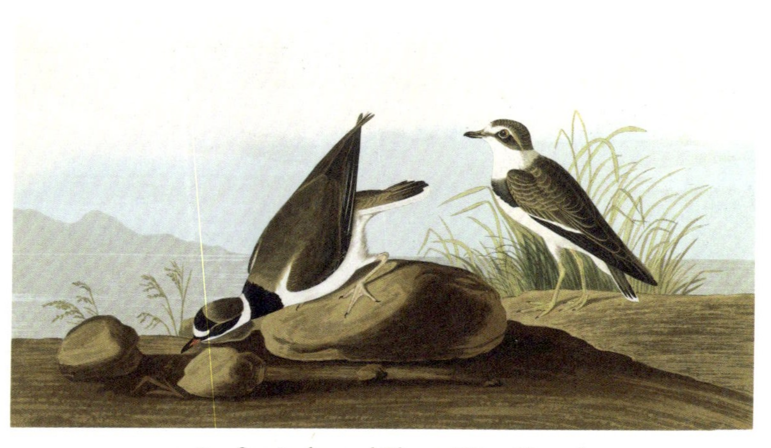

148   Semipalmated Plover [Ring Plover]
*Charadrius semipalmatus*

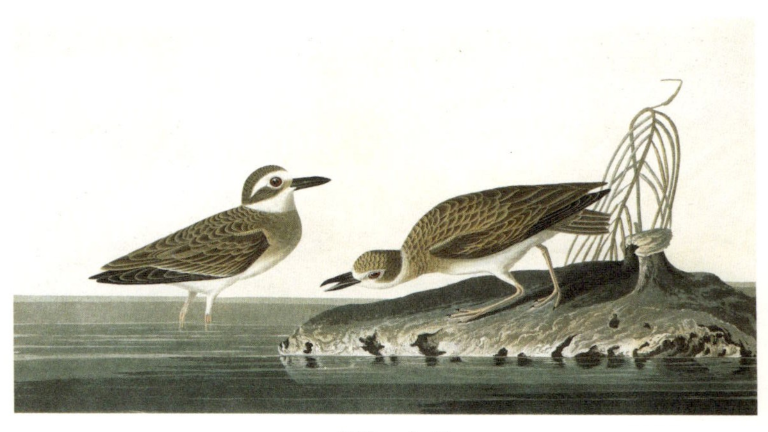

149 Wilson's Plover

*Charadrius wilsonia*

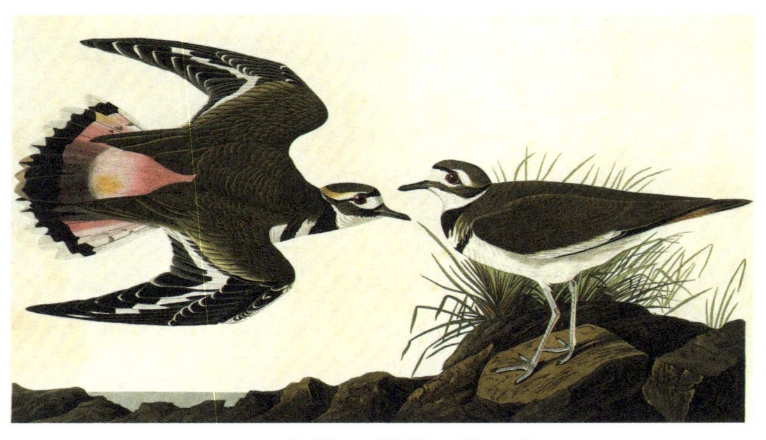

150  Killdeer [Kildeer Plover]
*Charadrius vociferus*

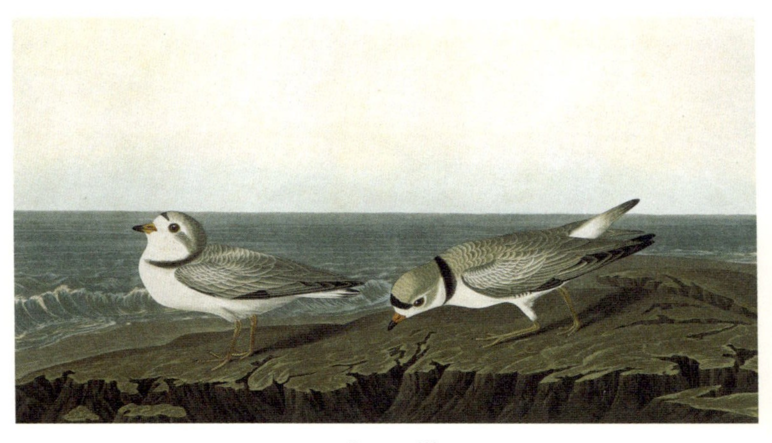

151    Piping Plover
*Charadrius melodus*

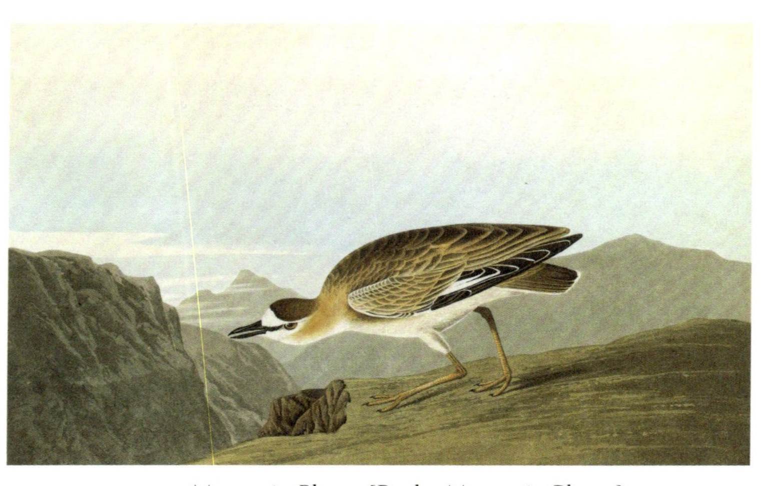

152 Mountain Plover [Rocky Mountain Plover]
*Charadrius montanus*

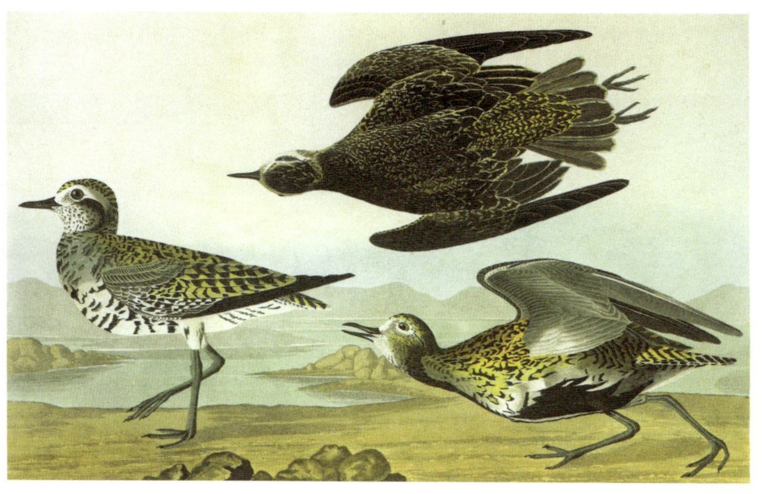

153 American Golden Plover
[Golden Plover]
*Pluvialis dominica*

European Golden Plover
[Golden Plover]
*Pluvialis apricaria*

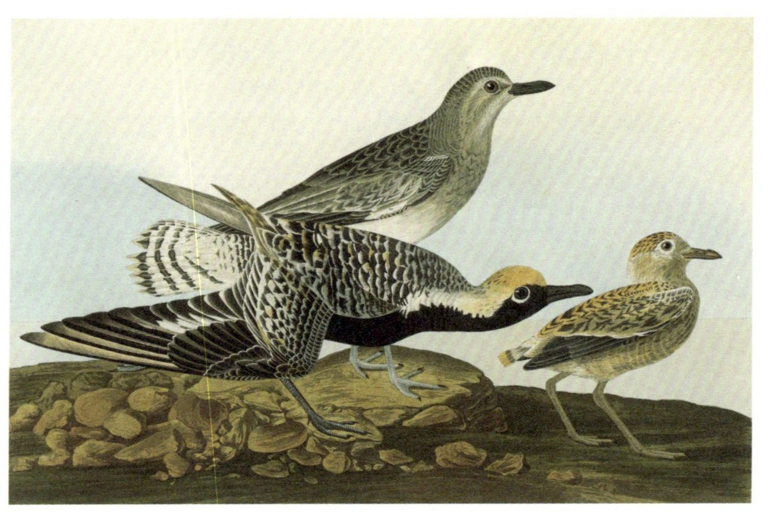

154  Black-bellied Plover
*Pluvialis squatarola*

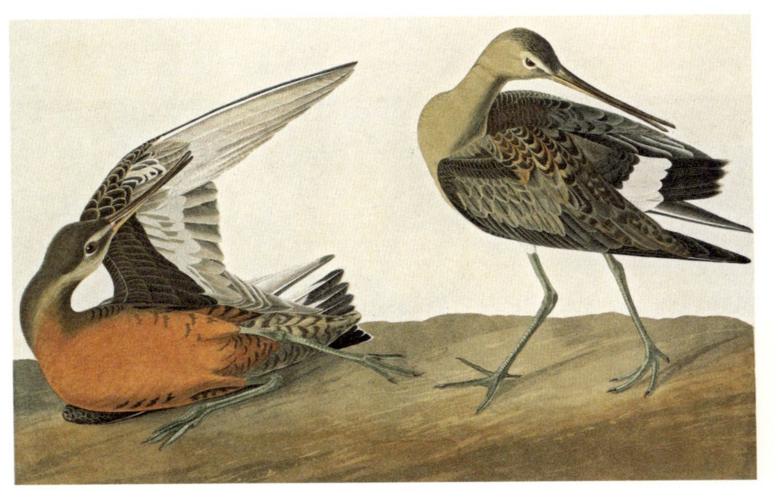

155  Hudsonian Godwit
*Limosa haemastica*

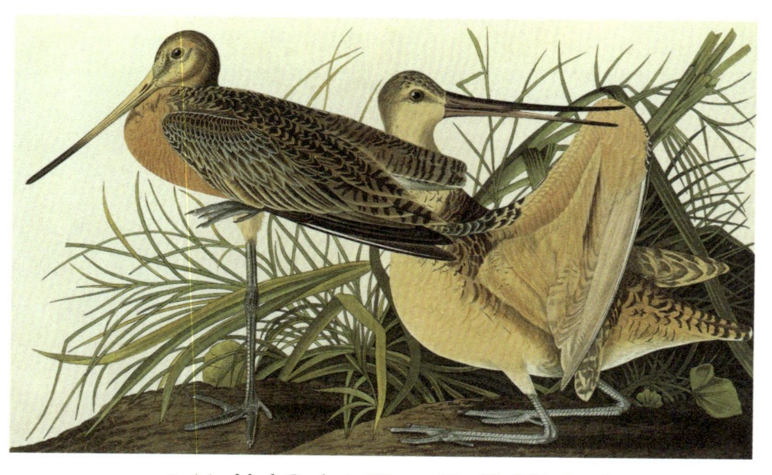

156 Marbled Godwit [Great Marbled Godwit]
*Limosa fedoa*

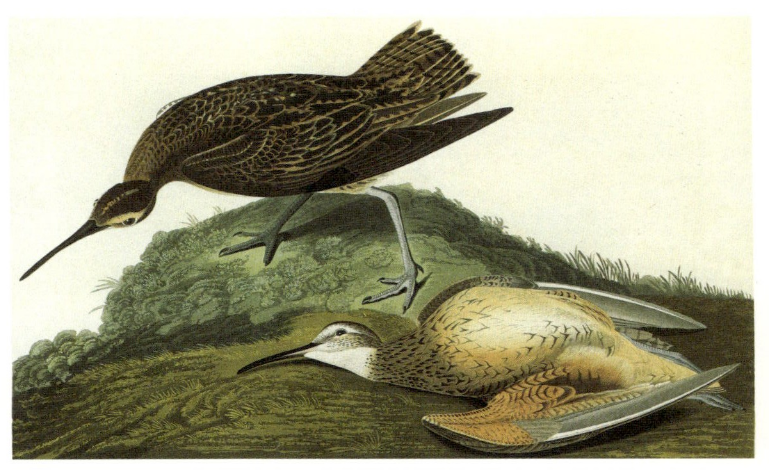

157  Eskimo Curlew [Esquimaux Curlew]
*Numenius borealis*

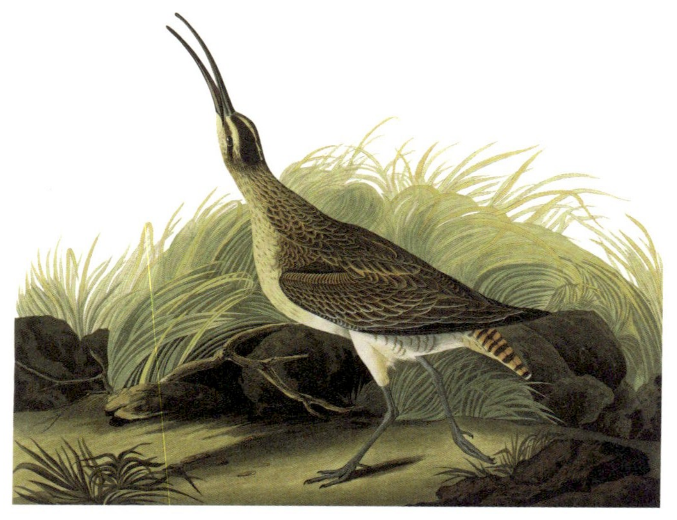

158  Whimbrel [Great Esquimaux Curlew]
*Numenius phaeopus*

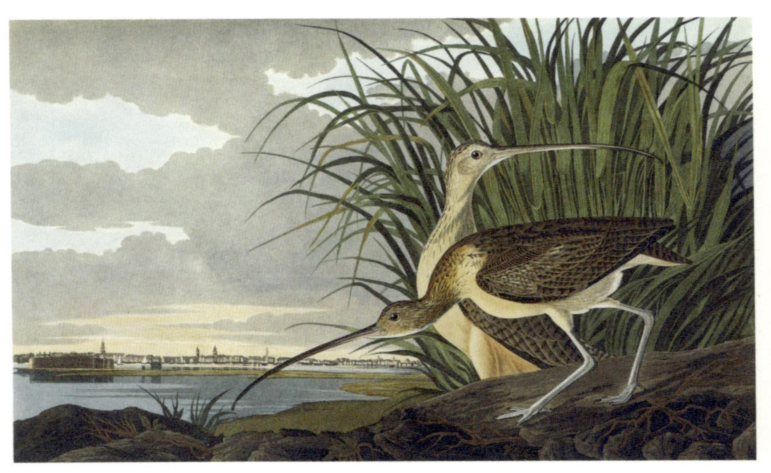

159  Long-billed Curlew
*Numenius americanus*

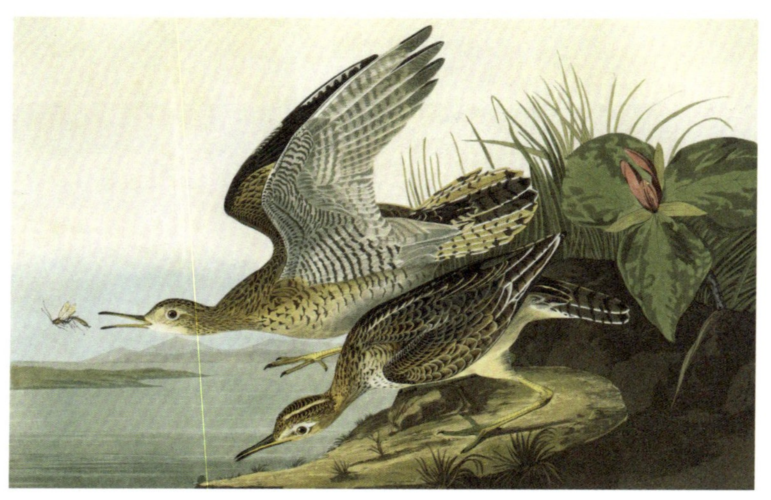

160  Upland Sandpiper [Bartram Sandpiper]
*Bartramia longicauda*

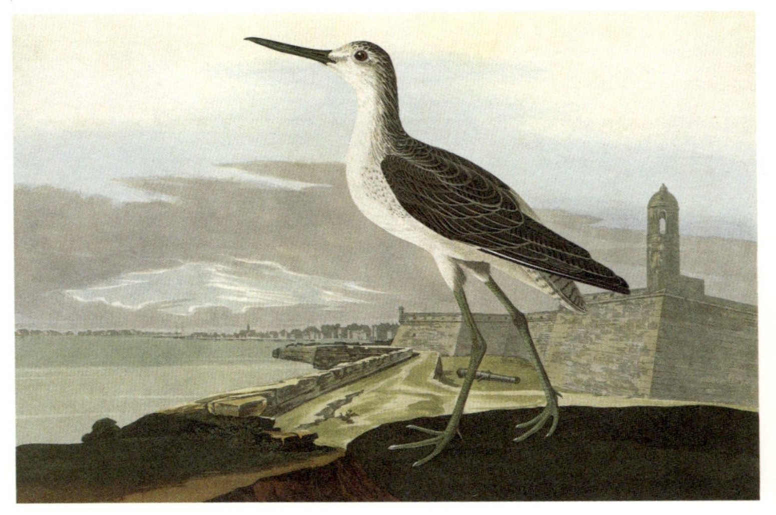

161  Greenshank
*Tringa nebularia*

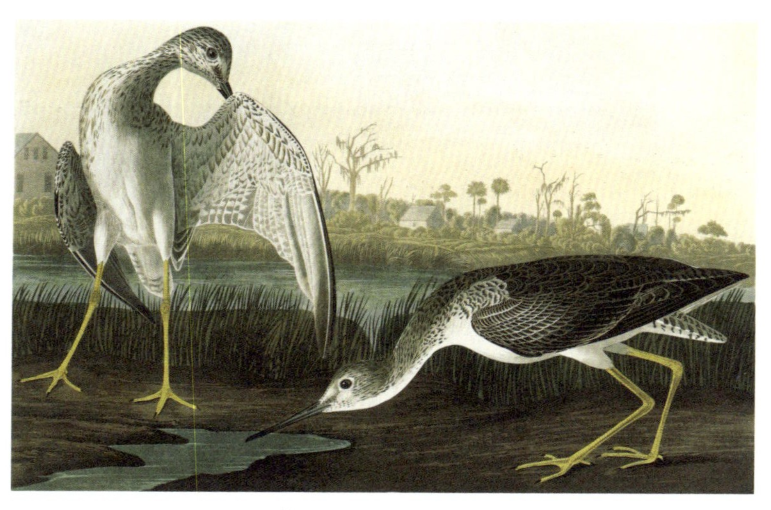

162  Greater Yellowlegs [Tell-tale Godwit or Snipe]
*Tringa melanoleuca*

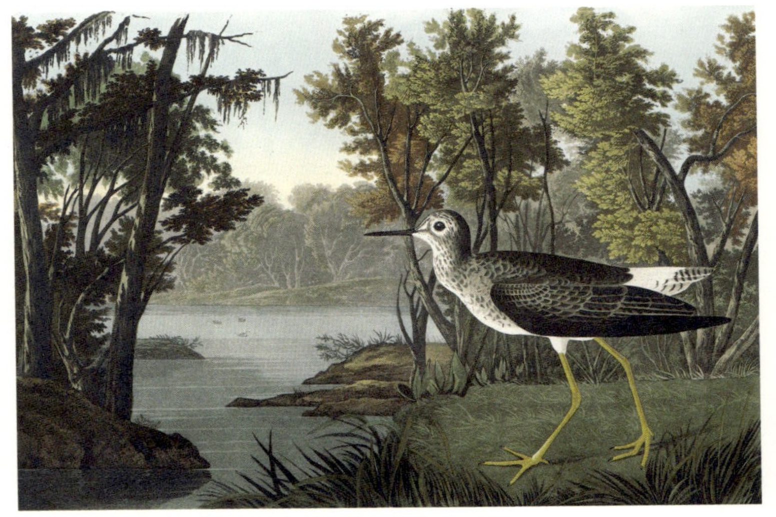

163  Lesser Yellowlegs [Yellow Shank]
*Tringa flavipes*

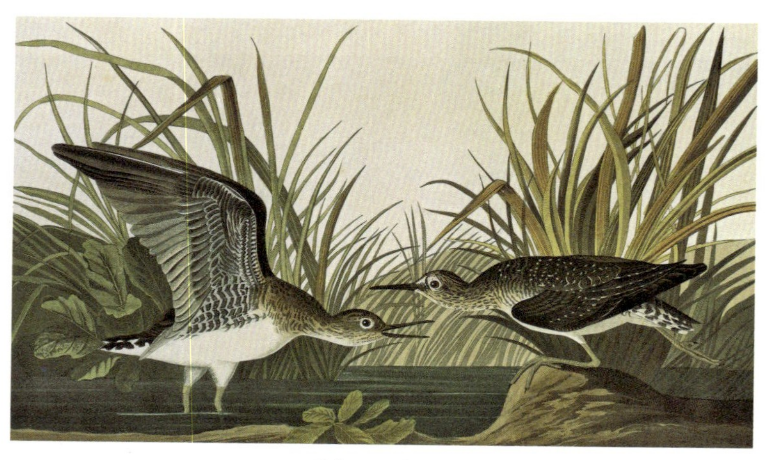

164  Solitary Sandpiper

*Tringa solitaria*

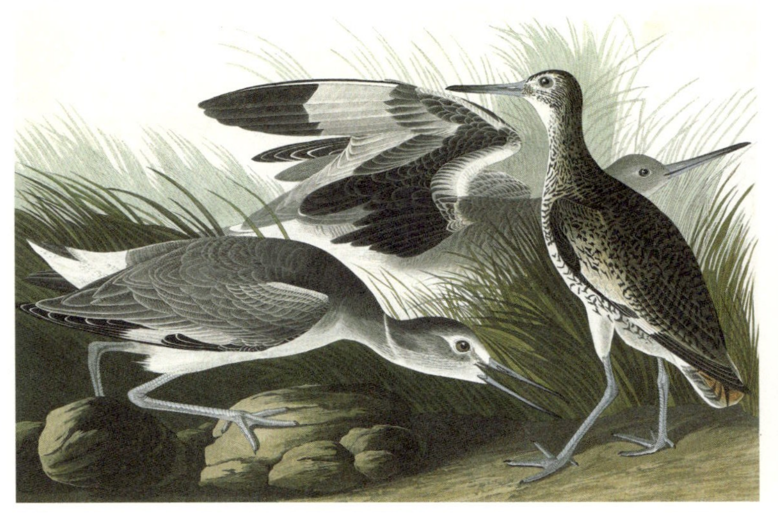

165  Willet [Semipalmated Snipe]
*Tringa semipalmata*

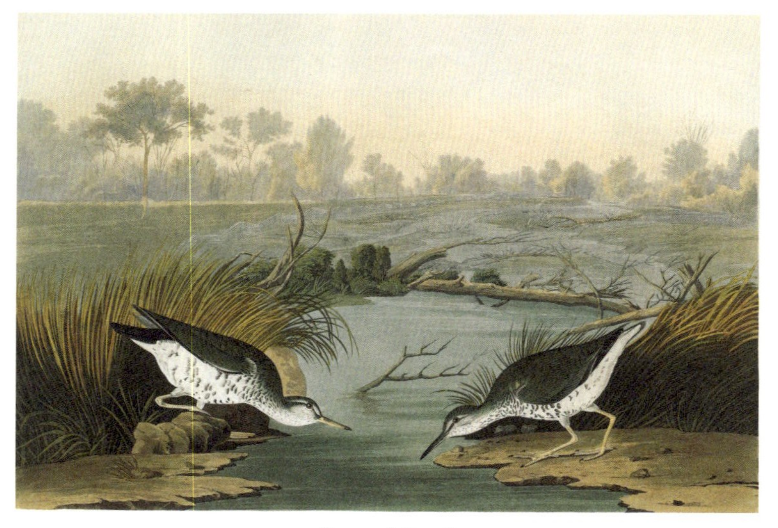

166  Spotted Sandpiper
*Actitis macularius*

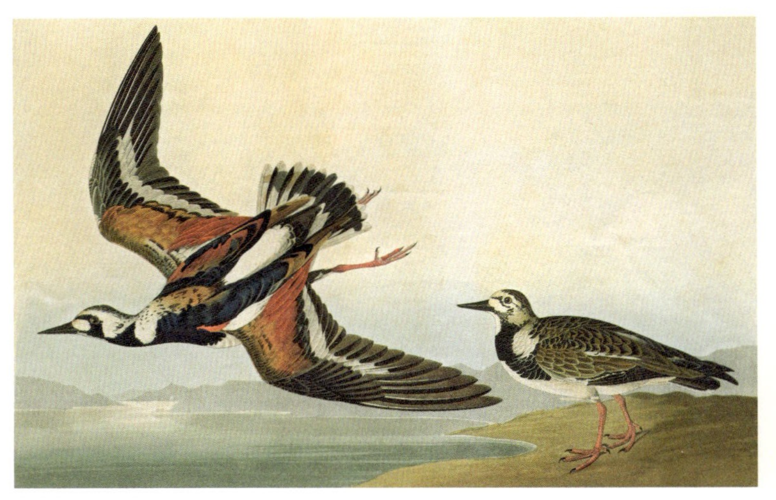

167  Ruddy Turnstone [Turn-stone]
*Arenaria interpres*

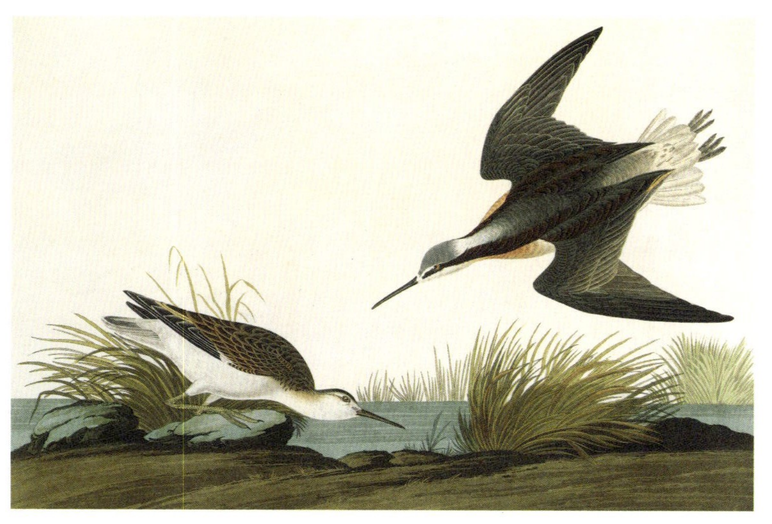

## 168  Wilson's Phalarope

*Phalaropus tricolor*

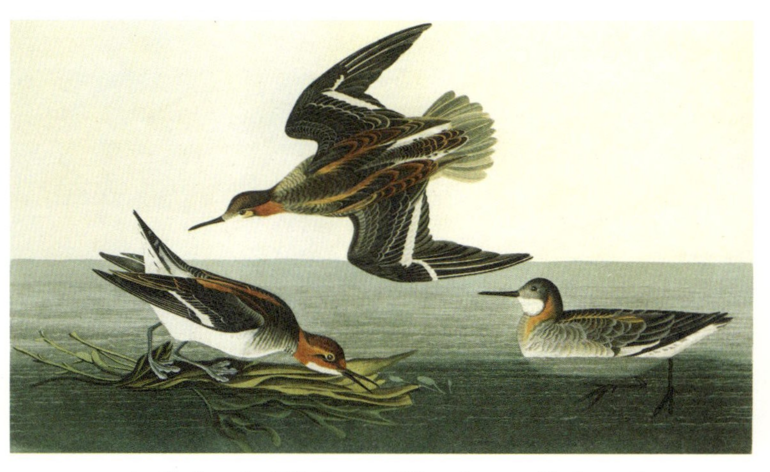

169  Red-necked Phalarope [Hyperborean Phalarope]
*Phalaropus lobatus*

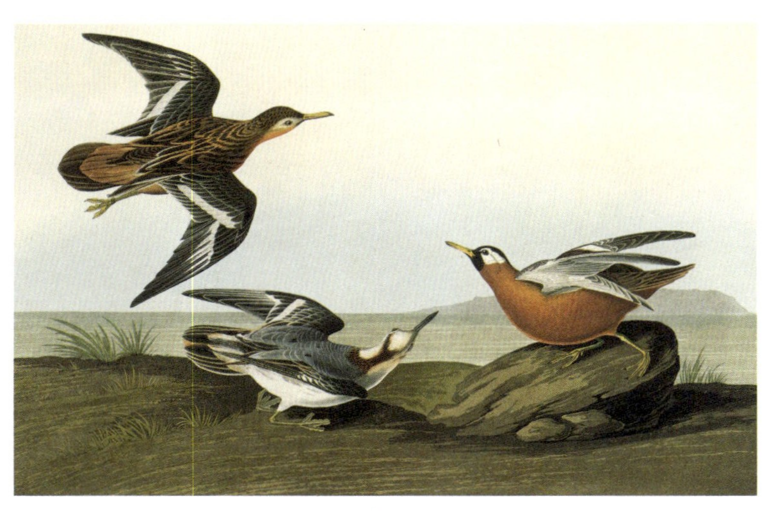

170  Red Phalarope
*Phalaropus fulicarius*

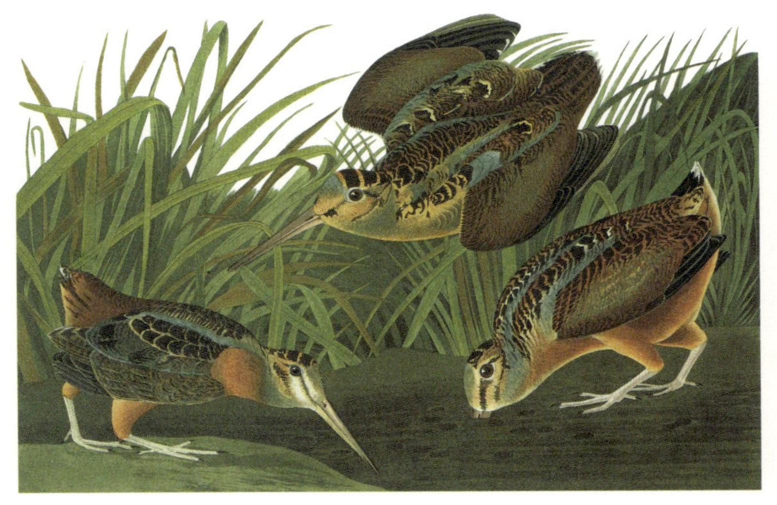

171  American Woodcock

*Scolopax minor*

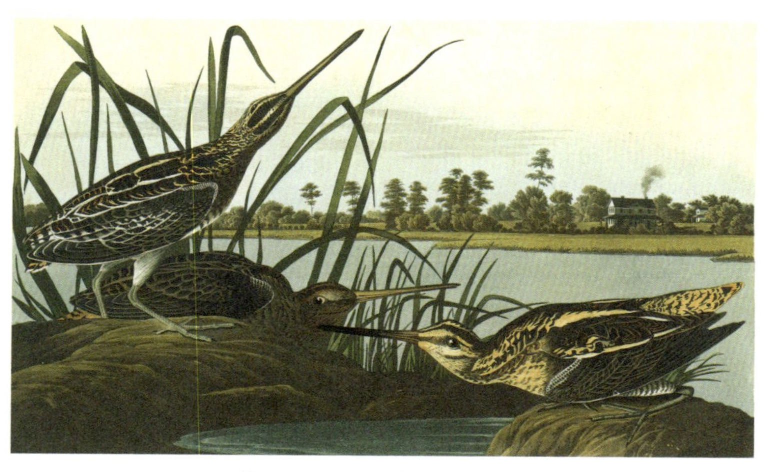

172  Common Snipe [American Snipe]
*Gallinago gallinago*

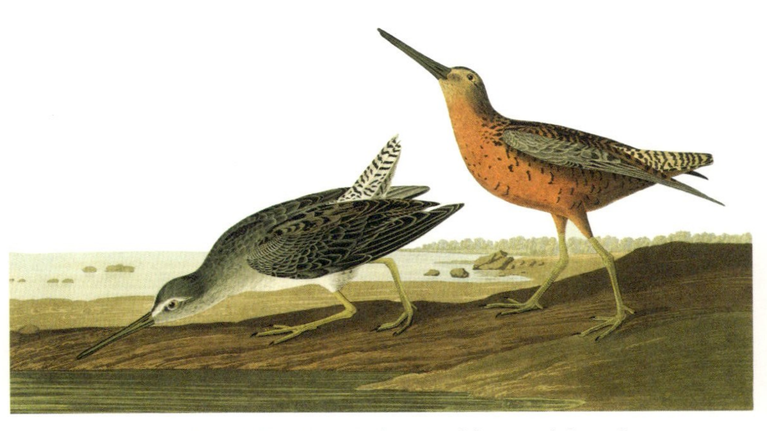

173  Short-billed Dowitcher [Red-breasted Snipe]
*Limnodromus griseus*

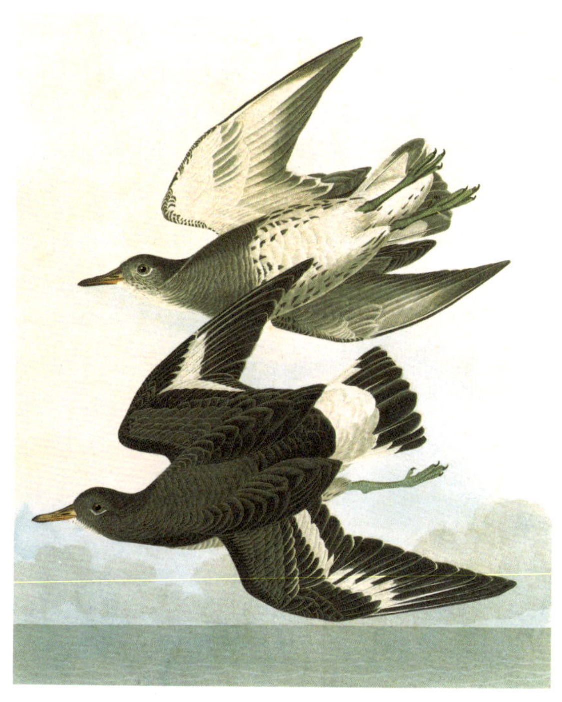

174  Surfbird [Townsend's Sandpiper]

*Calidris virgata*

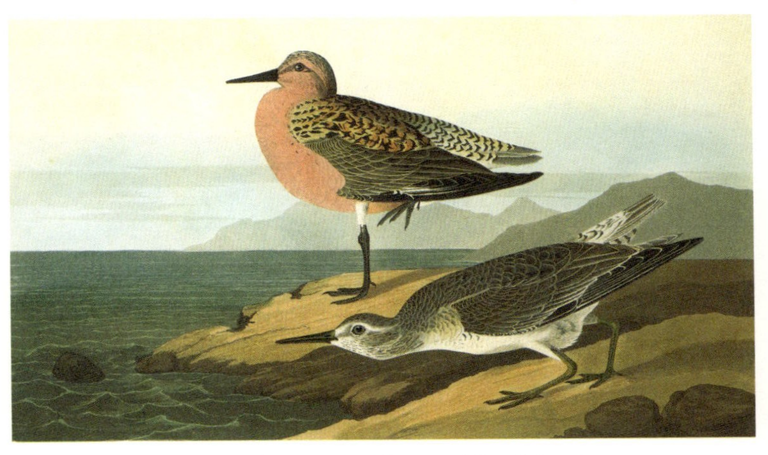

175  Red Knot [Red-breasted Sandpiper]
*Calidris canutus*

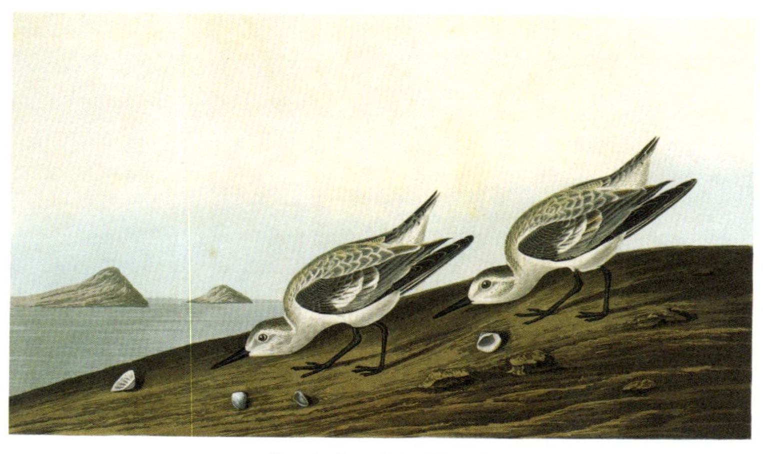

176  Sanderling [Ruddy Plover]
*Calidris alba*

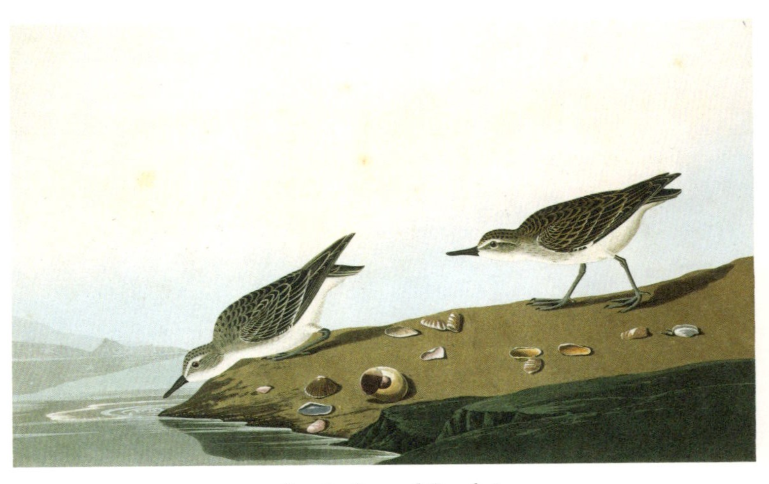

177 Semipalmated Sandpiper
*Calidris pusilla*

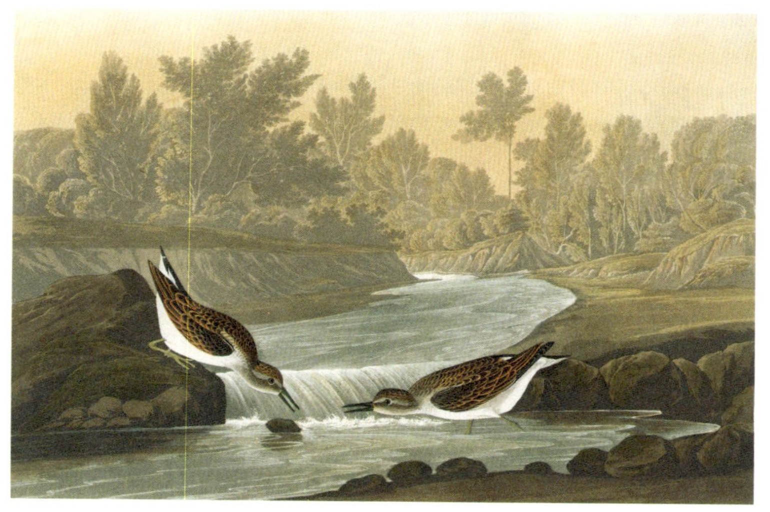

178  Least Sandpiper [Little Sandpiper]
*Calidris minutilla*

PLEASE NOTE: THIS PLATE IS OUT OF PHYLOGENETIC SEQUENCE.

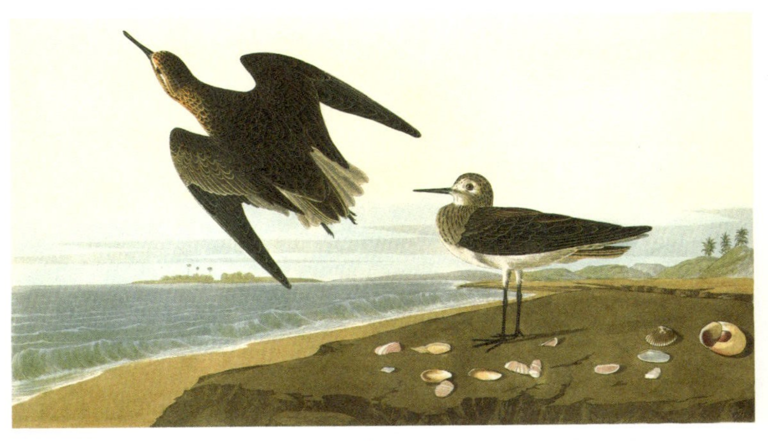

179  White-rumped Sandpiper [Schinz's Sandpiper]
*Calidris fusicollis*

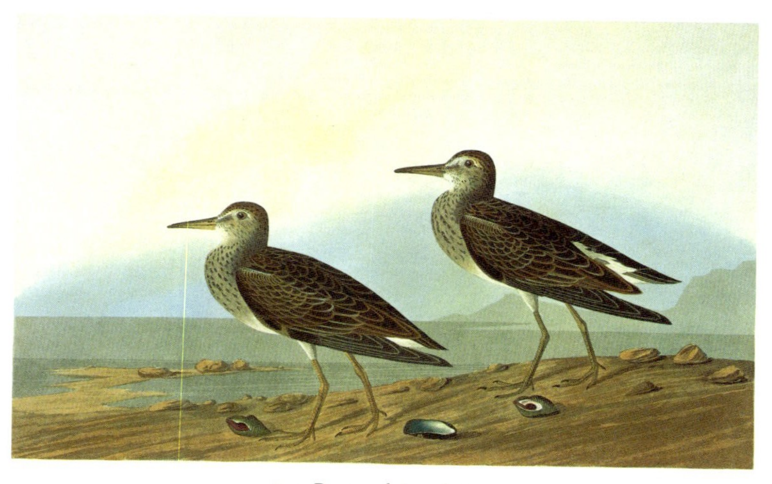

180  Pectoral Sandpiper
*Calidris melanotos*

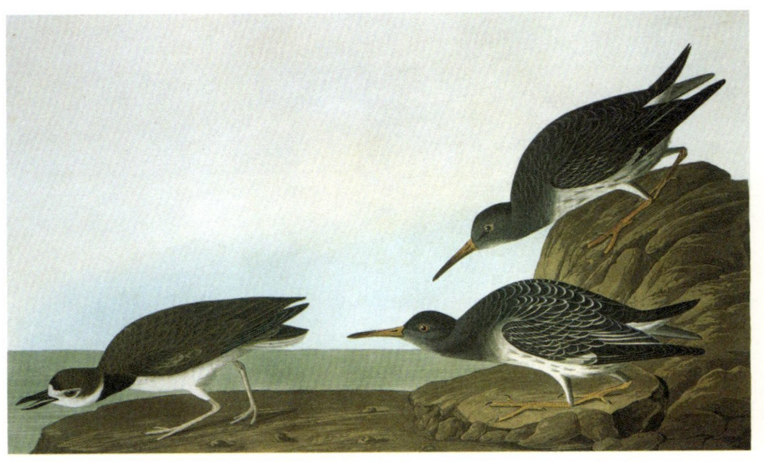

181  Wilson's Plover
*Charadrius wilsonia*

Purple Sandpiper
*Calidris maritima*

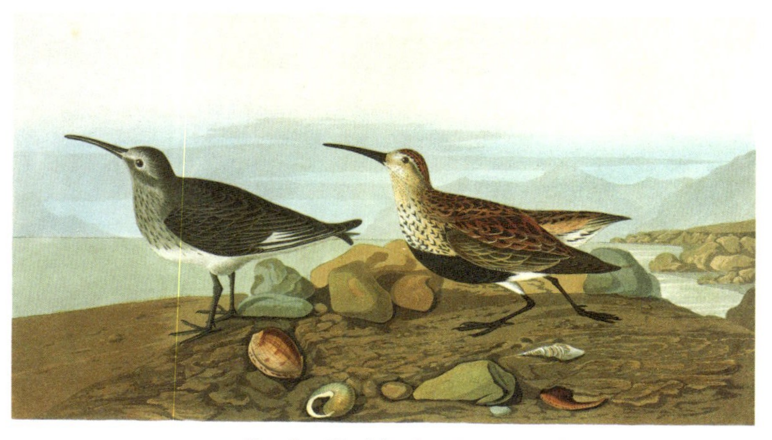

182  Dunlin [Red-backed Sandpiper]
*Calidris alpina*

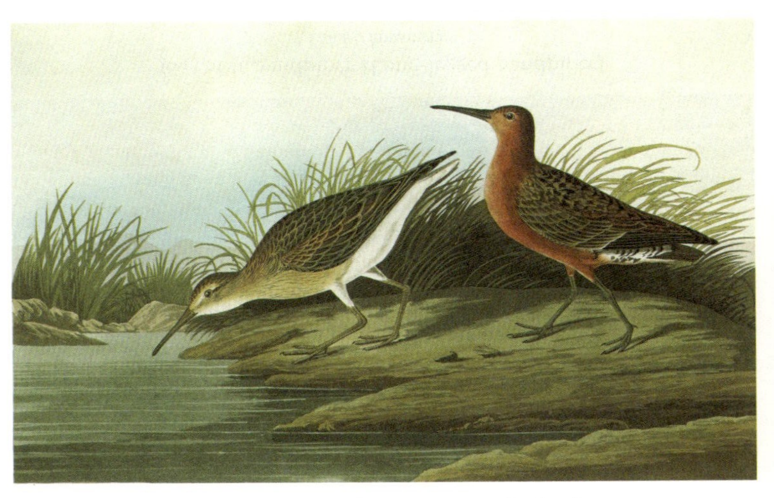

183  Curlew Sandpiper [Pigmy Curlew]
*Calidris ferruginea*

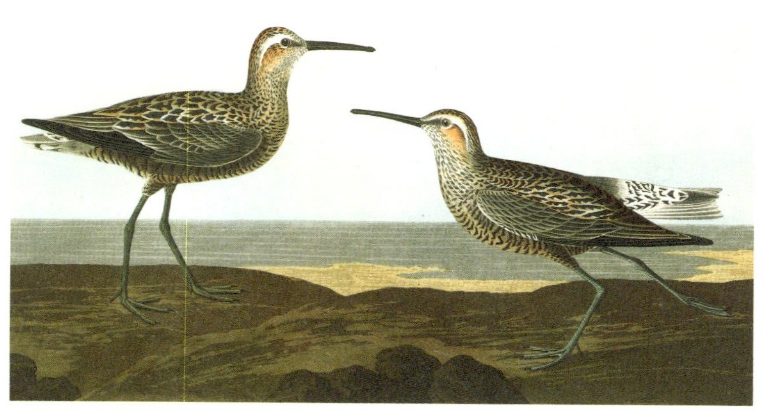

184  Stilt Sandpiper [Long-legged Sandpiper]
*Calidris himantopus*

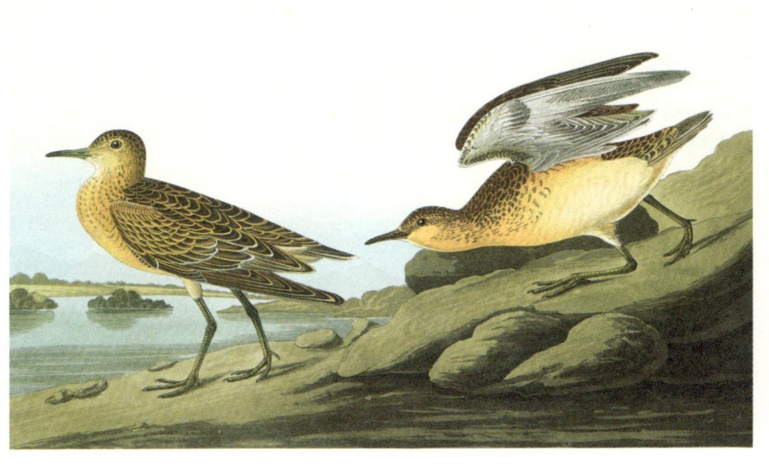

185  Buff-breasted Sandpiper
*Calidris subruficollis*

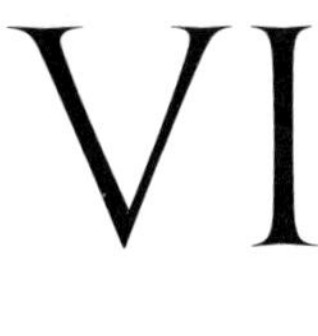

# SEABIRDS

Jaegers, Gulls, Terns, Skimmers, and Auks

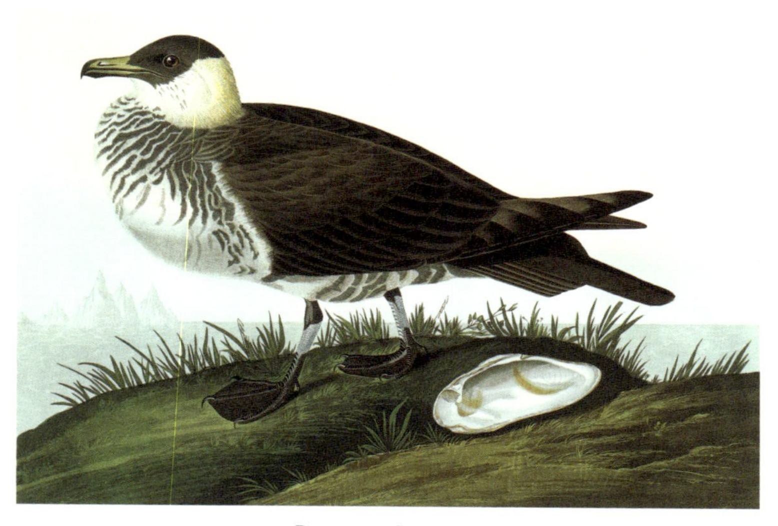

186  Pomarine Jaeger [Jager]
*Stercorarius pomarinus*

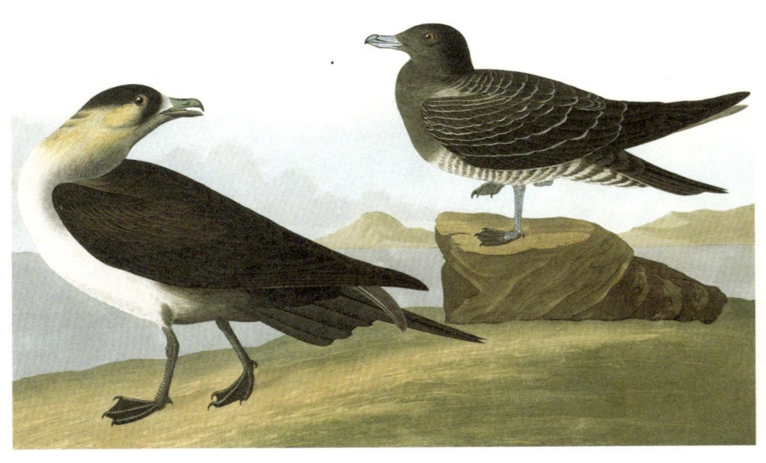

187  Parasitic Jaeger [Richardson's Jager]
*Stercorarius parasiticus*

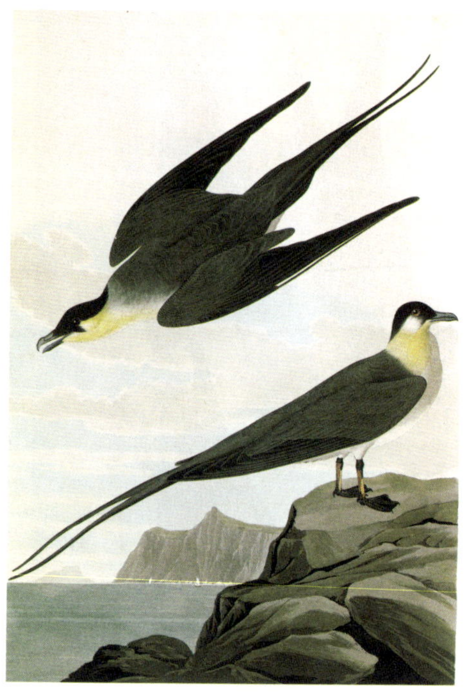

188  Long-tailed Jaeger [Arctic Jager]
*Stercorarius longicaudus*

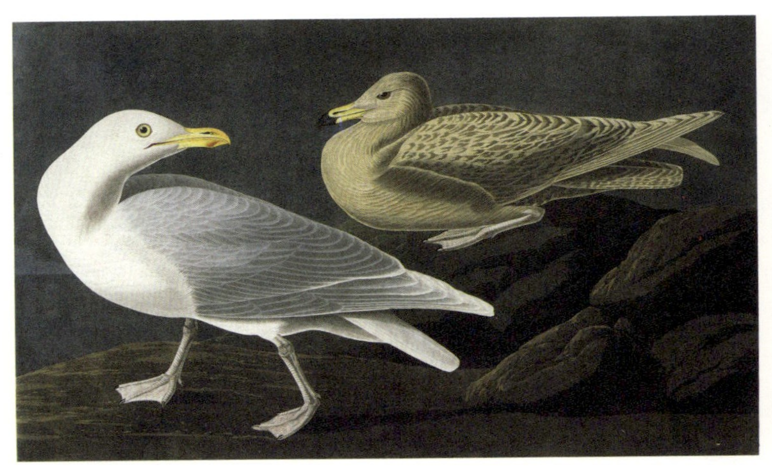

189  Glaucous Gull [Burgomaster Gull]
*Larus hyperboreus*

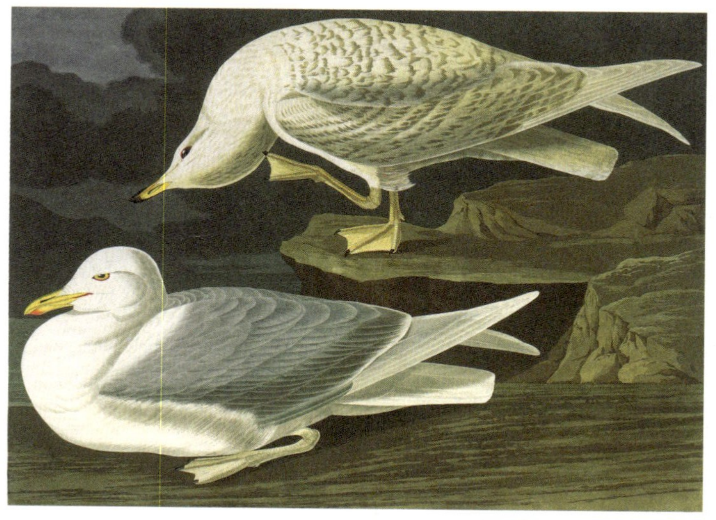

190  Iceland Gull [White-winged Silvery Gull]
*Larus glaucoides*

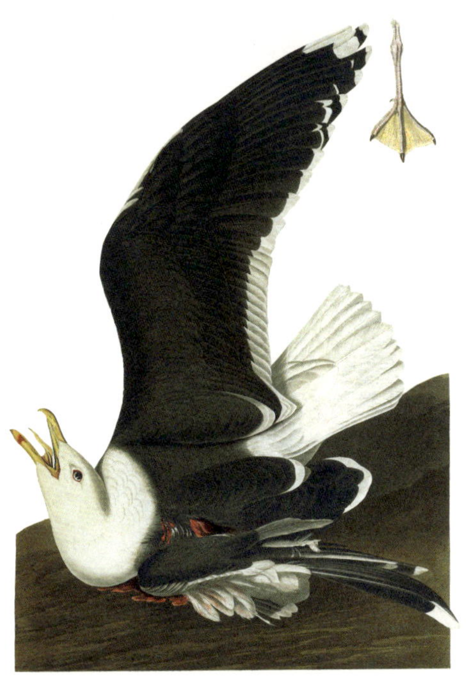

191 Great Black-backed Gull [Black-backed Gull]
*Larus marinus*

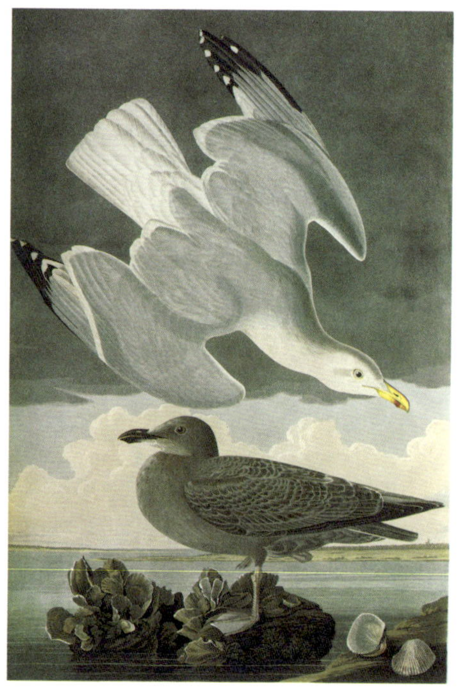

192  Herring Gull

*Larus argentatus*

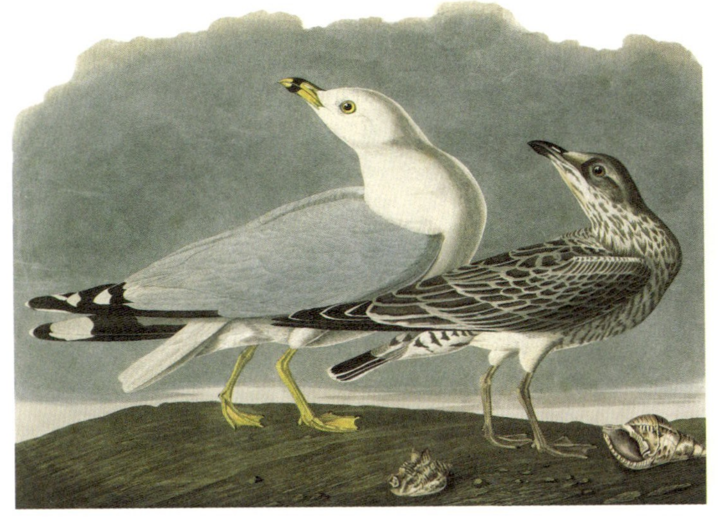

193  Ring-billed Gull [Common Gull]
*Larus delawarensis*

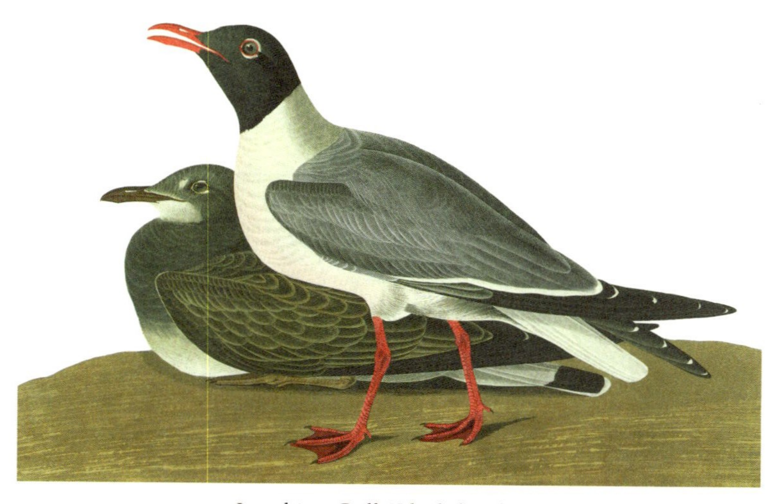

194 Laughing Gull [Black-headed Gull]
*Leucophaeus atricilla*

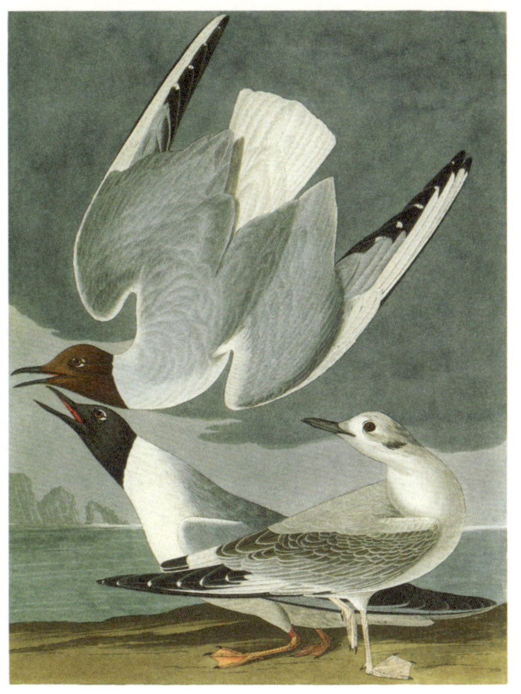

195  Bonaparte's Gull [Bonapartian Gull]
*Chroicocephalus philadelphia*

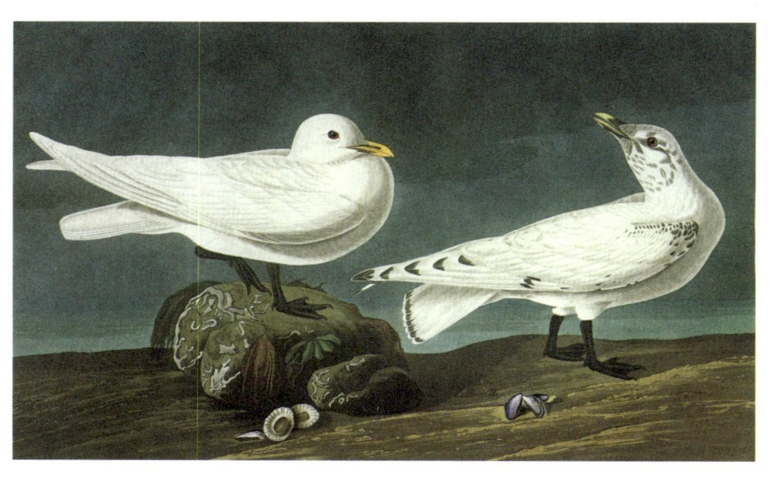

196  Ivory Gull

*Pagophila eburnea*

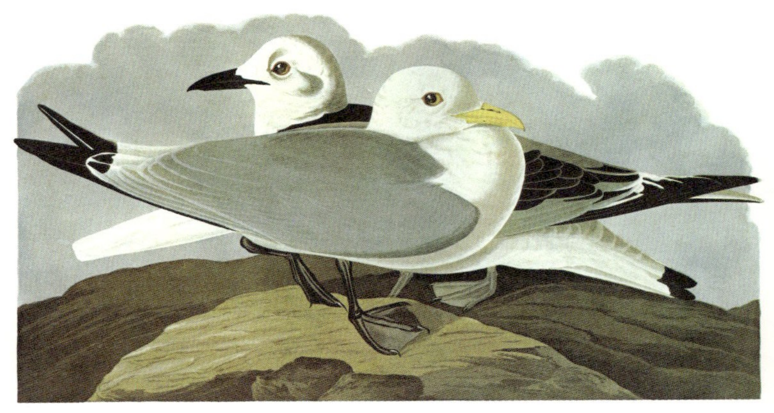

197  Black-legged Kittiwake [Kittiwake Gull]
*Rissa tridactyla*

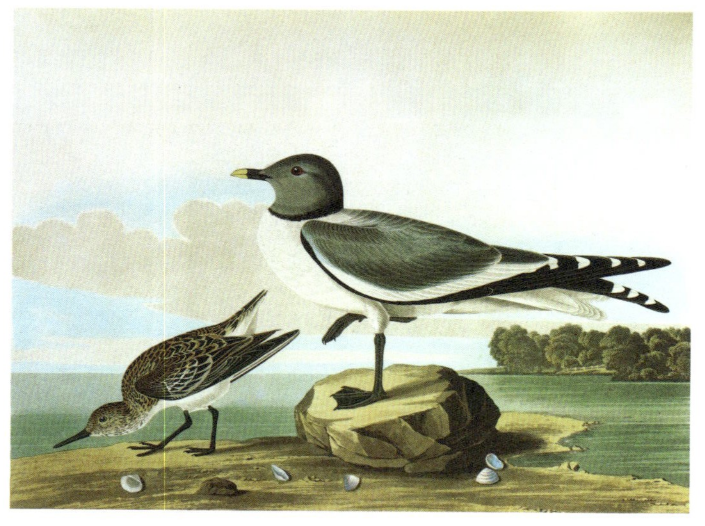

198  Sanderling
*Calidris alba*

Sabine's Gull [Forked-tailed Gull]
*Xema sabini*

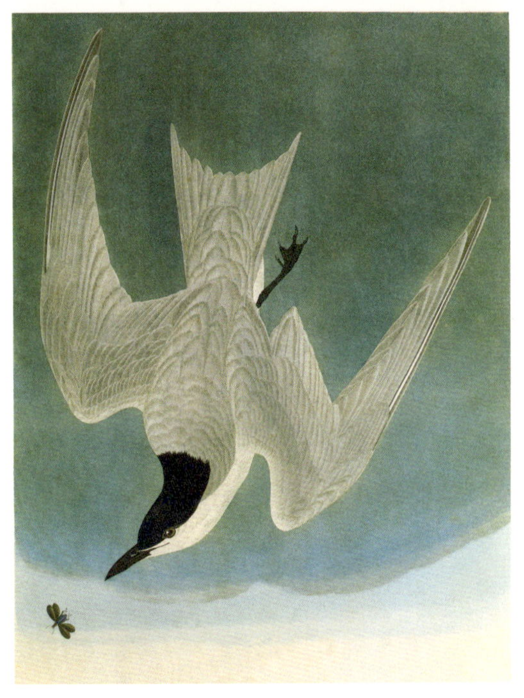

199  Gull-billed Tern [Marsh Tern]
*Sterna niloctica*

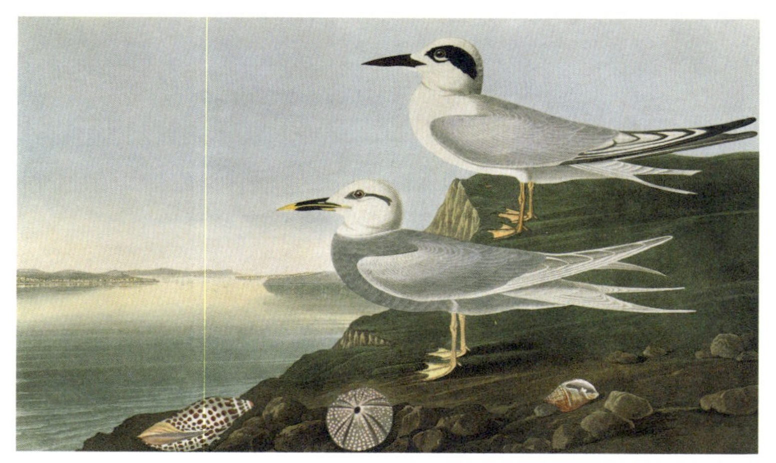

200  Forster's Tern [Havell's Tern]
*Sterna forsteri*

Trudeau's Tern
*Sterna trudeaui*

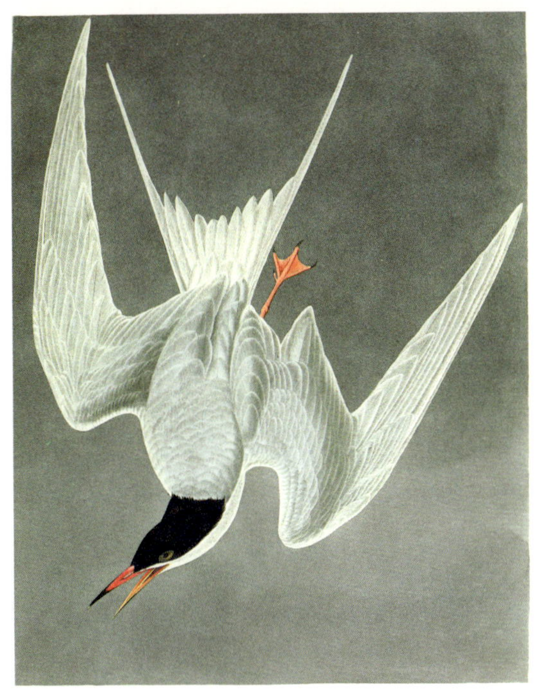

201  Common Tern [Great Tern]
*Sterna hirundo*

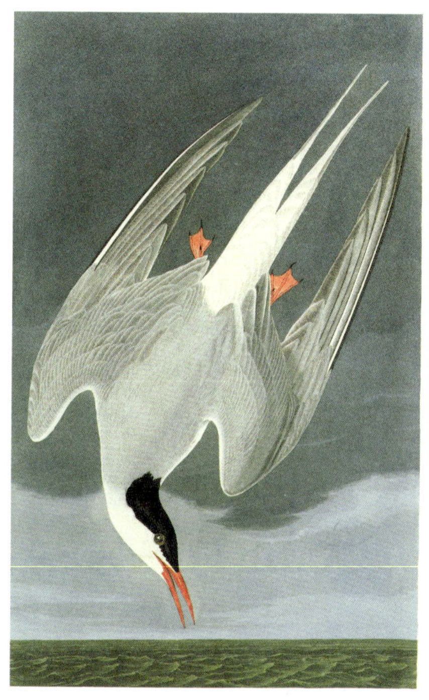

## 202  Arctic Tern
*Sterna paradisaea*

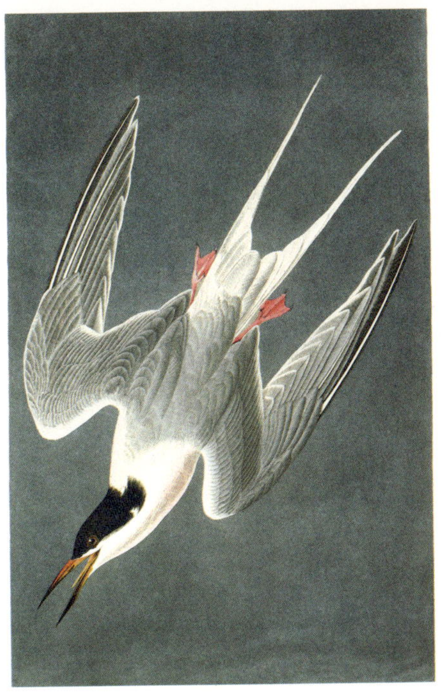

**203  Roseate Tern**
*Sterna dougallii*

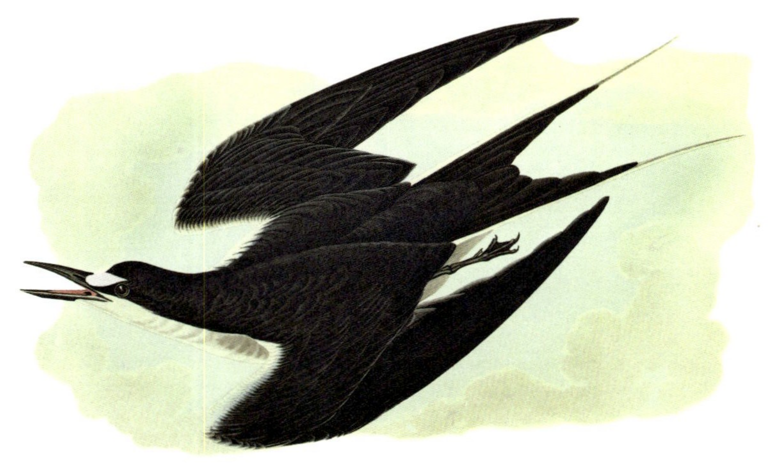

204  Sooty Tern
*Onychoprion fuscatus*

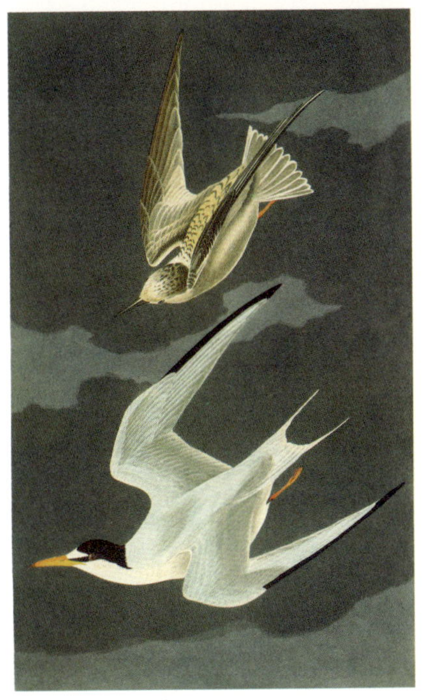

**205  Least Tern [Lesser Tern]**

*Sternula antillarum*

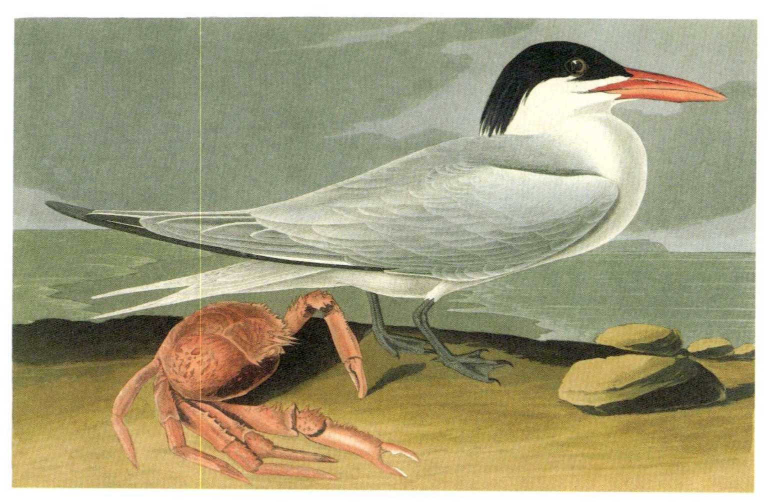

206  Royal Tern [Cayenne Tern]
*Thalasseus maximus*

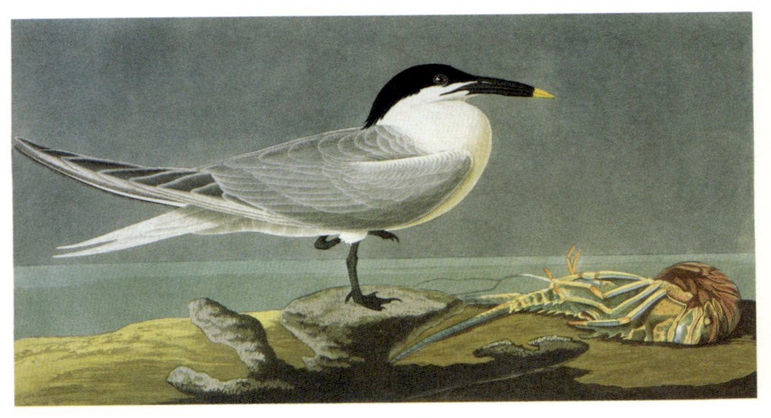

207  Sandwich Tern
*Thalasseus sandvicensis*

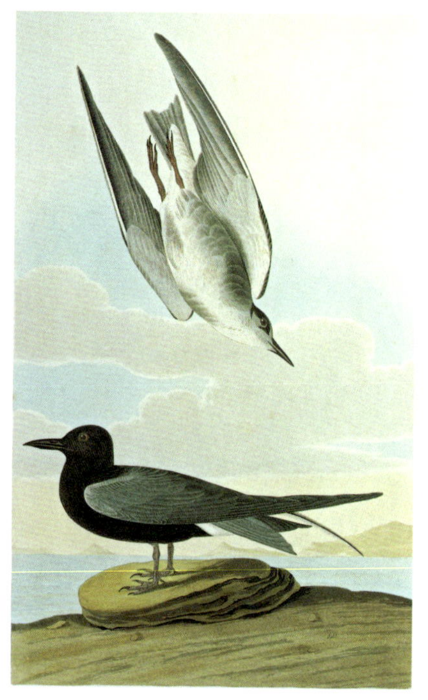

208  Black Tern

*Chlidonias niger*

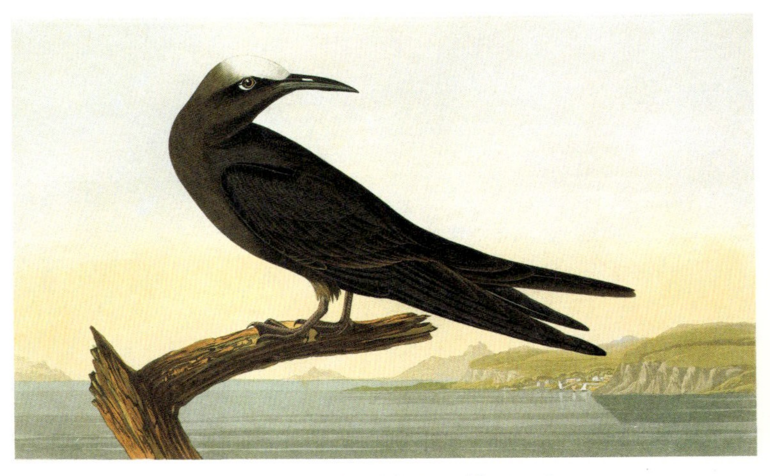

209  Brown Noddy [Noddy Tern]
*Anous stolidus*

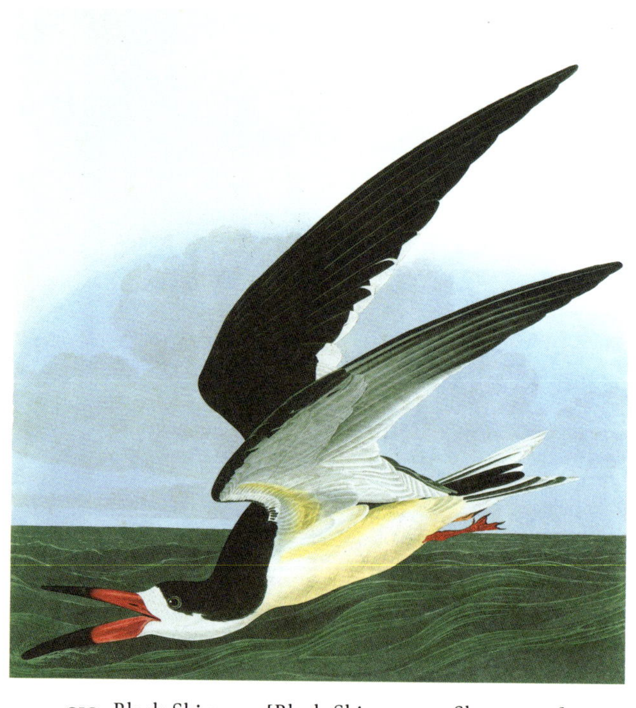

210  Black Skimmer [Black Skimmer or Shearwater]
*Rynchops niger*

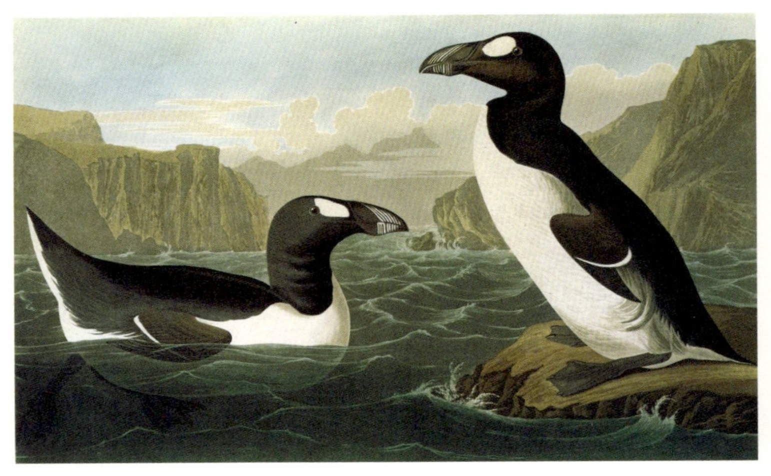

211 Great Auk

*Pinguinus impennis*

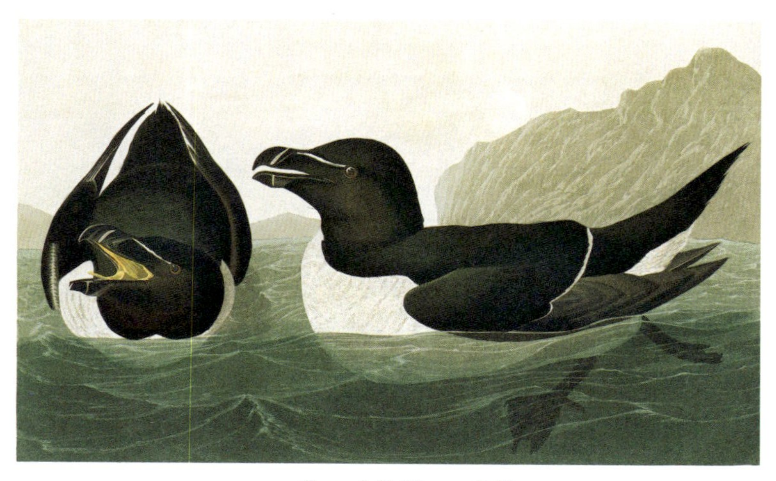

212  Razorbill [Razor Bill]
*Alca torda*

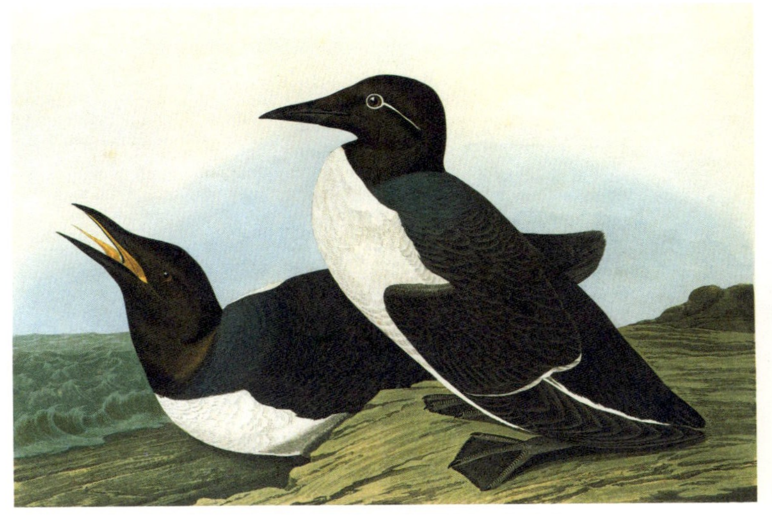

213  Common Murre [Foolish Guillemot]

*Uria aalge*

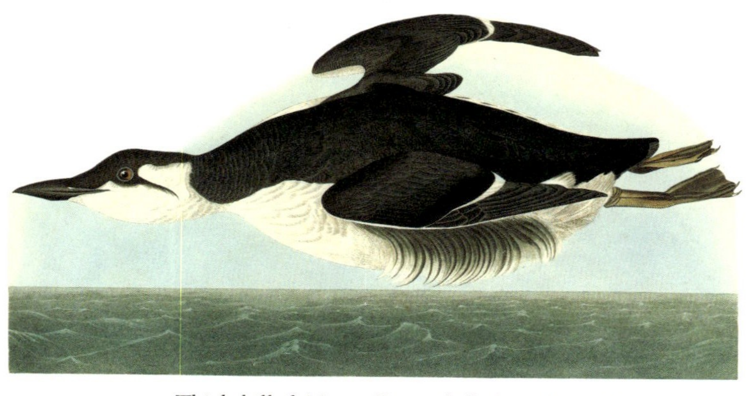

214  Thick-billed Murre [Large-billed Guillemot]
*Uria lomvia*

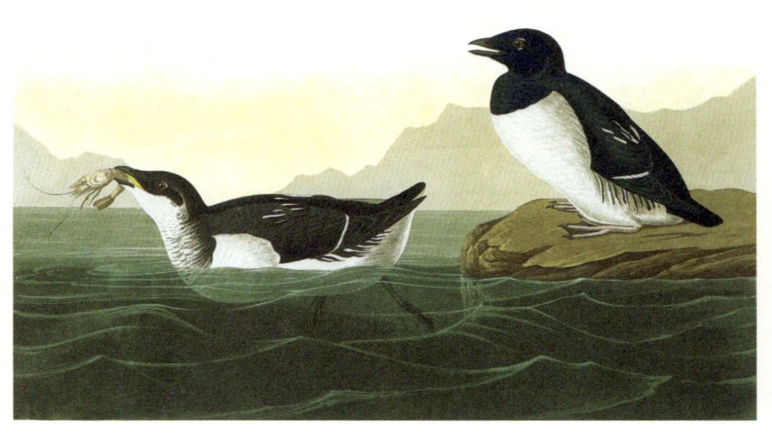

215 Dovekie [Little Auk]

*Alle alle*

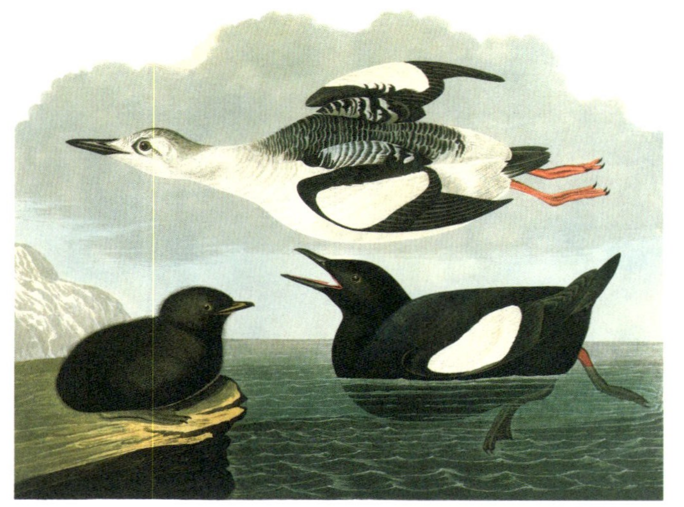

216  Black Guillemot

*Cepphus grylle*

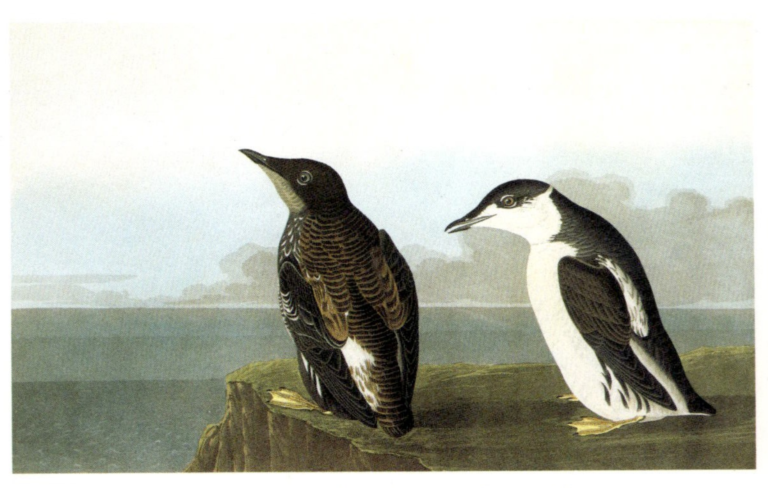

217  Marbled Murrelet [Slender-billed Guillemot]
*Brachyramphus marmoratus*

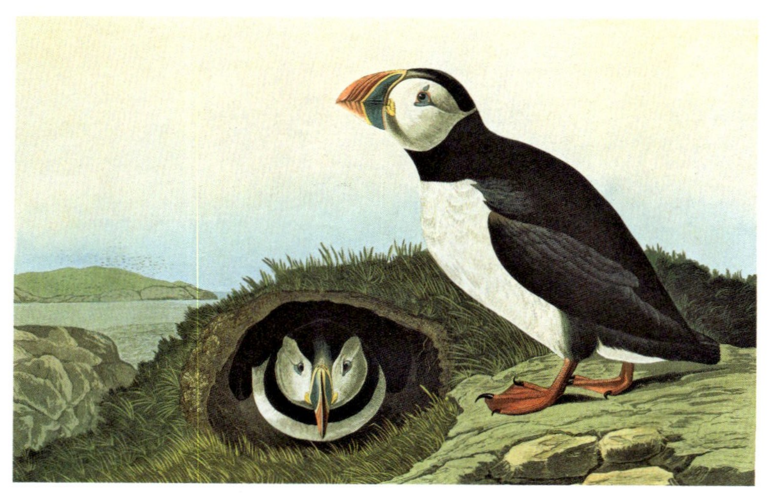

218  Atlantic Puffin [Puffin]
*Fratercula arctica*

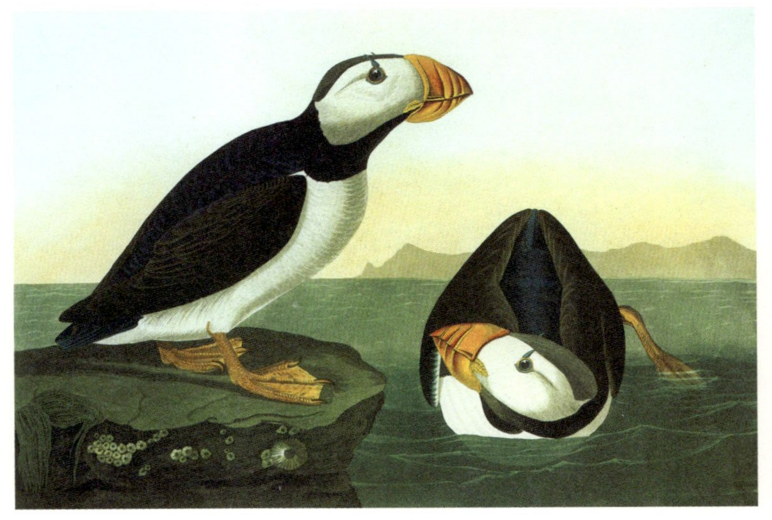

219  Horned Puffin [Large-billed Puffin]
*Fratercula corniculata*

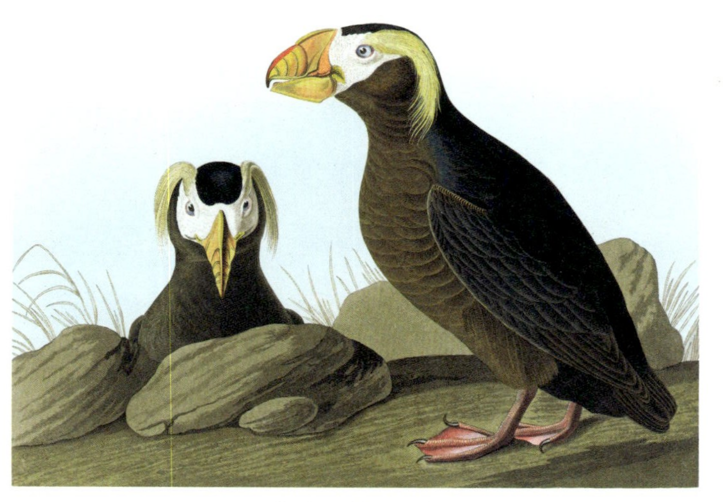

220  Tufted Puffin [Tufted Auk]
*Fratercula cirrhata*

Overleaf from left to right

221  Five Alcids [Auks]

Ancient Murrelet [Black-throated Guillemot]
*Synthliboramphus antiquus*

Marbled Murrelet [Black-throated Guillemot]
*Brachyramphus marmoratus*

Least Auklet [Nobbed-billed Phaleris]
*Aethia pusilla*

Crested Auklet [Curled-crested Phaleris]
*Aethia cristatella*

Rhinoceros Auklet [Horned-billed Guillemot]
*Cerorhinca monocerata*

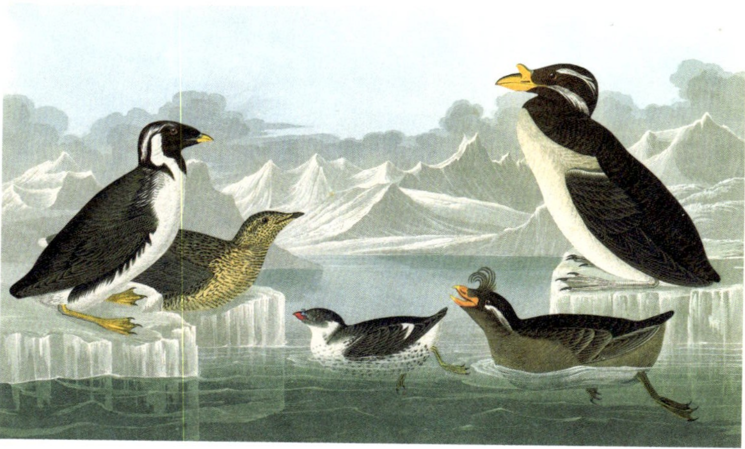

# VII

## SHOWY BIRDS, NOCTURNAL HUNTERS, AND SUPERB AERIALISTS

Pigeons, Parrots, Cuckoos, Owls, Nightjars,

Swifts, and Hummingbirds

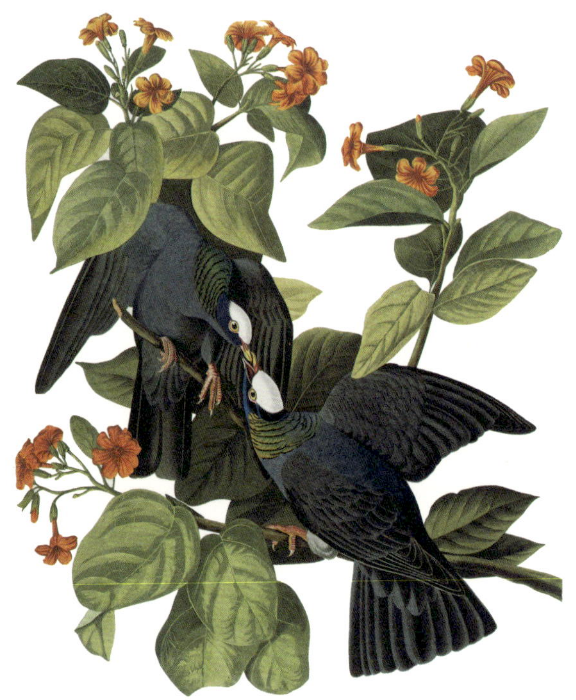

222 White-crowned Pigeon

*Patagioenas leucocephala*

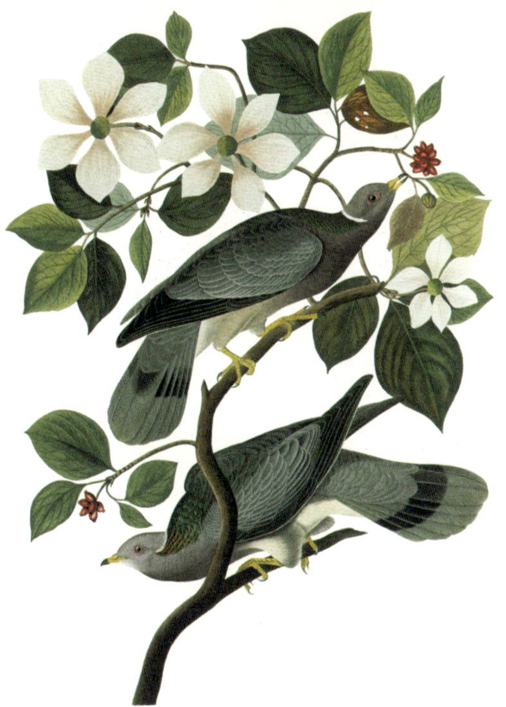

223  Band-tailed Pigeon
*Patagioenas fasciata*

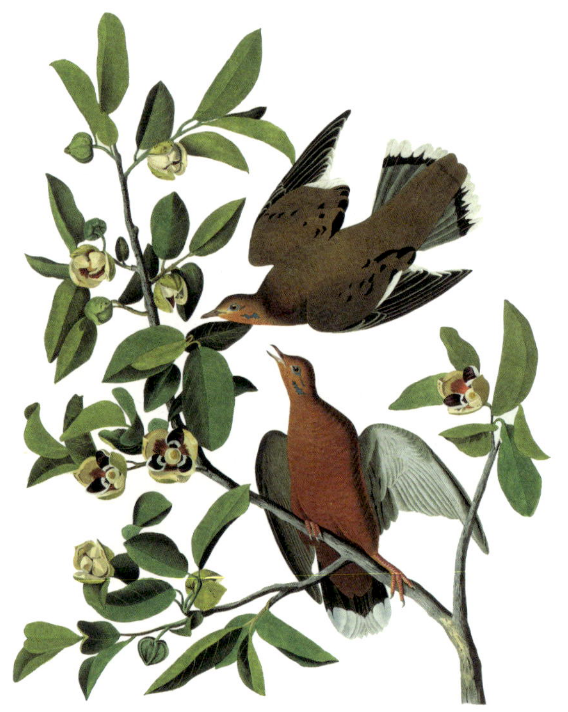

224  Zenaida Dove

*Zenaida aurita*

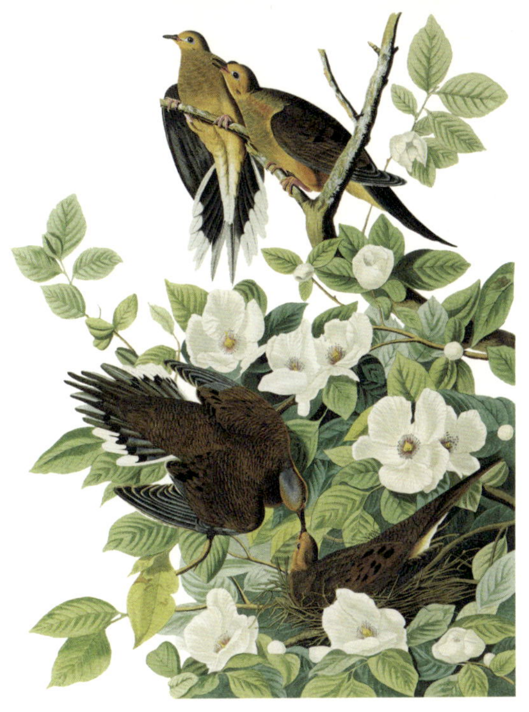

225  Mourning Dove [Carolina Turtle Dove or Carolina Pigeon]
*Zenaida macroura*

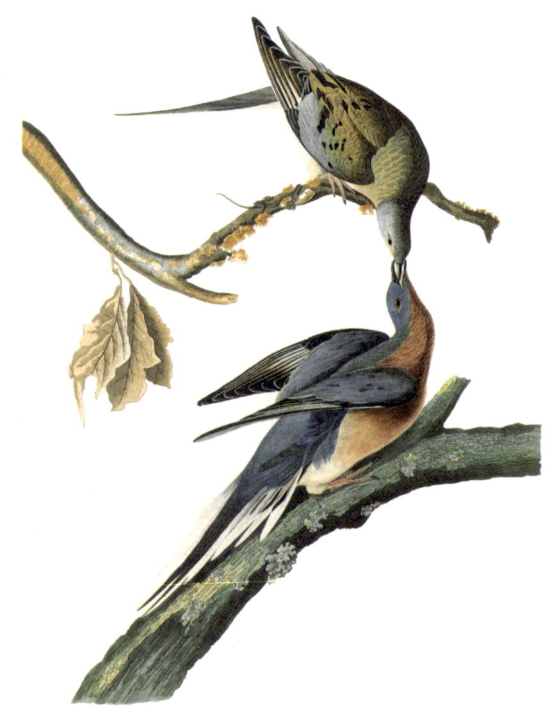

226  Passenger Pigeon
*Ectopistes migratorius*

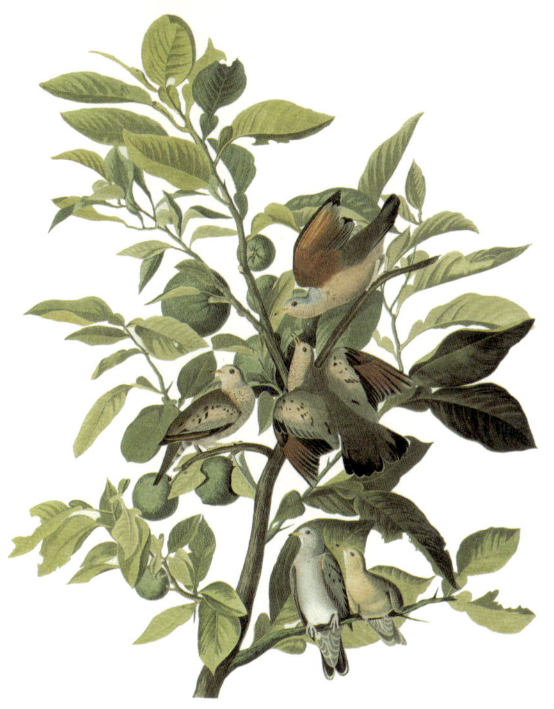

227  Common Ground Dove [Ground Dove]
*Columbina passerina*

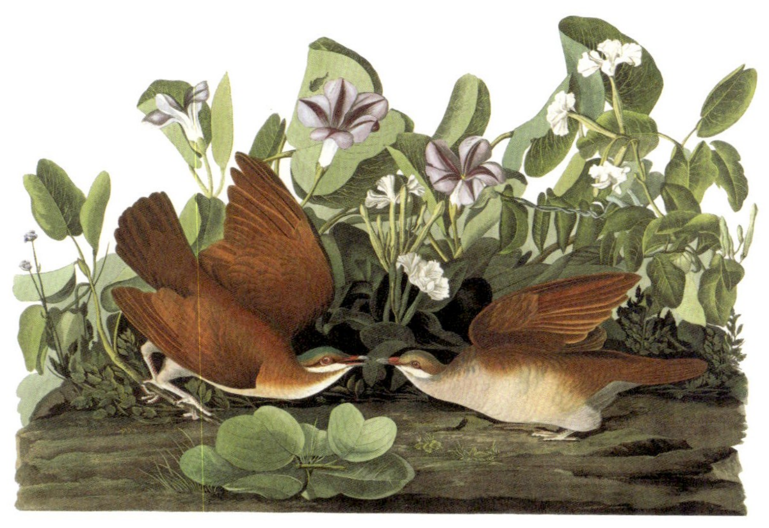

228 Key West Quail Dove [Key West Dove]
*Geotrygon chrysia*

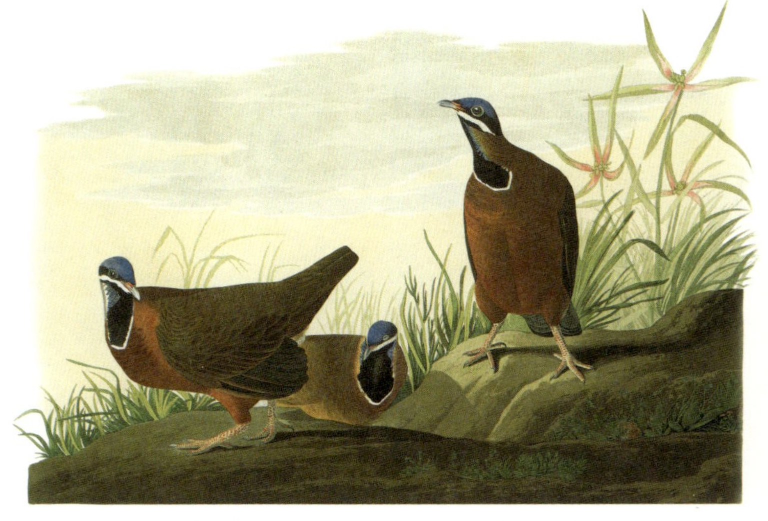

229  Blue-headed Quail Dove [Blue-headed Pigeon]
*Starnoenas cyanocephala*

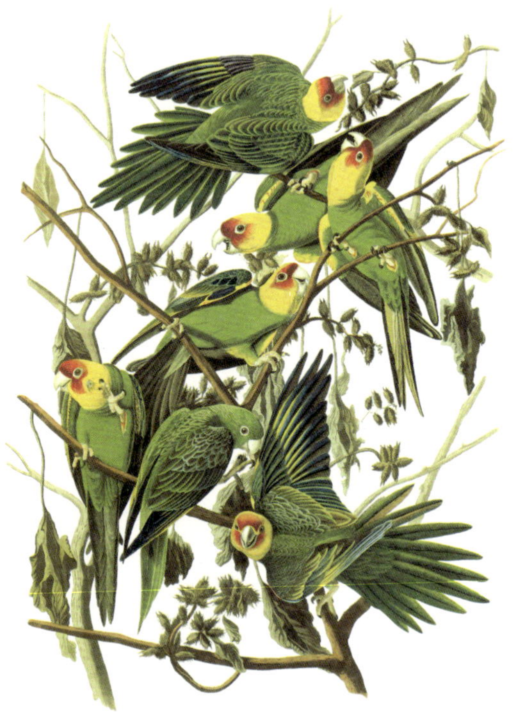

230  Carolina Parakeet [Carolina Parrot]
*Conuropsis carolinensis*

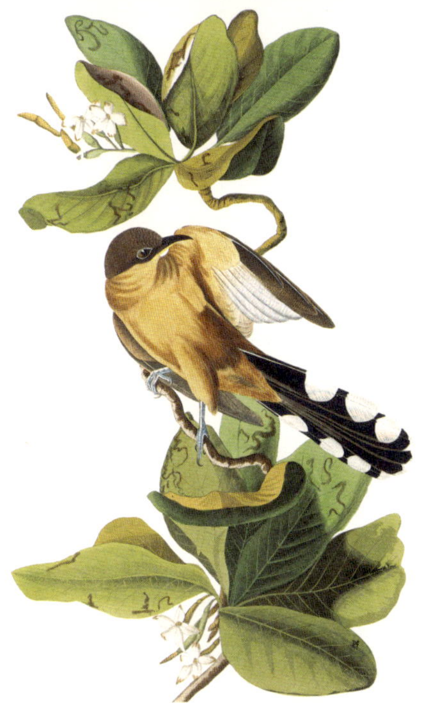

231  Mangrove Cuckoo
*Coccyzus minor*

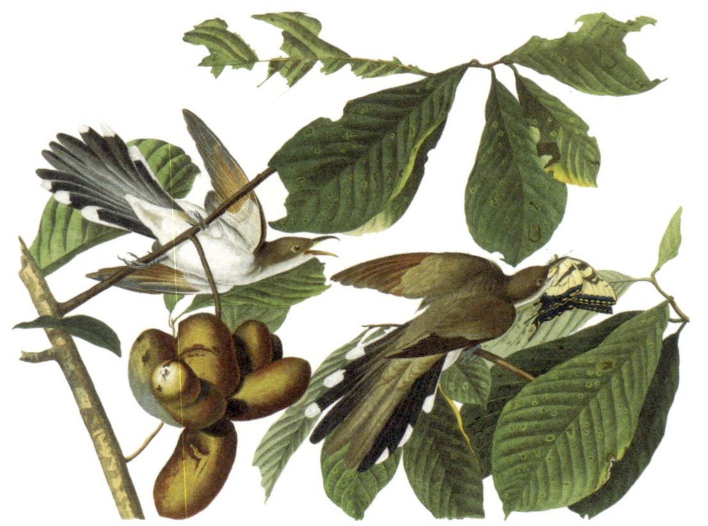

232  Yellow-billed Cuckoo
*Coccyzus americanus*

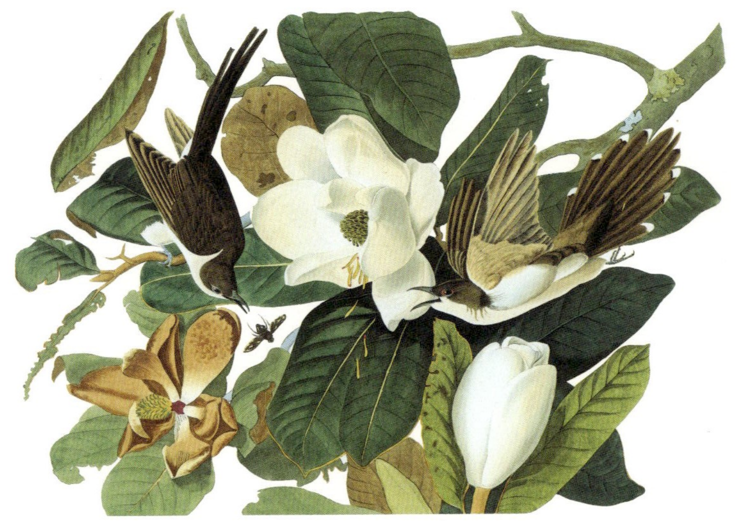

233  Black-billed Cuckoo
*Coccyzus erythropthalmus*

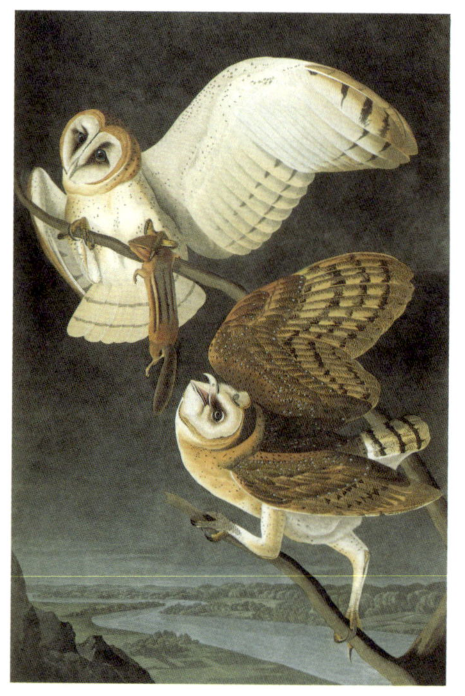

## 234  Barn Owl
*Tyto alba*

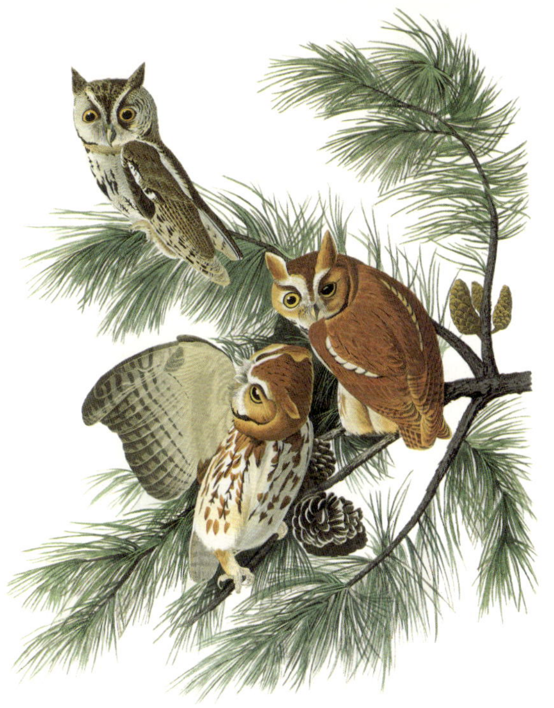

235  Eastern Screech-Owl [Mottled Owl]

*Megascops asio*

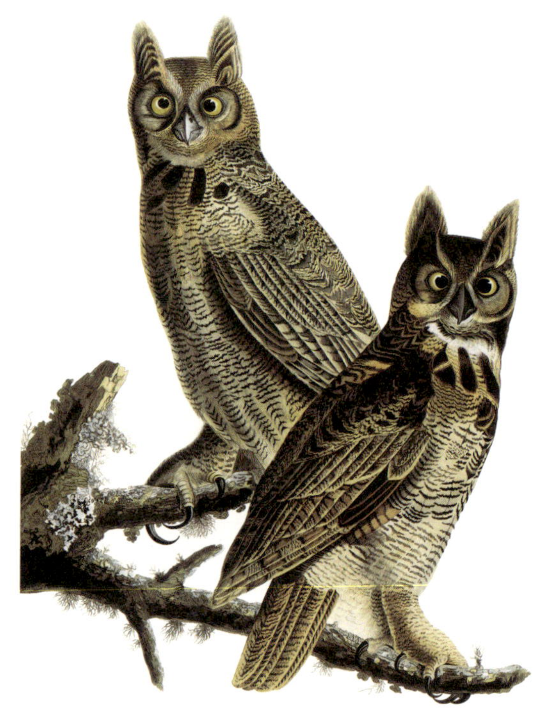

236  Great Horned Owl
*Bubo virginianus*

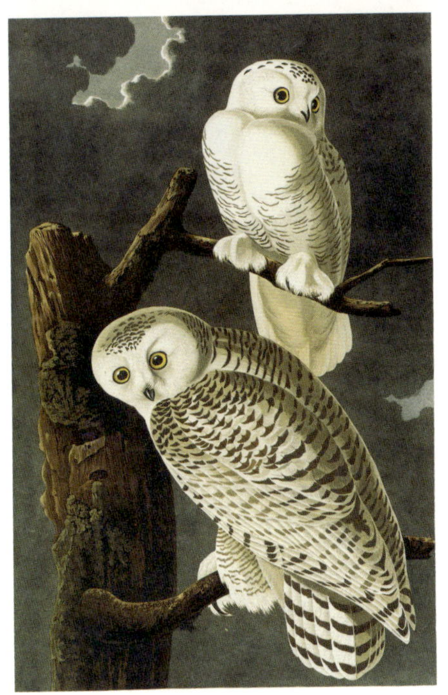

237  Snowy Owl
*Bubo scandiacus*

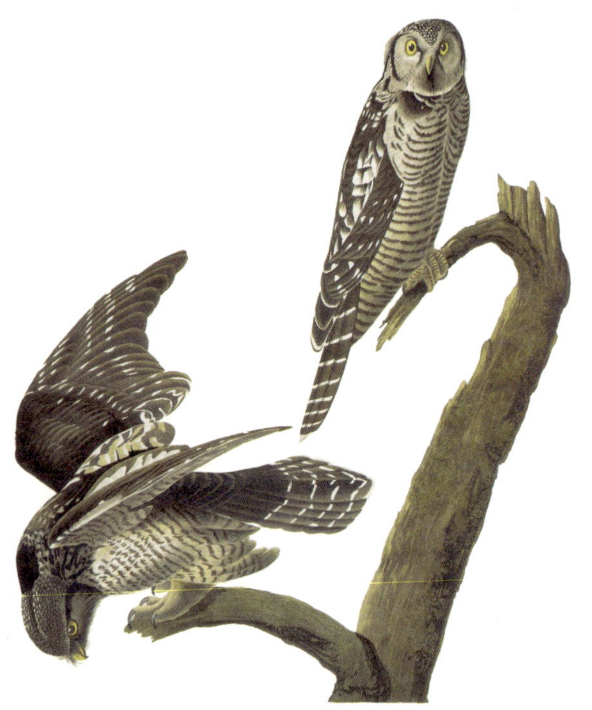

238  Northern Hawk-Owl
*Surnia ulula*

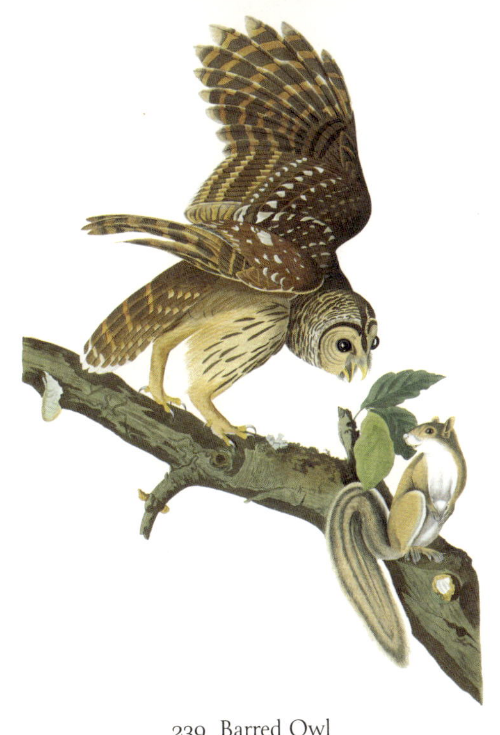

**239  Barred Owl**
*Strix varia*

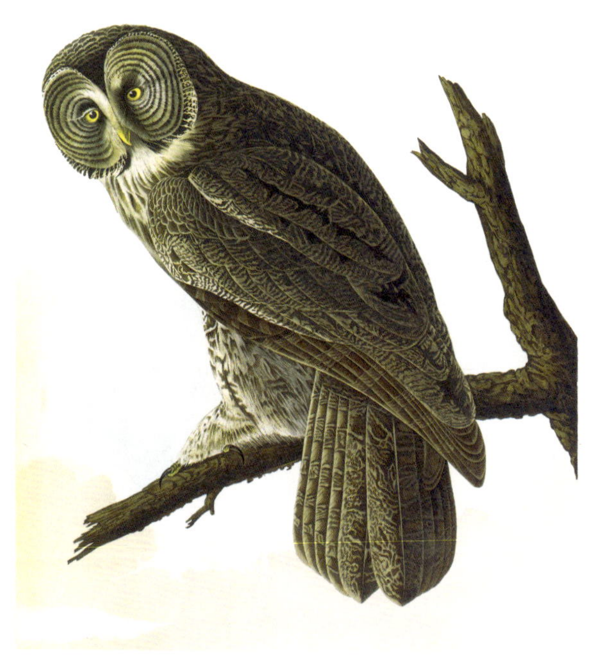

240  Great Gray Owl [Great Cinereous Owl]
*Strix nebulosa*

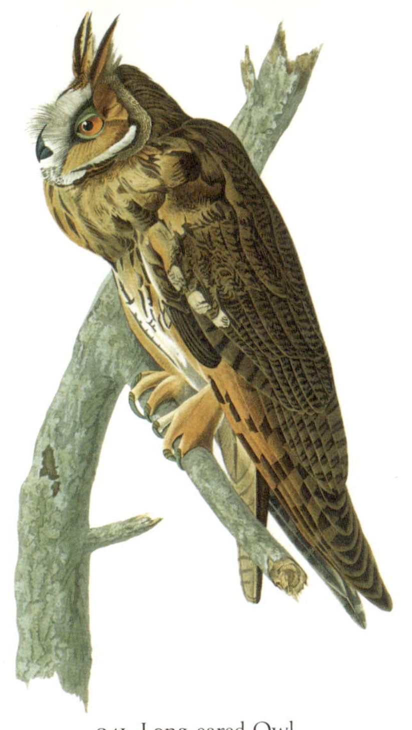

241  Long-eared Owl
*Asio otus*

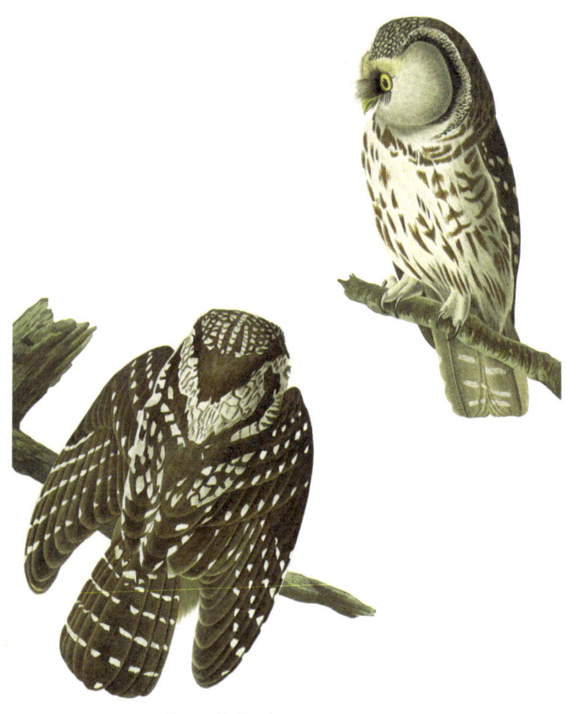

242  Boreal Owl [Tengmalm's Owl]
*Aegolius funereus*

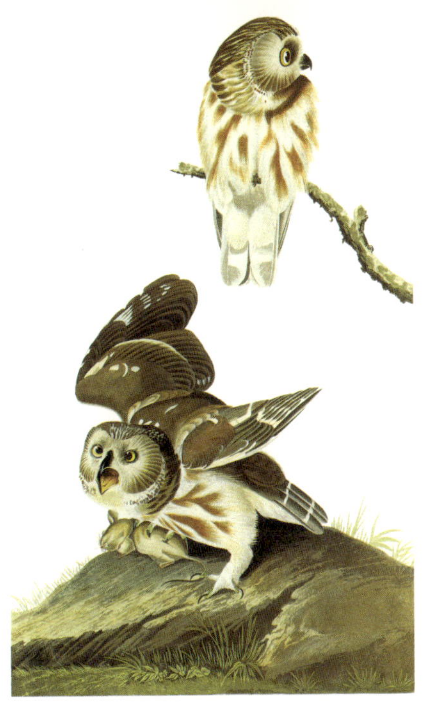

243  Saw-whet Owl [Little Owl]
*Aegolius acadicus*

Following page clockwise from left

244  Burrowing Owl [Large-headed Burrowing Owl]
*Athene cunicularia*

Little Owl? [Little Night Owl]
*Athene noctua?*

Northern Pygmy Owl [Columbian Owl]
*Glaucidium gnoma*

Short-eared Owl
*Asio flammeus*

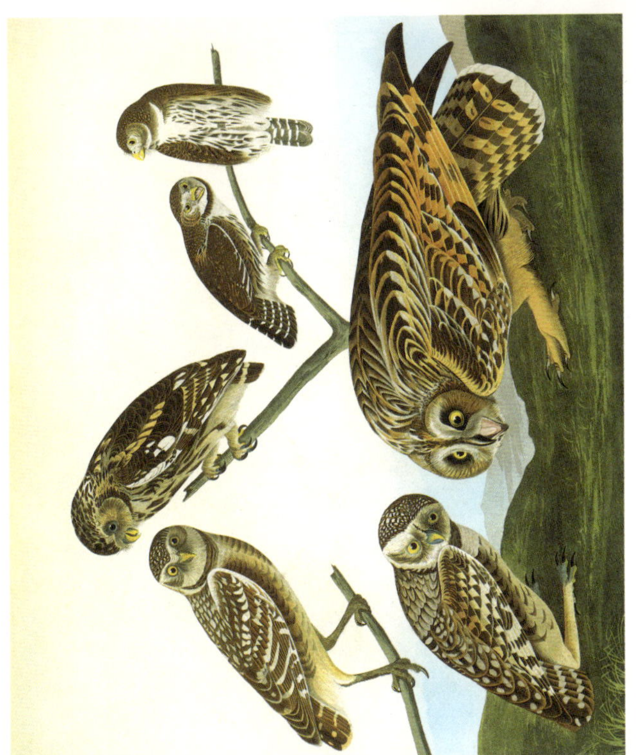

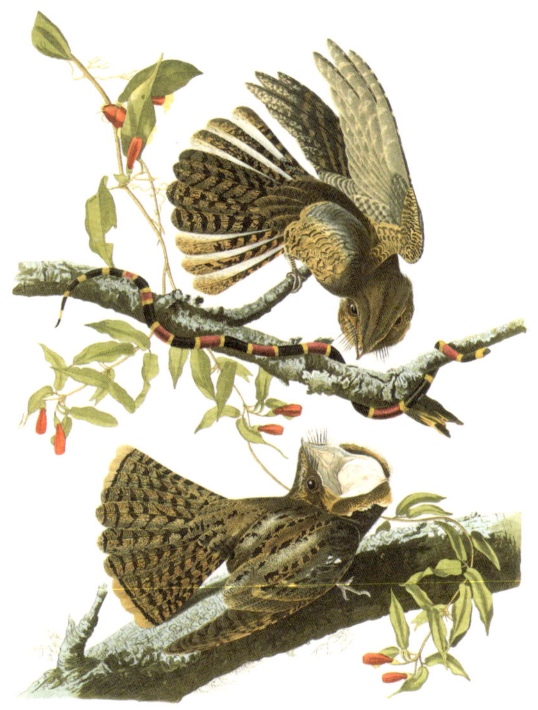

245  Chuck-will's-widow [Chuck Will's Widow]
*Antrostomus carolinensis*

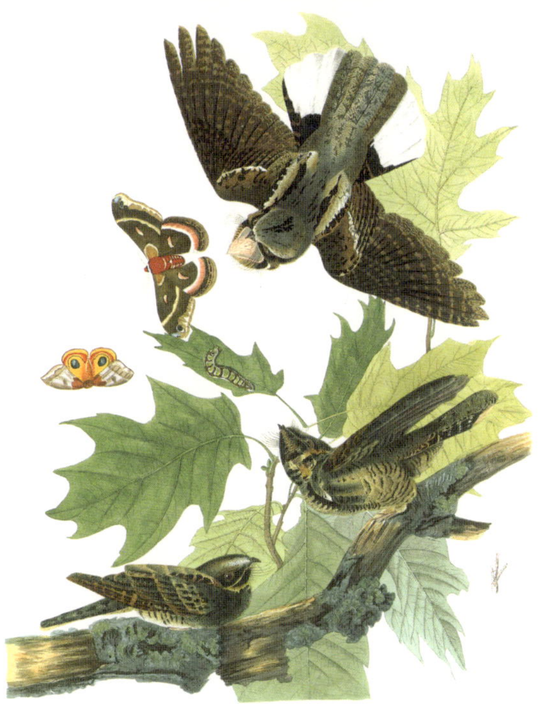

246 Whip-poor-will
*Antrostomus vociferus*

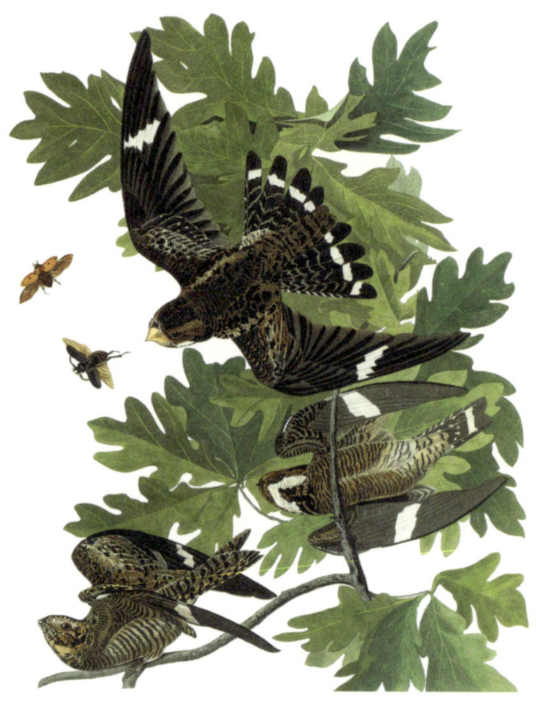

247  Common Nighthawk [Night Hawk]
*Chordeiles minor*

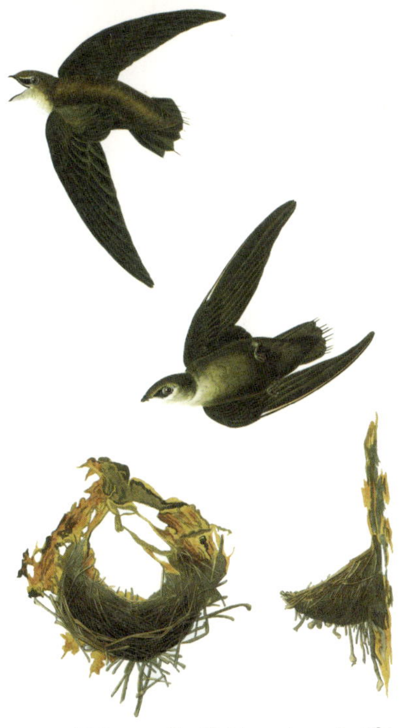

248  Chimney Swift [American Swift]
*Chaetura pelagica*

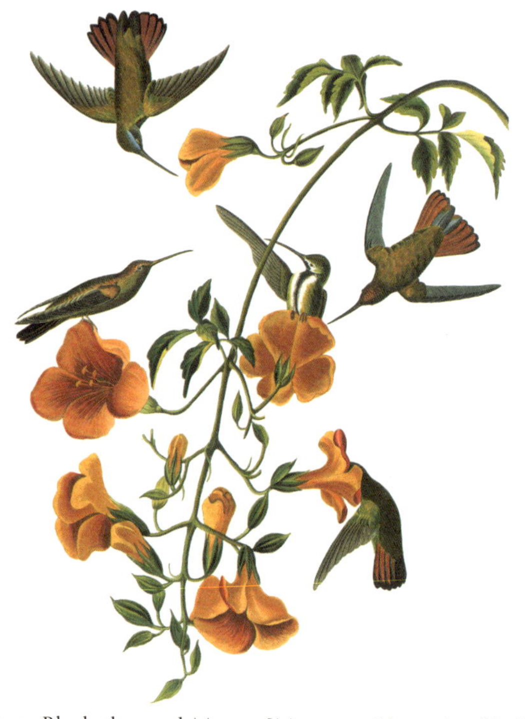

249  Black-throated Mango [Mangrove Humming Bird]
*Anthracothorax nigricollis*

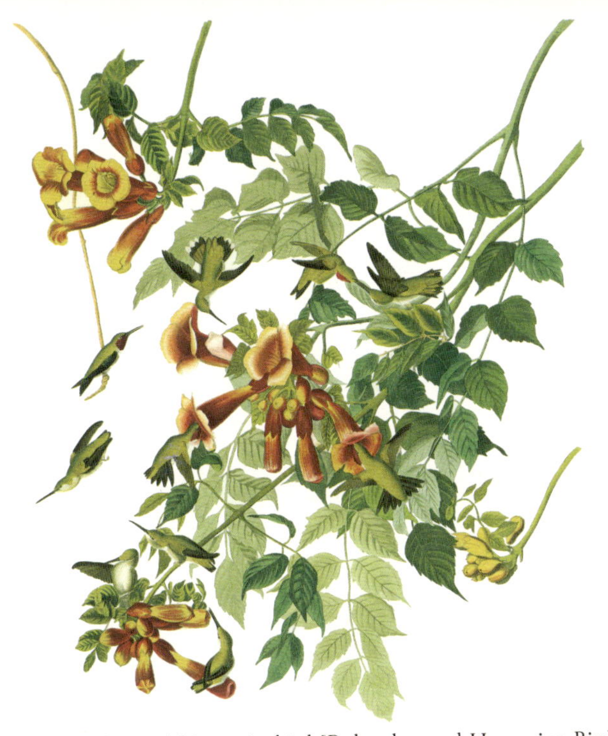

250  Ruby-throated Hummingbird [Ruby-throated Humming Bird]
*Archilochus colubris*

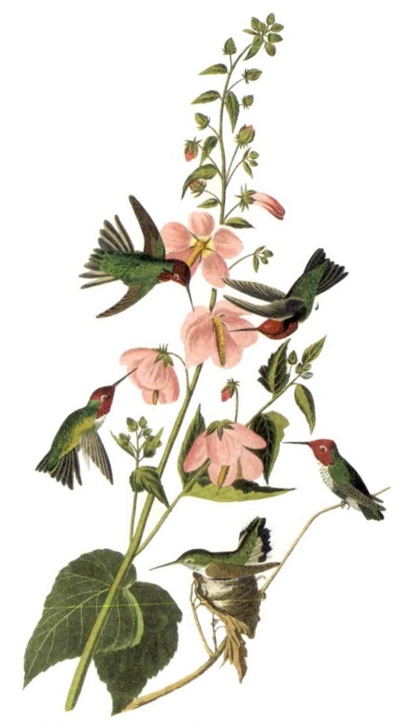

251  Anna's Hummingbird [Columbian Humming Bird]
*Calypte anna*

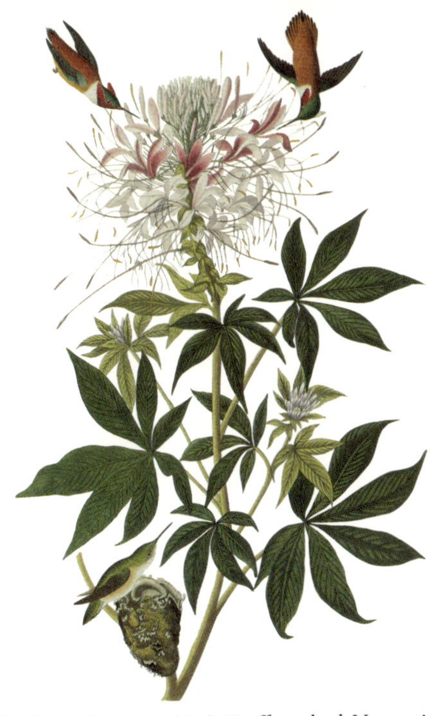

252  Rufous Hummingbird [Ruff-necked Humming-bird]
*Selasphorus rufus*

# VIII

## GLEANERS OF FOREST
## AND MEADOW

Kingfishers, Woodpeckers, Tyrant Flycatchers,

Larks, Swallows, Jays, Magpies, Crows,

Titmice, and Nuthatches

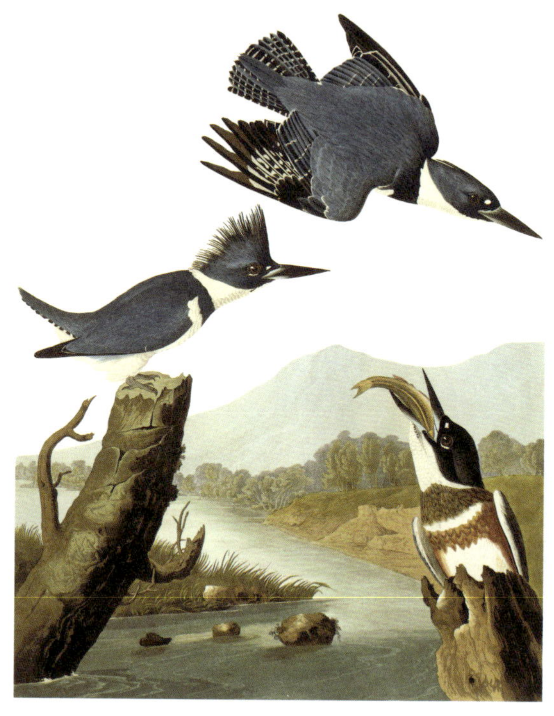

253  Belted Kingfisher

*Megaceryle alcyon*

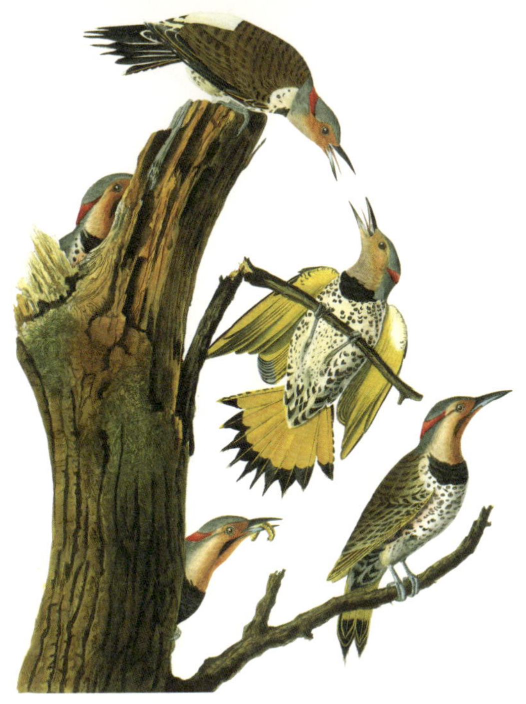

254  Northern Flicker [Golden-winged Woodpecker]
*Colaptes auratus*

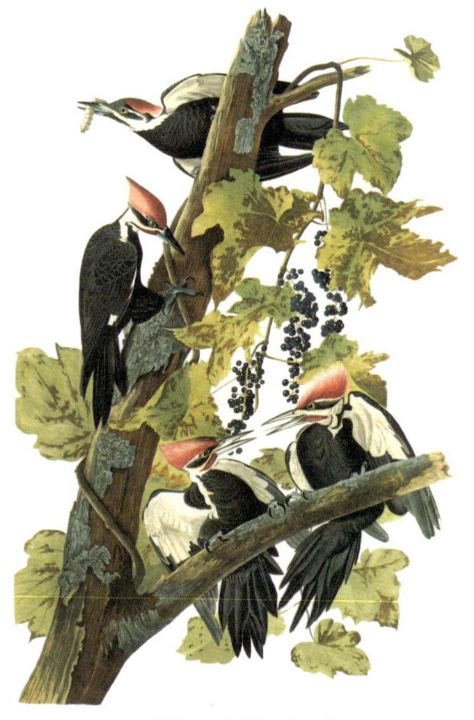

**255  Pileated Woodpecker**
*Dryocopus pileatus*

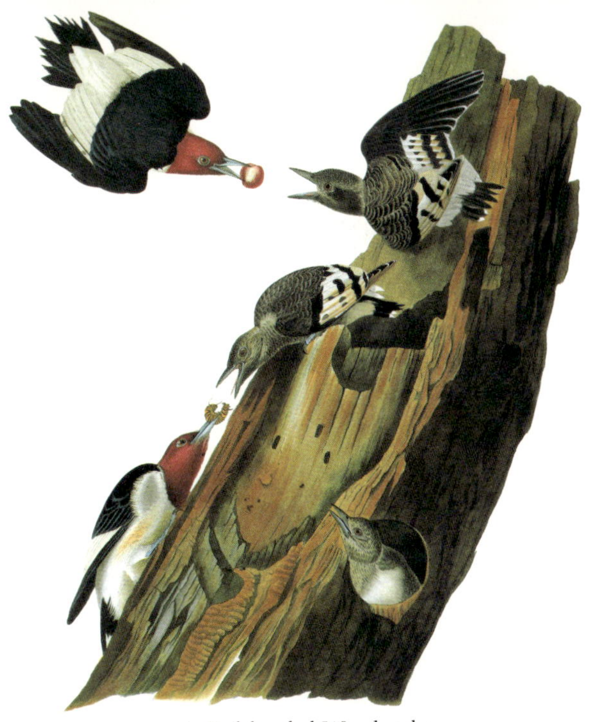

256  Red-headed Woodpecker
*Melanerpes erythrocephalus*

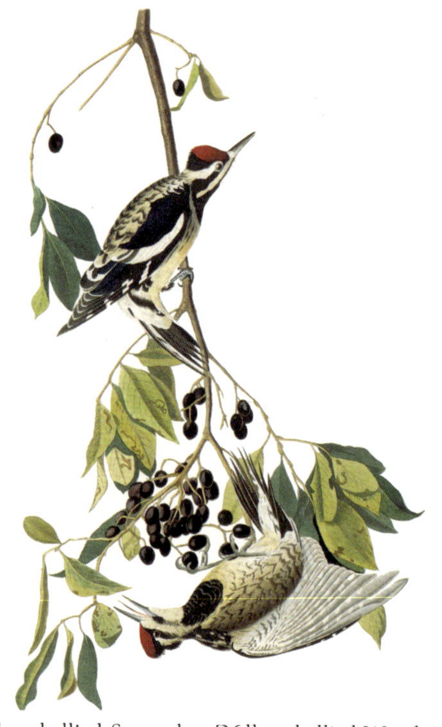

257  Yellow-bellied Sapsucker [Yellow-bellied Woodpecker]
*Sphyrapicus varius*

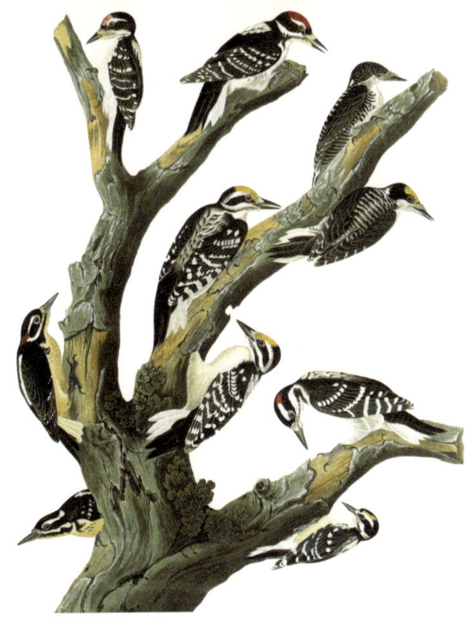

258  Hairy Woodpecker [Maria's, Phillips's, Canadian, Harris's and Audubon's Woodpeckers]
*Dryobates villosus*

Three-toed Woodpecker [Banded Three-toed Woodpecker]
*Picoides dorsalis*

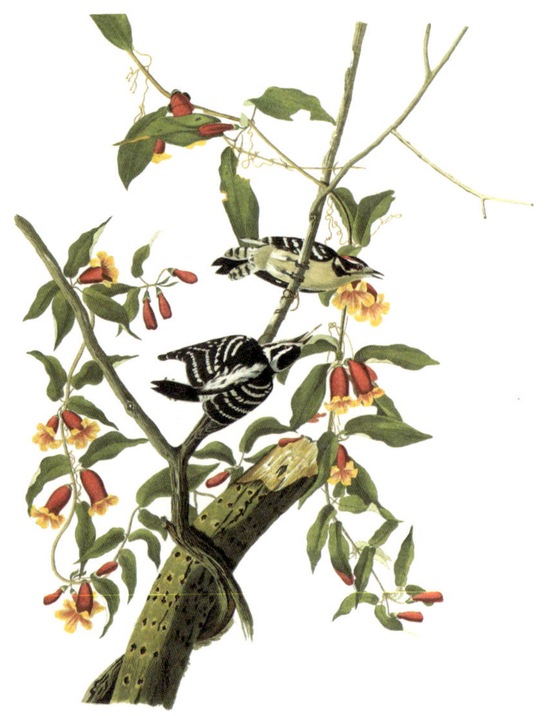

259  Downy Woodpecker
*Dryobates pubescens*

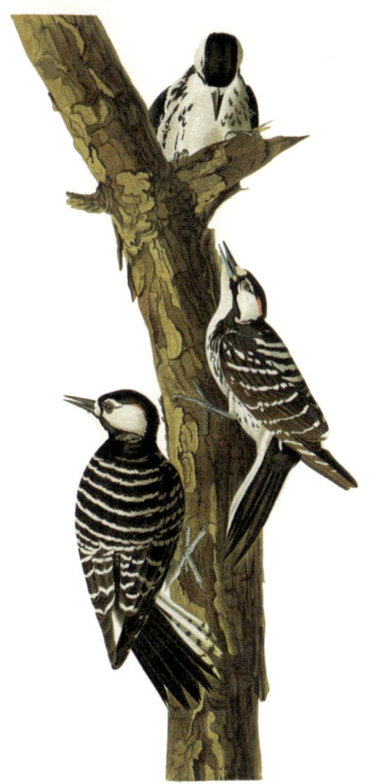

260 Red-cockaded Woodpecker
*Dryobates borealis*

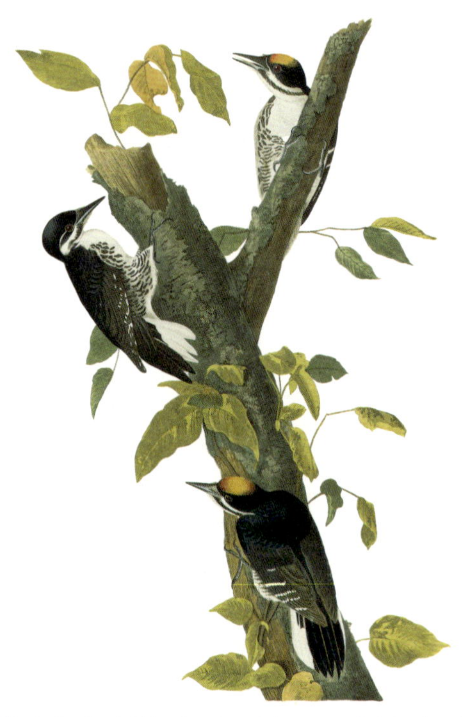

261  Black-backed Woodpecker [Three-toed Woodpecker]
*Picoides arcticus*

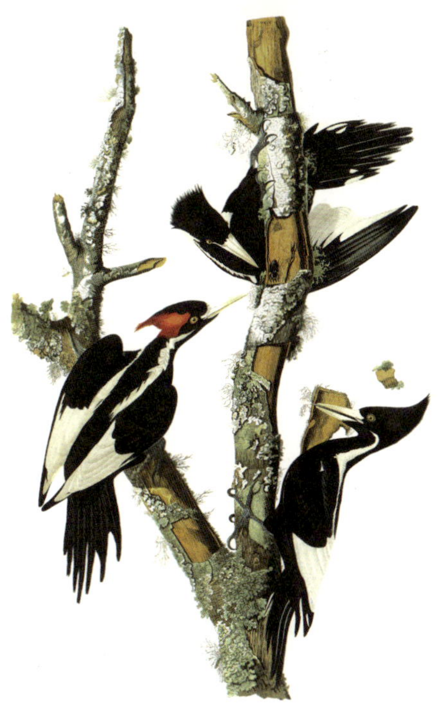

262  Ivory-billed Woodpecker
*Campephilus principalis*

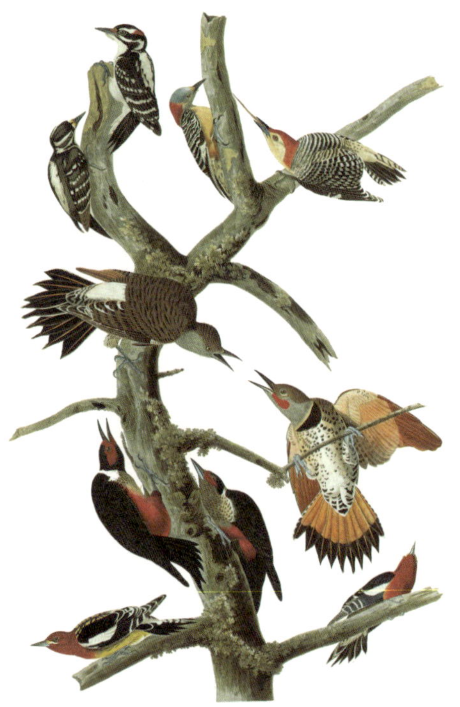

263  Hairy Woodpecker
*Dryobates villosus*

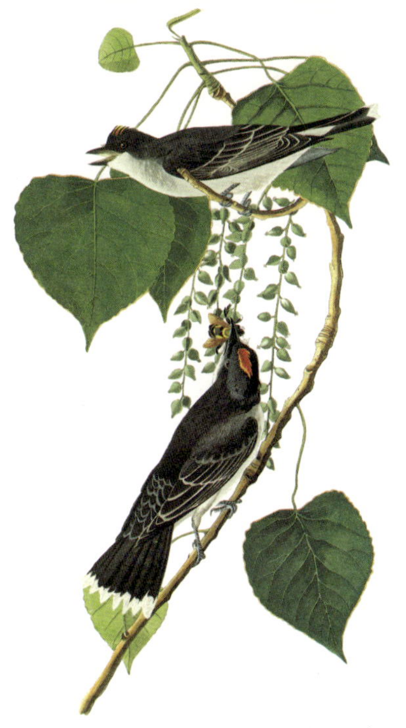

264  Eastern Kingbird [Tyrant Flycatcher]
*Tyrannus tyrannus*

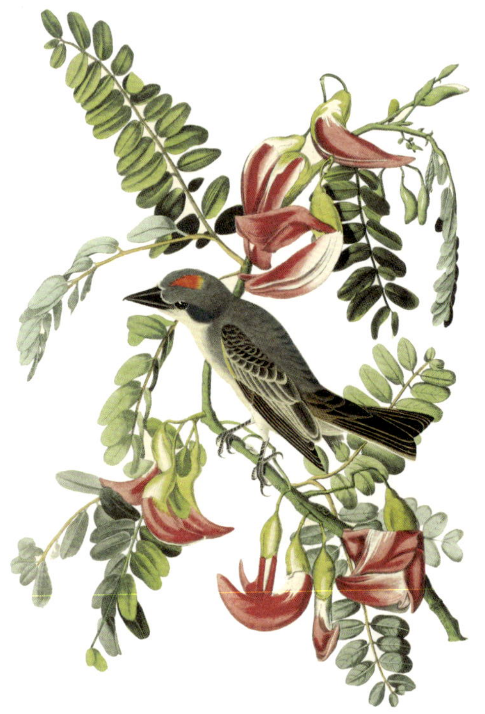

265  Gray Kingbird [Gray Tyrant]
*Tyrannus dominicensis*

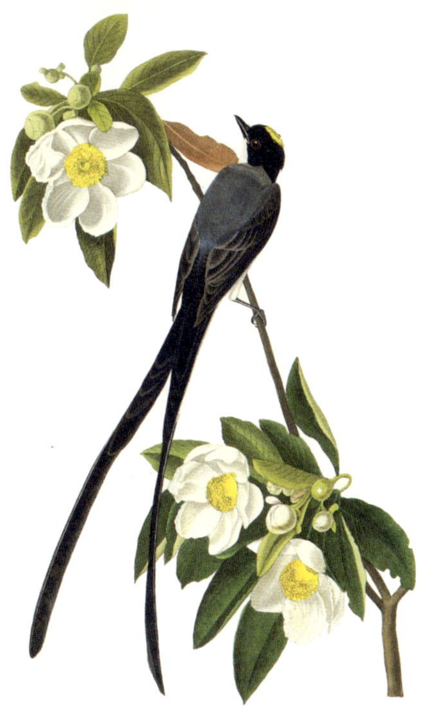

266  Fork-tailed Flycatcher
*Tyrannus savana*

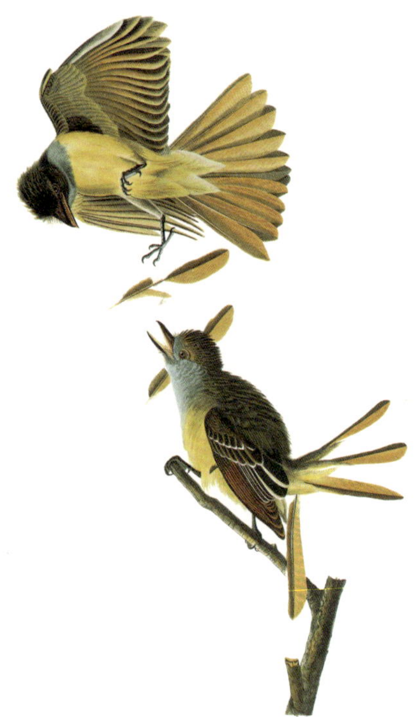

267  Great Crested Flycatcher
*Myiarchus crinitus*

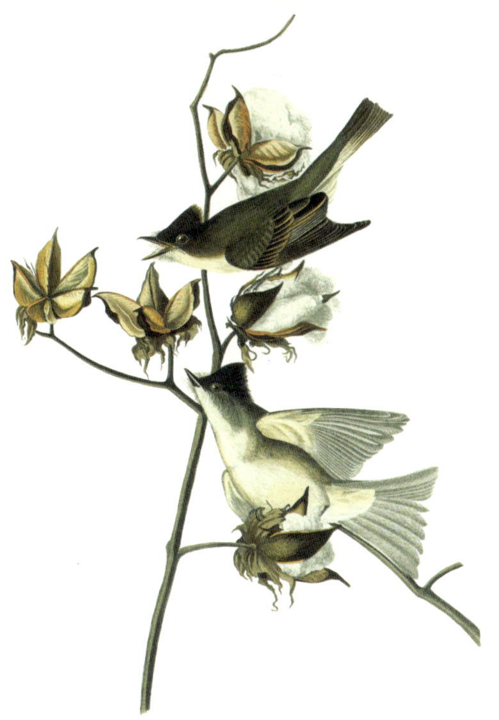

268  Eastern Phoebe [Pewit Flycatcher]
*Sayornis phoebe*

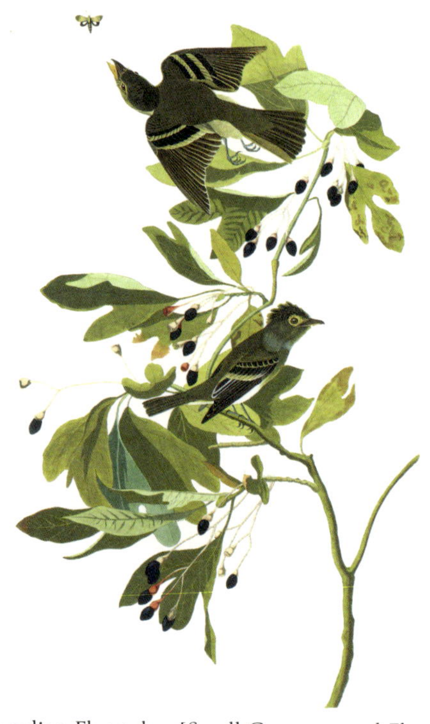

269  Acadian Flycatcher [Small Green-crested Flycatcher]
*Empidonax virescens*

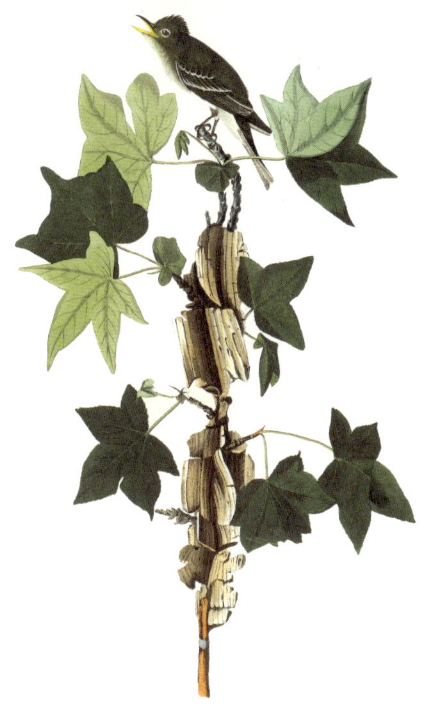

270  Willow Flycatcher [Traill's Flycatcher]
*Empidonax traillii*

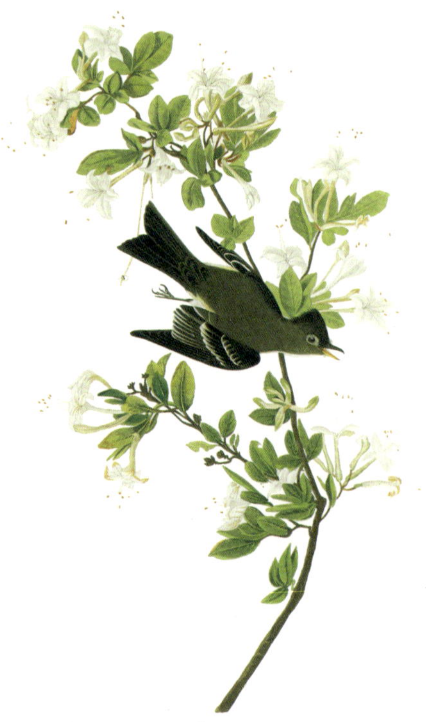

271  Eastern Wood-Pewee [Wood Pewee]

*Contopus virens*

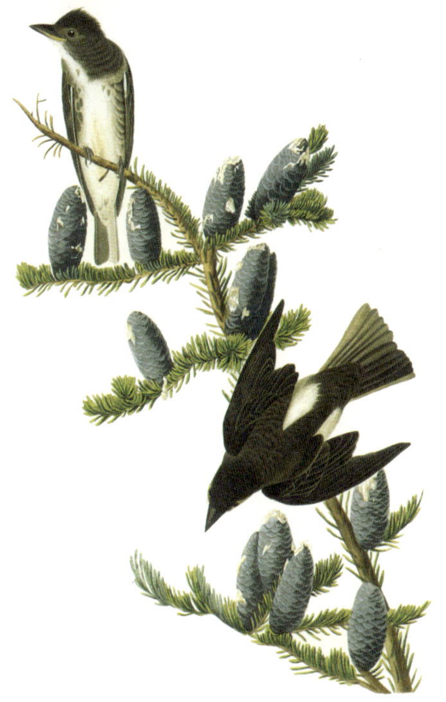

272  Olive-sided Flycatcher

*Contopus cooperi*

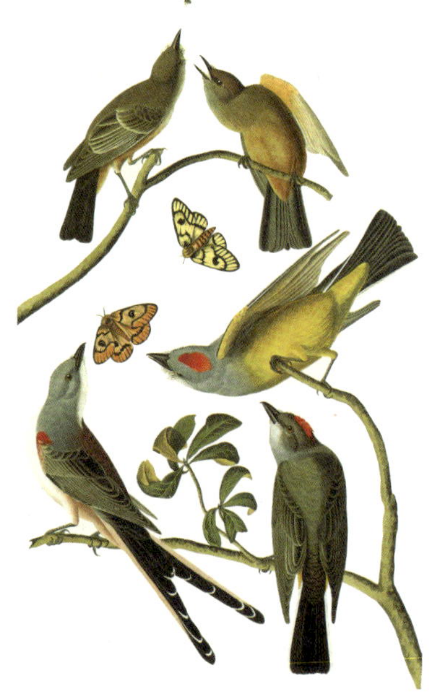

273  Say's Phoebe [Say's Flycatcher]
*Sayornis saya*

Western Kingbird
[Arkansaw Flycatcher]
*Tyrannus verticalis*

Scissor-tailed Flycatcher
[Swallow-tailed Flycatcher]
*Tyrannus forficatus*

Following page clockwise from top

274  "Blue Mountain Warbler"
*Dendroica montana*

Yellow-green Vireo [Bartram's Vireo]
*Vireo flavoviridis*

Least Flycatcher [Little Tyrant Flycatcher]
*Empidonax minimus*

Black Phobe [Rocky Mountain Flycatcher]
*Sayornis nigricans*

"Small-headed Warbler" [Small-headed Flycatcher]
*Wilsonia[?] microcephala*

Alder Flycatcher [Short-legged Pewee]
*Empidonax alnorum*

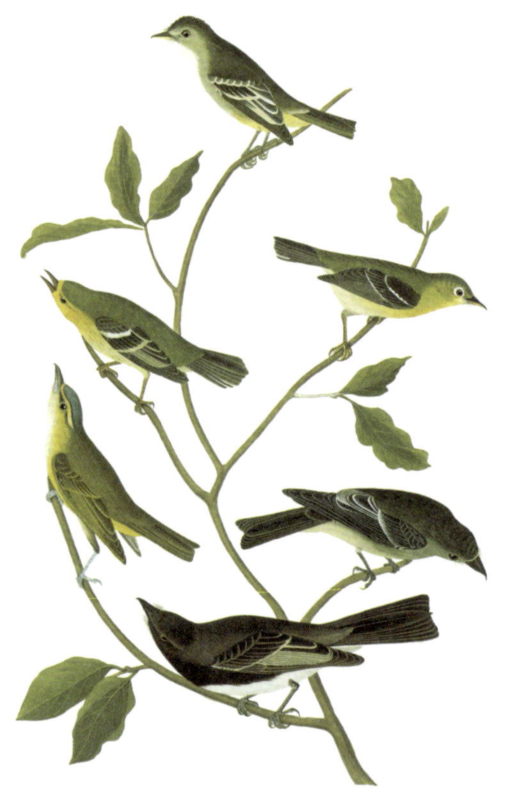

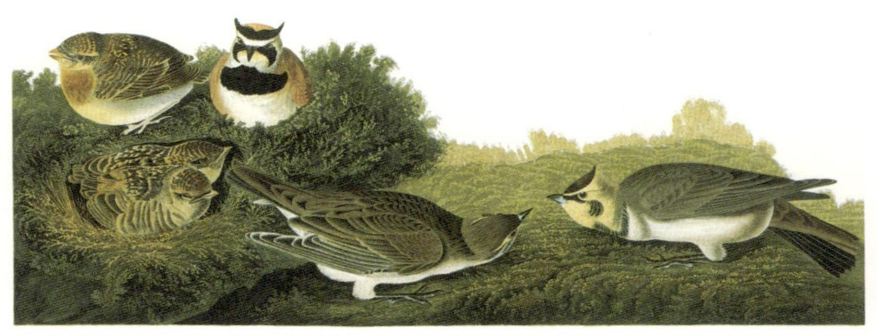

275  Horned Lark [Shore Lark]
*Eremophila alpestris*

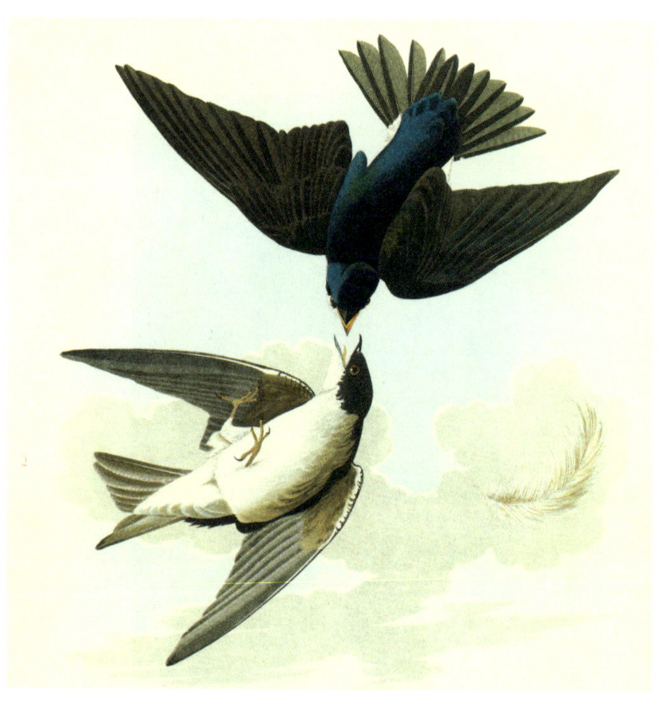

276 Tree Swallow [White-bellied Swallow or Green-blue Swallow]
*Tachycineta bicolor*

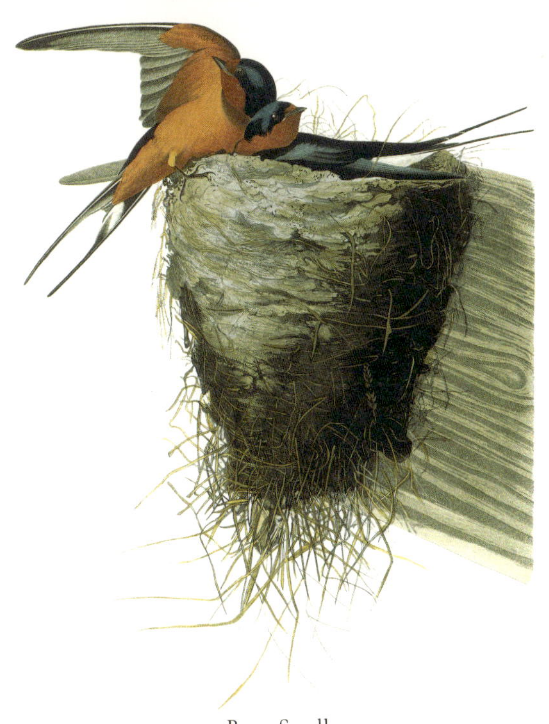

## 277 Barn Swallow
*Hirundo rustica*

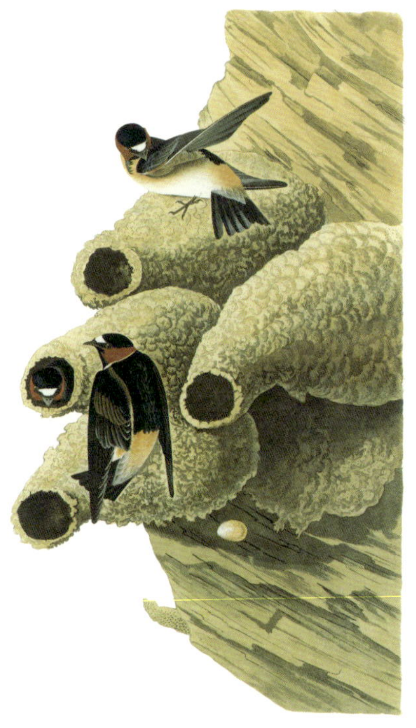

278  Cliff Swallow [Republican Cliff Swallow]
*Petrochelidon pyrrhonota*

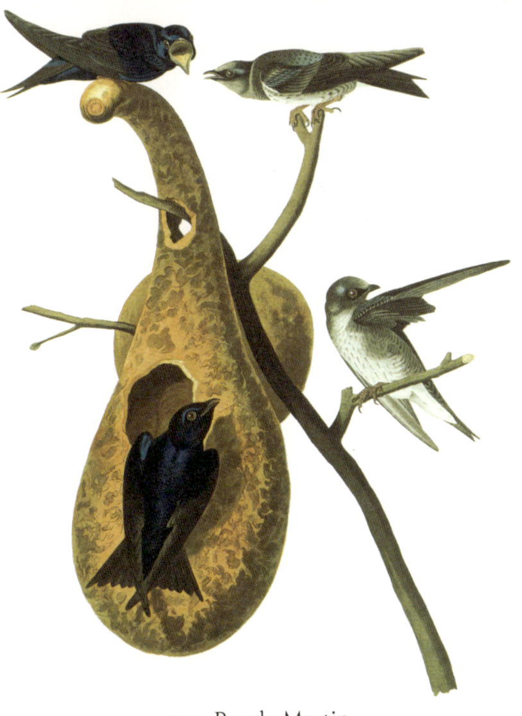

279  Purple Martin
*Progne subis*

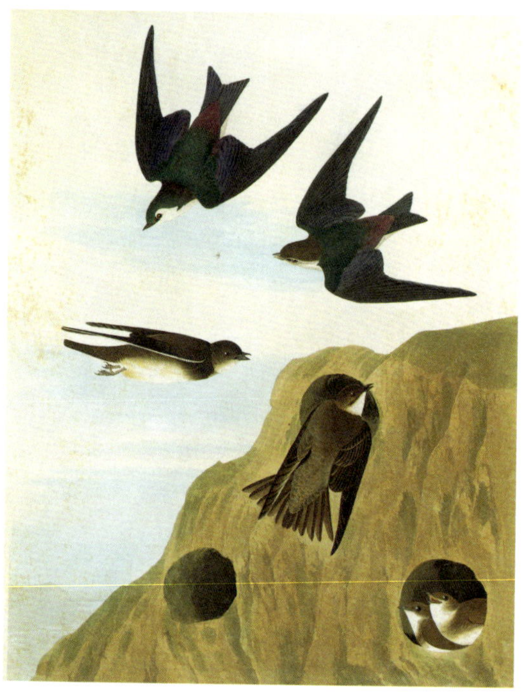

280 Violet-green Swallow
*Tachycineta thalassina*

Bank Swallow
*Riparia riparia*

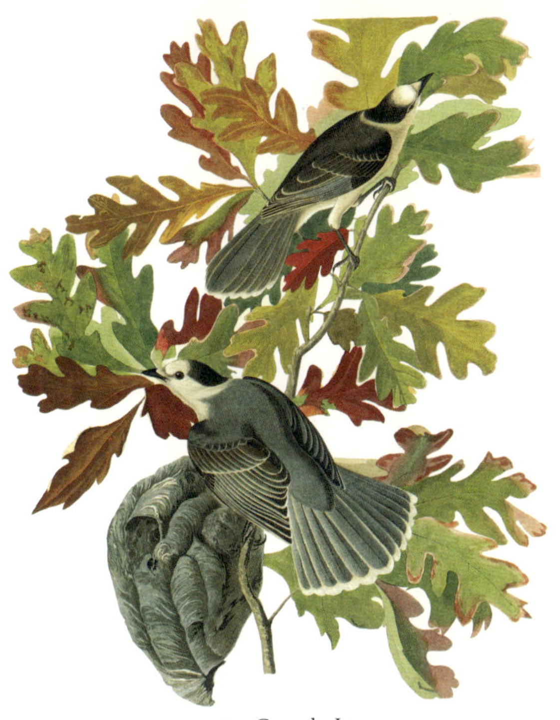

281  Canada Jay

*Perisoreus canadensis*

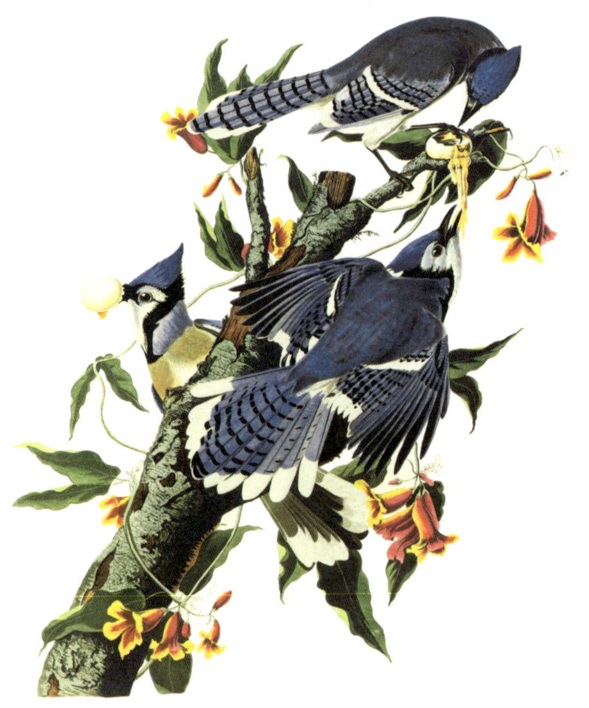

**282  Blue Jay**
*Cyanocitta cristata*

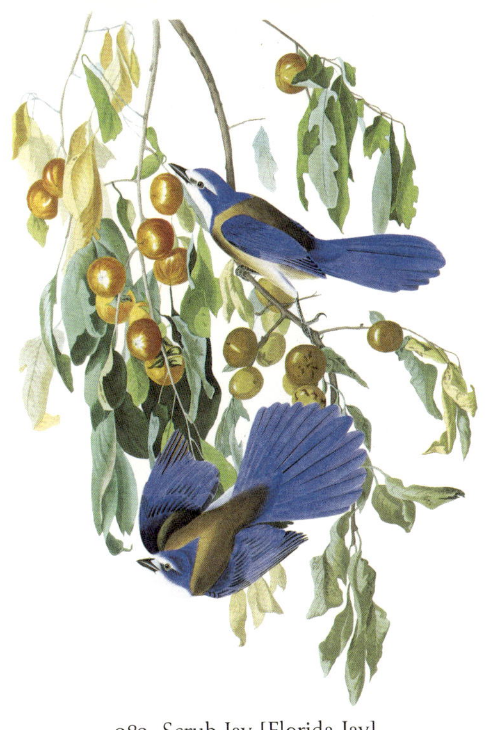

**283  Scrub Jay [Florida Jay]**

*Aphelocoma coerulescens*

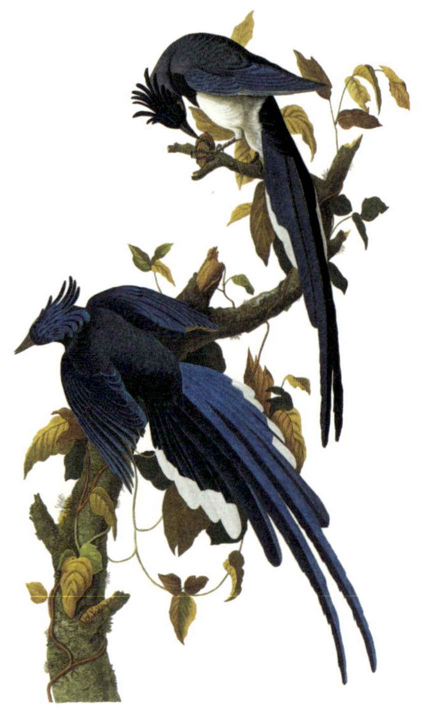

284  Black-throated Magpie-jay
*Calocitta colliei*

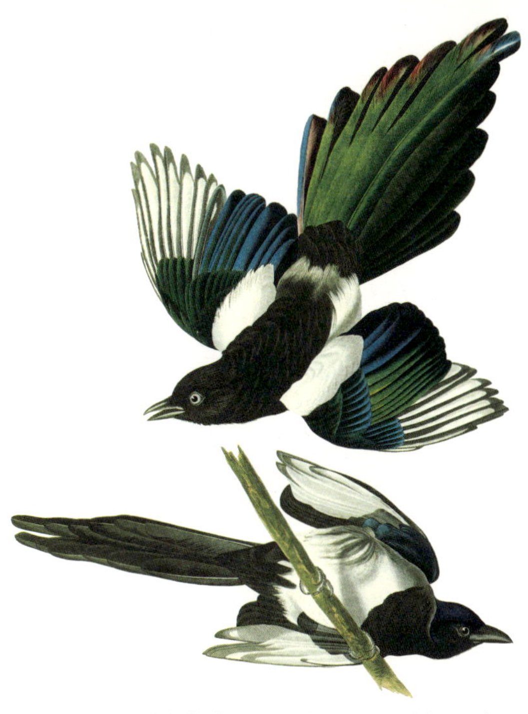

285  Black-billed Magpie [American Magpie]
*Pica hudsonia*

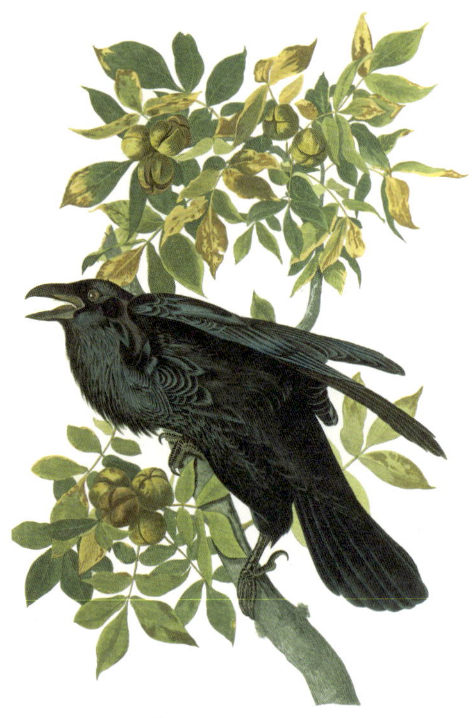

**286  Common Raven [Raven]**

*Corvus corax*

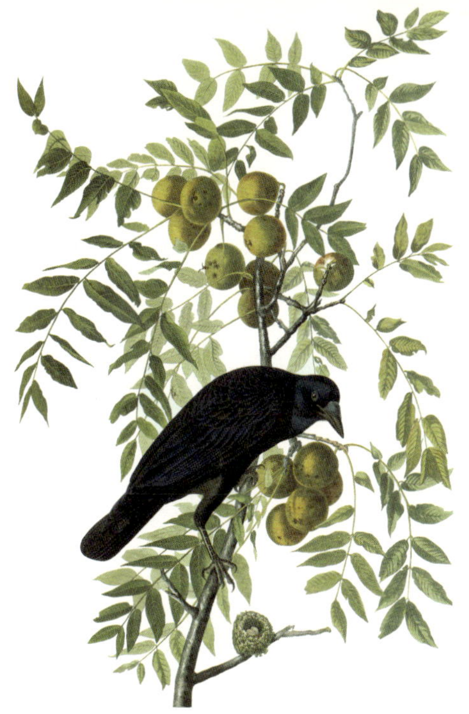

287  American Crow
*Corvus brachyrhynchos*

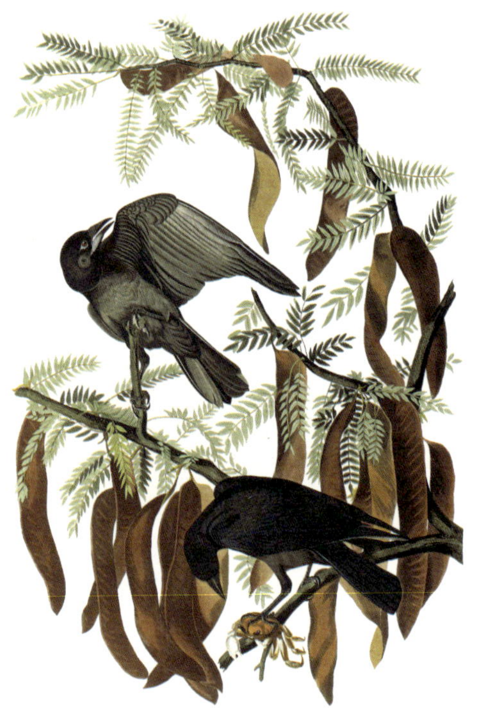

## 288  Fish Crow

*Corvus ossifragus*

Following page from top to bottom

289  Scrub Jay [Ultramarine Jay]
*Aphelocoma coerulescens*

Steller's Jay
*Cyanocitta stelleri*

Yellow-billed Magpie
*Pica nuttalli*

Clark's Nutcracker [Clark's Crow]
*Nucifraga columbiana*

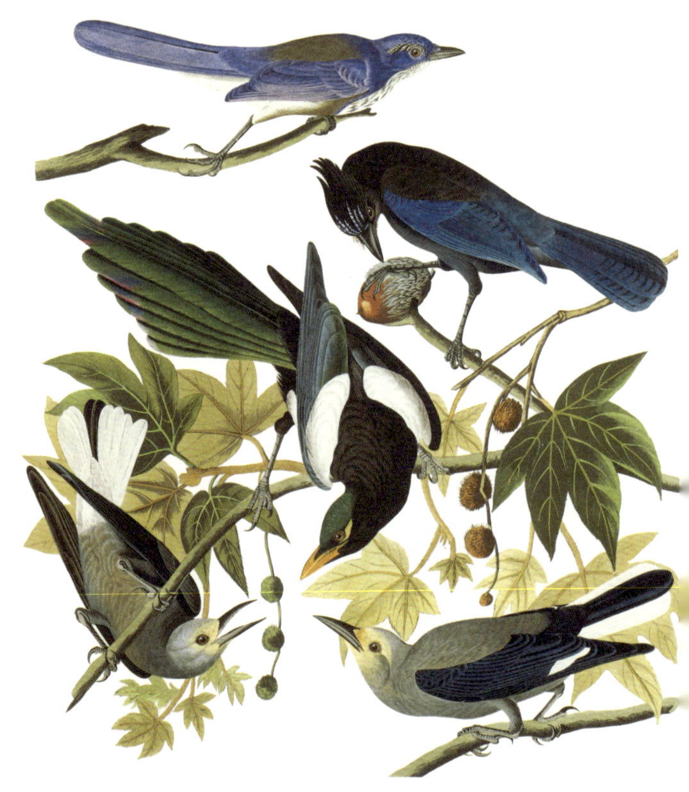

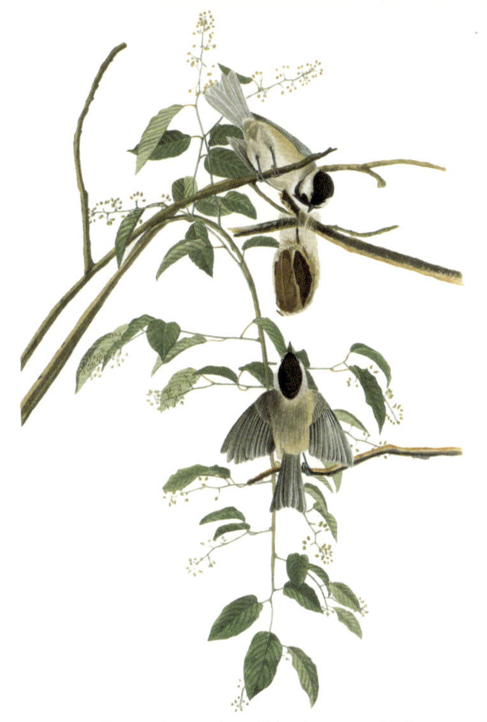

290  Carolina Chickadee [Black-capped Titmouse]
*Poecile carolinensis*

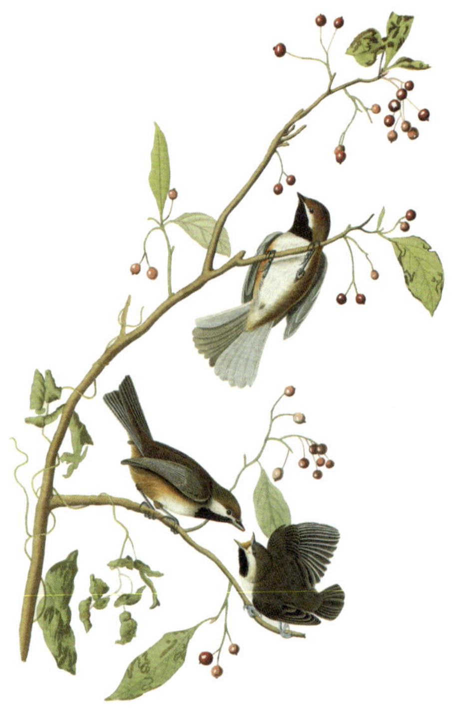

291  Boreal Chickadee [Canadian Titmouse]
*Poecile hudsonicus*

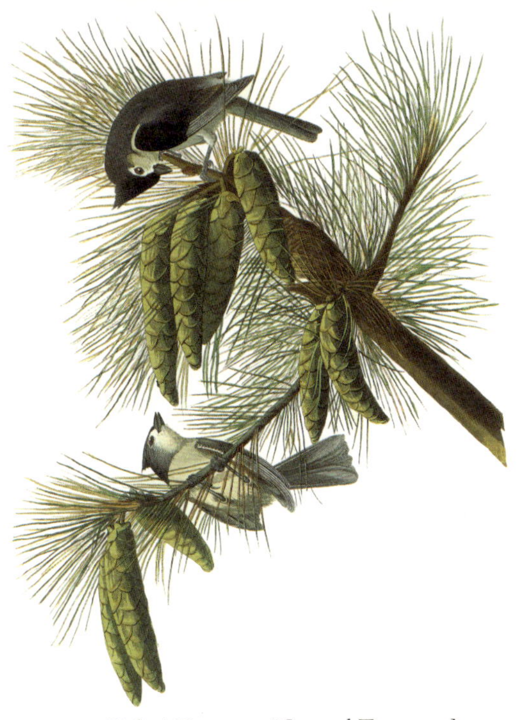

292  Tufted Titmouse [Crested Titmouse]
*Baeolophus bicolor*

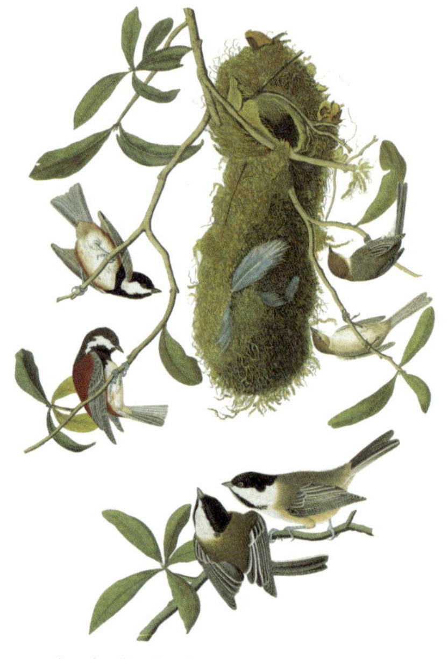

293  Chestnut-backed Chickadee [Chestnut-backed Titmouse]
*Poecile rufescens*

Bushtit
[Chestnut-crowned Titmouse]
*Psaltriparus minimus*

Black-capped Chickadee
[Black-capt Titmouse]
*Poecile atricapillus*

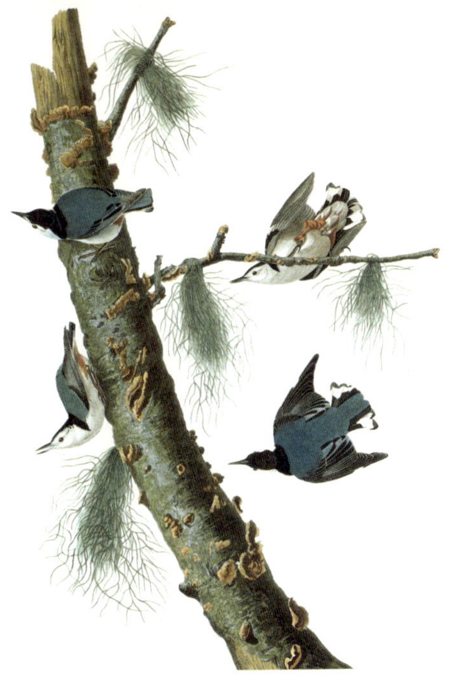

294 White-breasted Nuthatch
[White-breasted Black-capped Nuthatch]
*Sitta carolinensis*

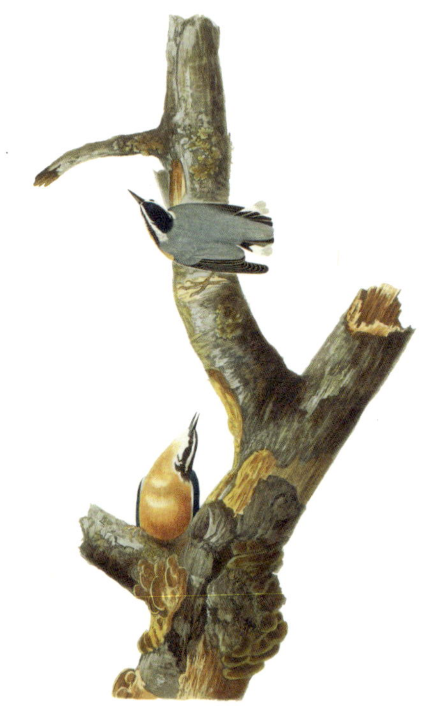

**295  Red-breasted Nuthatch**
*Sitta canadensis*

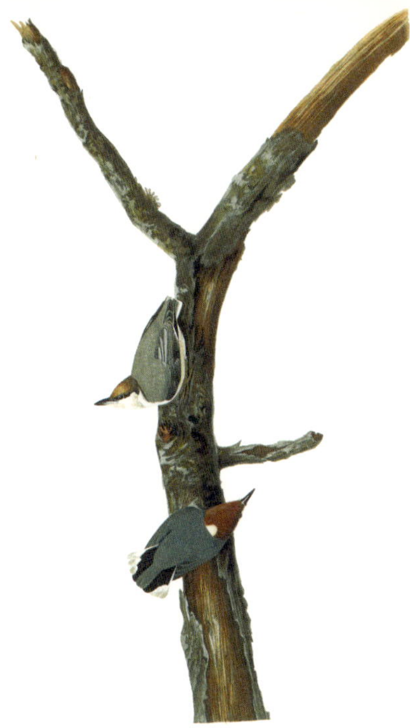

**296  Brown-headed Nuthatch**
*Sitta pusilla*

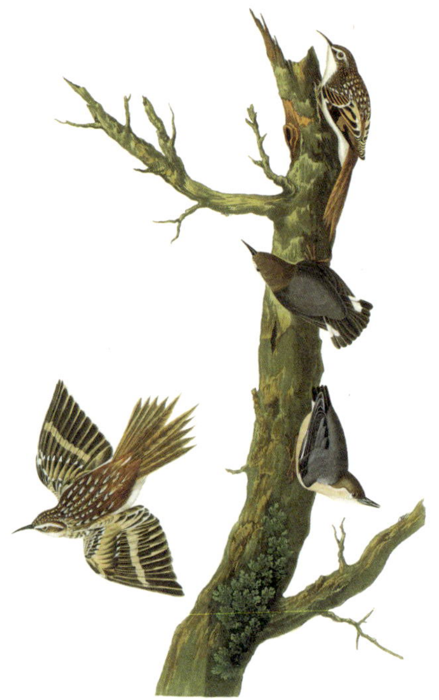

297  Brown Creeper
*Certhia americana*

Pygmy Nuthatch
[Californian Nuthatch]
*Sitta pygmaea*

# IX

## SONGSTERS AND MIMICS

Dippers, Wrens, Mockingbirds, Thrashers,
Thrushes, Gnatcatchers, Kinglets, Pipits,
Waxwings, and Shrikes

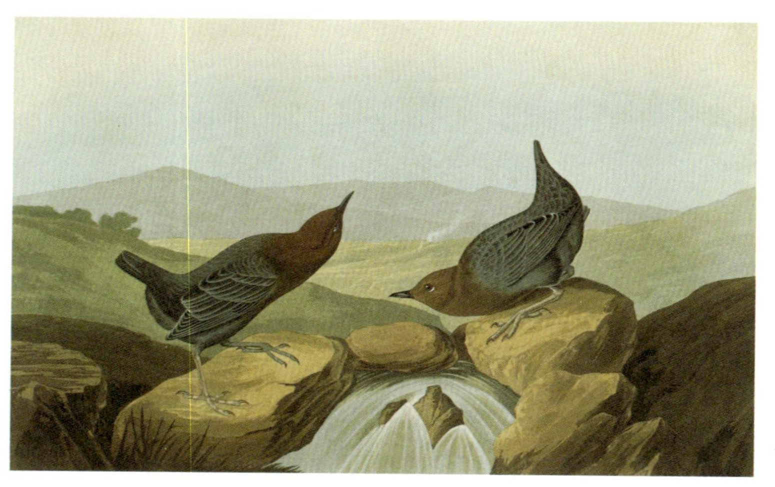

298  North American Dipper [American Water Ouzel]
*Cinclus mexicanus*

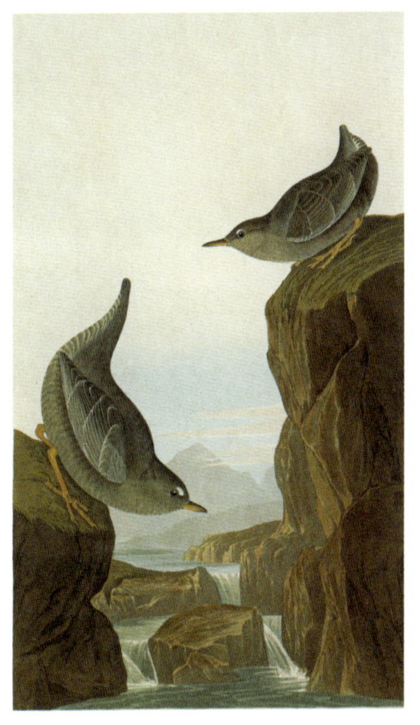

299  American Dipper [Columbian and Arctic Water Ouzels]
*Cinclus mexicanus*

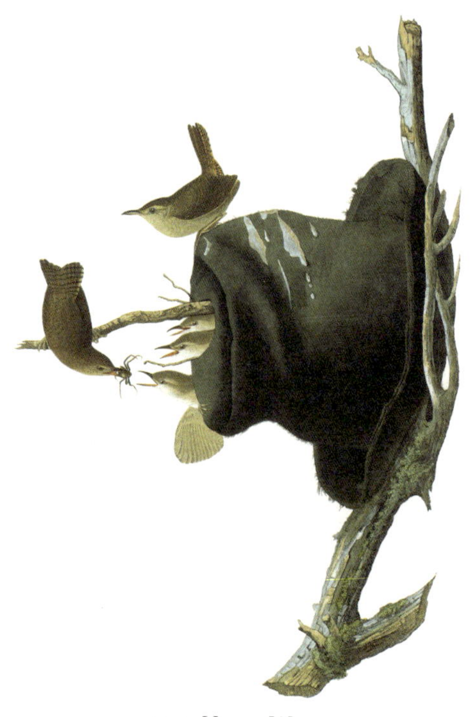

300  House Wren
*Troglodytes aedon*

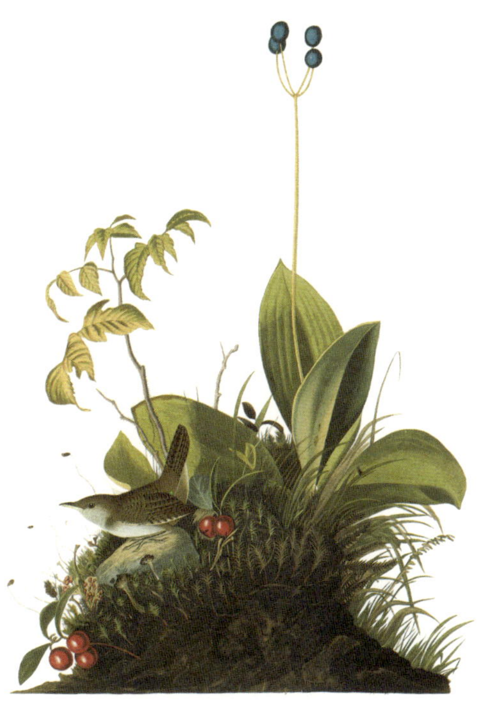

301  House Wren [Wood Wren]

*Troglodytes aedon*

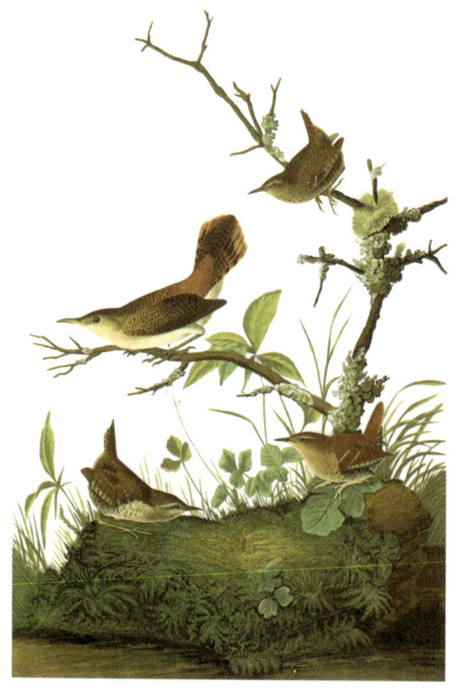

302  Winter Wren
*Troglodytes hiemalis*

Rock Wren
*Salpinctes obsoletus*

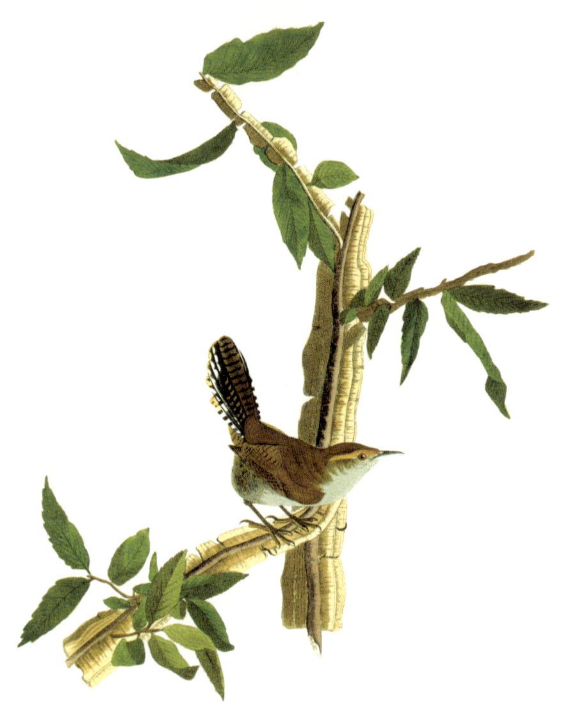

303  Bewick's Wren [Bewick's Long-tailed Wren]
*Thryomanes bewickii*

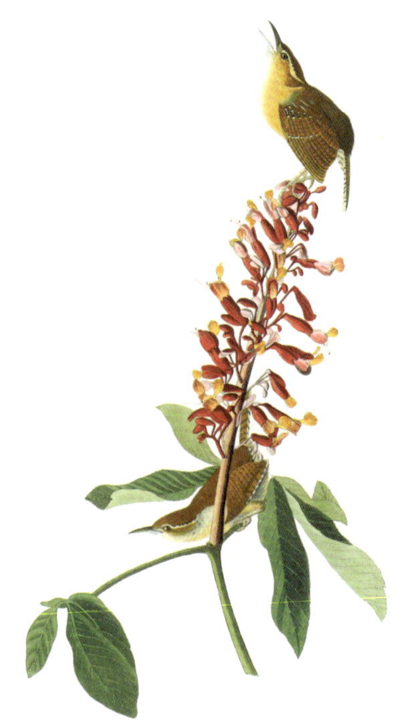

304  Carolina Wren [Great Carolina Wren]
*Thryothorus ludovicianus*

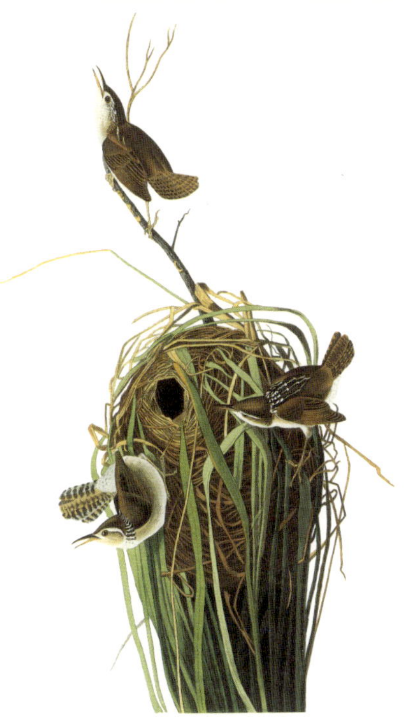

305  Marsh Wren

*Cistothorus palustris*

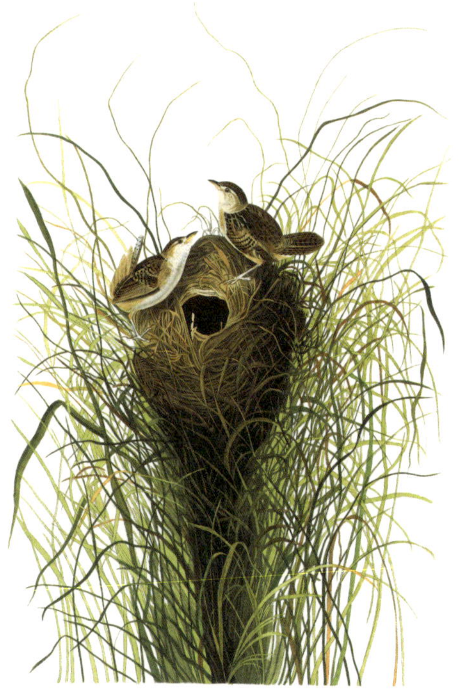

306  Sedge Wren [Nuttall's Lesser Marsh Wren]
*Cistothorus stellaris*

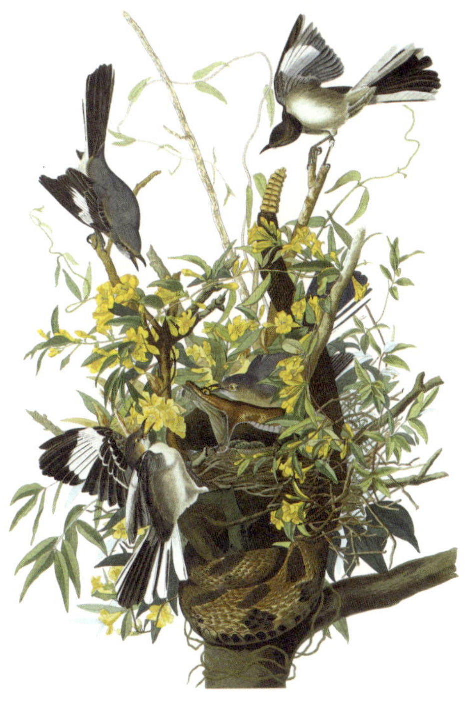

307  Northern Mockingbird [Mocking Bird]
*Mimus polyglottos*

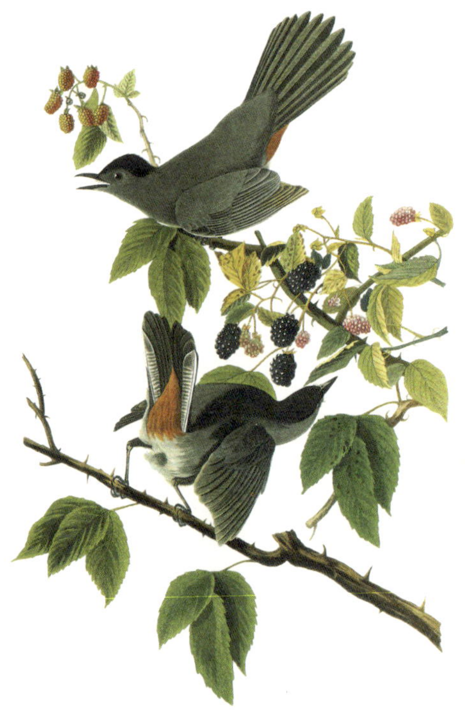

## 308  Gray Catbird [Cat Bird]
*Dumetella carolinensis*

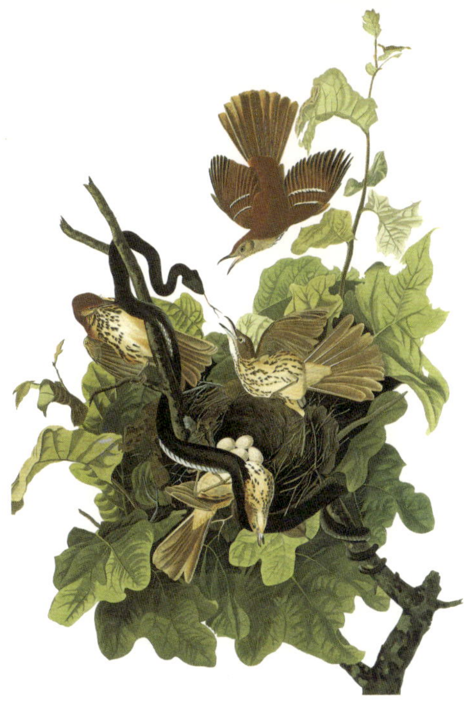

309  Brown Thrasher [Ferruginous Thrush]
*Toxostoma rufum*

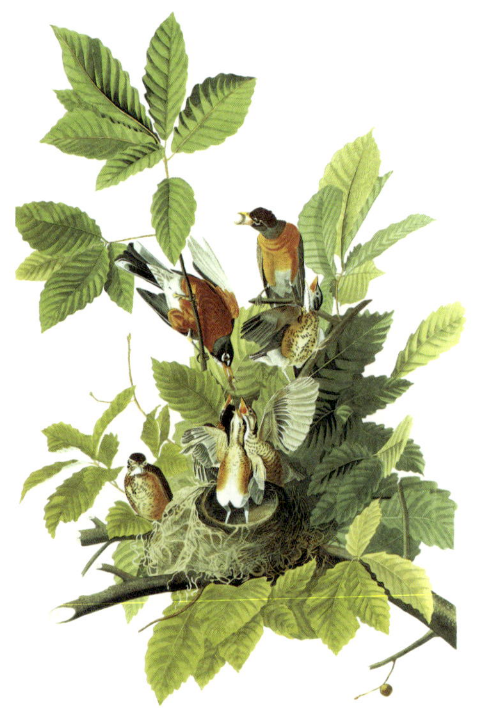

310  American Robin

*Turdus migratorius*

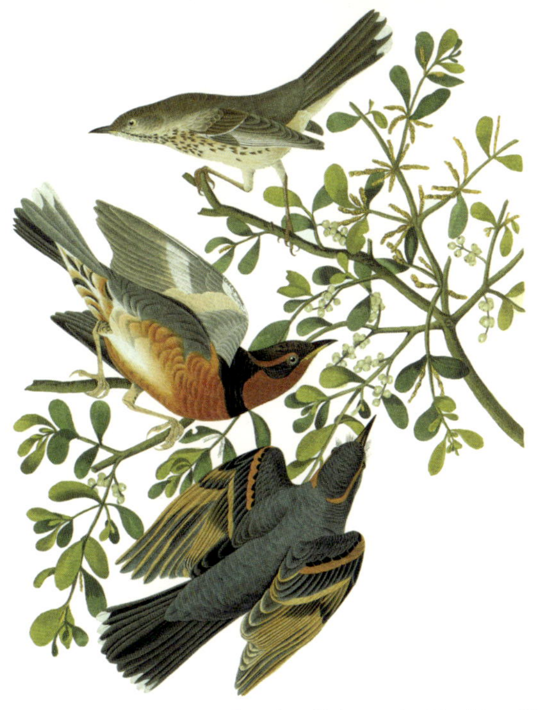

311 Varied Thrush
*Ixoreus naevius*

Sage Thrasher [Mountain Mocking Bird]
*Oreoscoptes montanus*

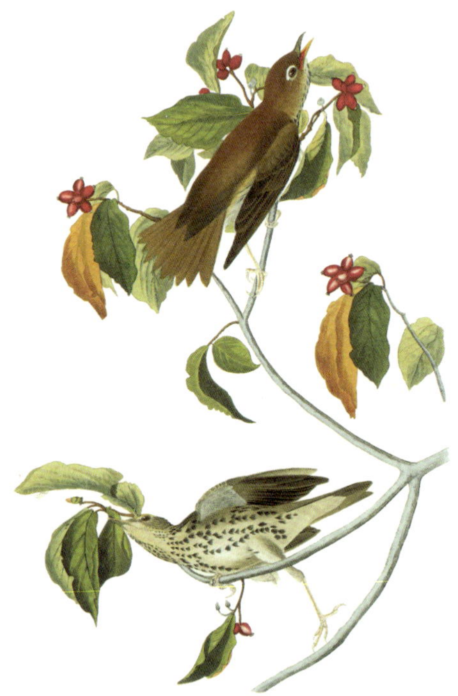

**312  Wood Thrush**

*Hylocichla mustelina*

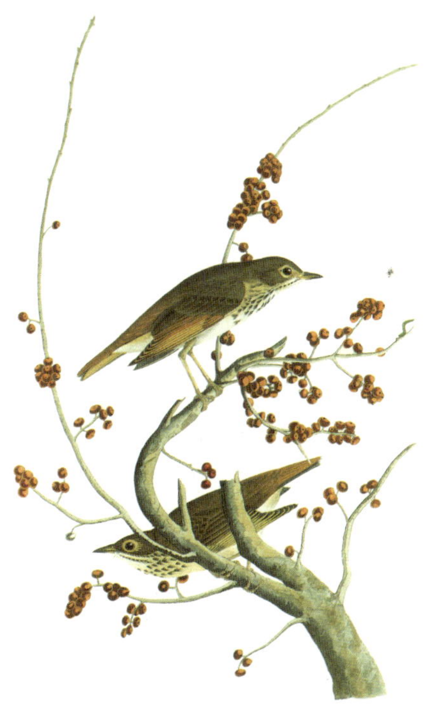

313  Hermit Thrush
*Catharus guttatus*

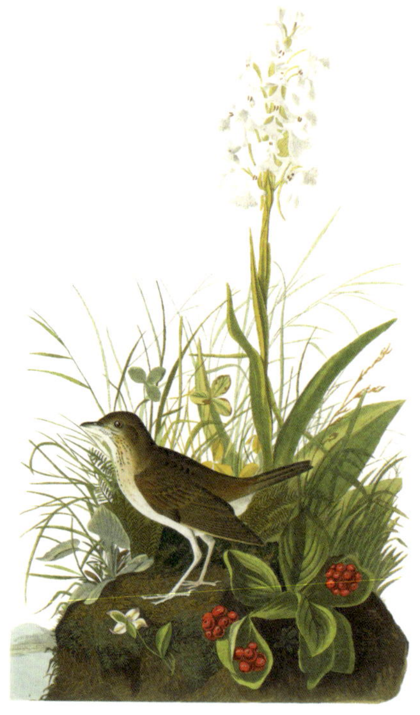

314  Veery [Tawny Thrush]
*Catharus fuscescens*

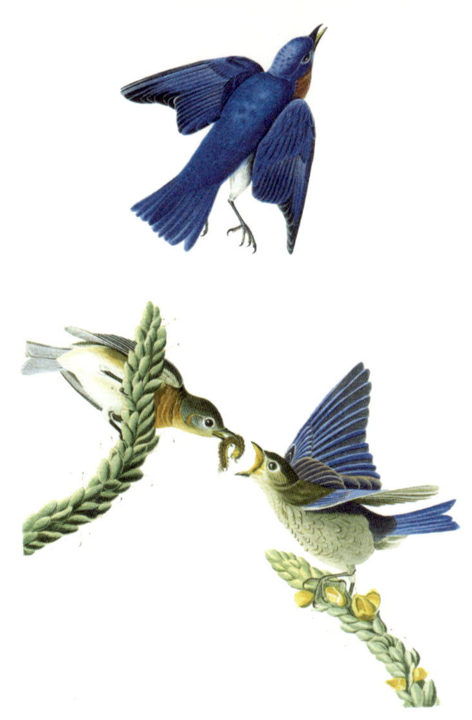

315  Eastern Bluebird [Blue-bird]
*Sialia sialis*

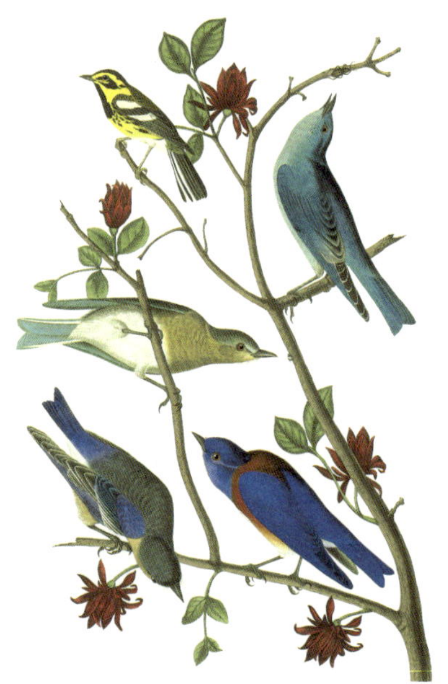

316 Townsend's Warbler
*Dendroica townsendi*

Mountain Bluebird
[Arctic Blue Bird]
*Sialia currucoides*

Western Bluebird
[Western Blue Bird]
*Sialia mexicana*

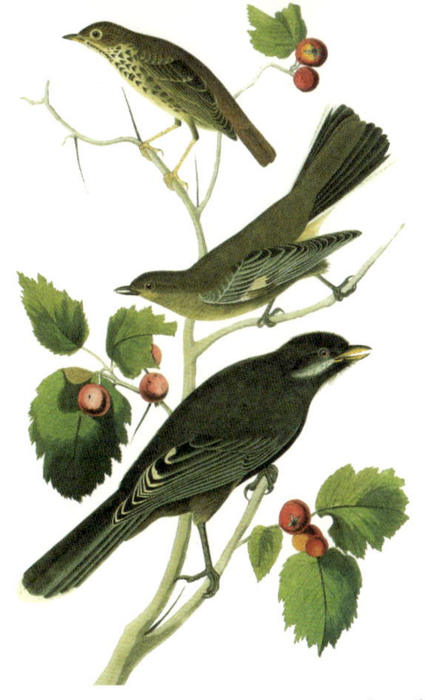

317  Hermit Thrush [Little Tawny Thrush]
*Catharus guttatus*

Townsend's Solitaire
[Townsend's Ptilogonys]
*Myadestes townsendi*

Canada Jay
*Perisoreus canadensis*

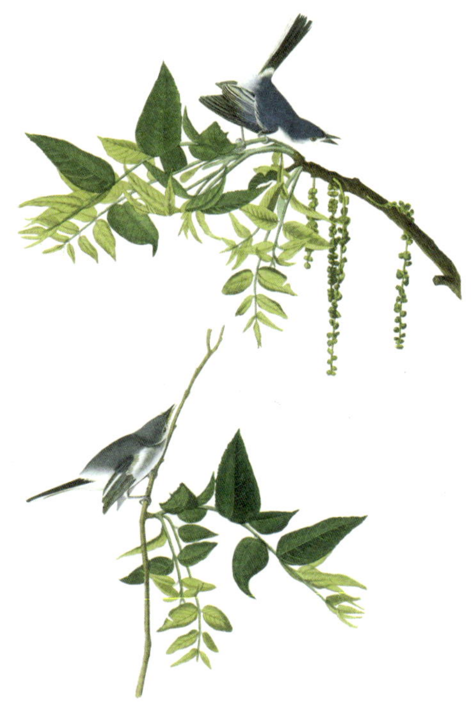

318  Blue-gray Gnatcatcher [Blue-grey Flycatcher]
*Polioptila caerulea*

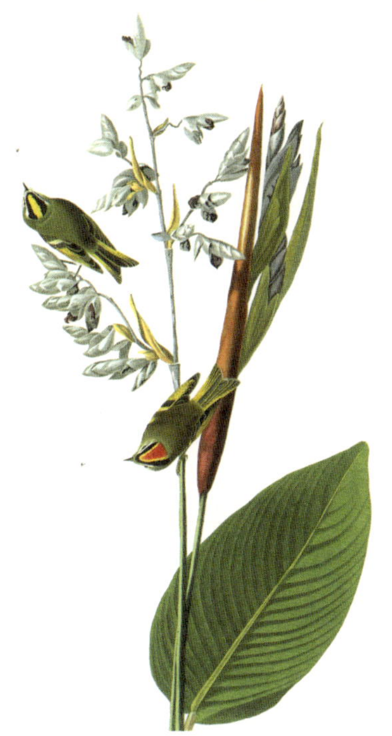

319  Golden-crowned Kinglet [Golden-crested Wren]
*Regulus satrapa*

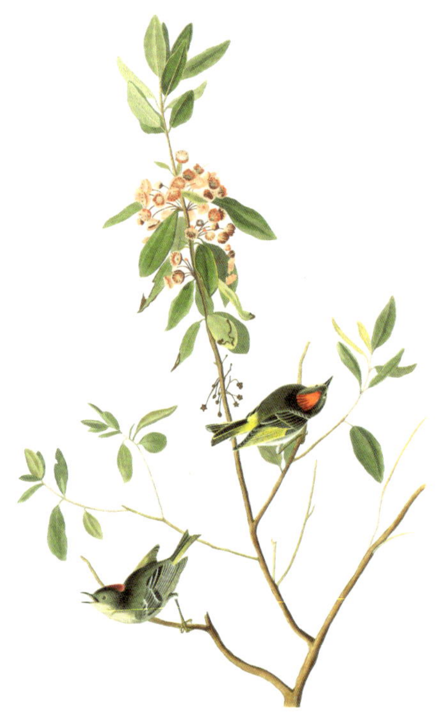

320  Ruby-crowned Kinglet [Ruby-crowned Wren]
*Regulus calendula*

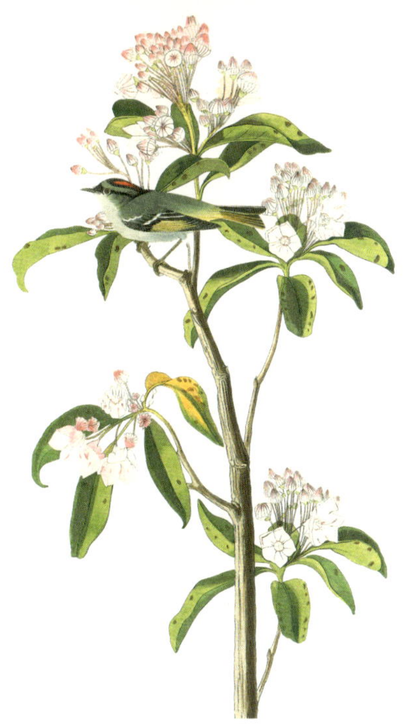

321  "Cuvier's Kinglet" [Cuvier's Wren]
*"Regulus cuvieri"*

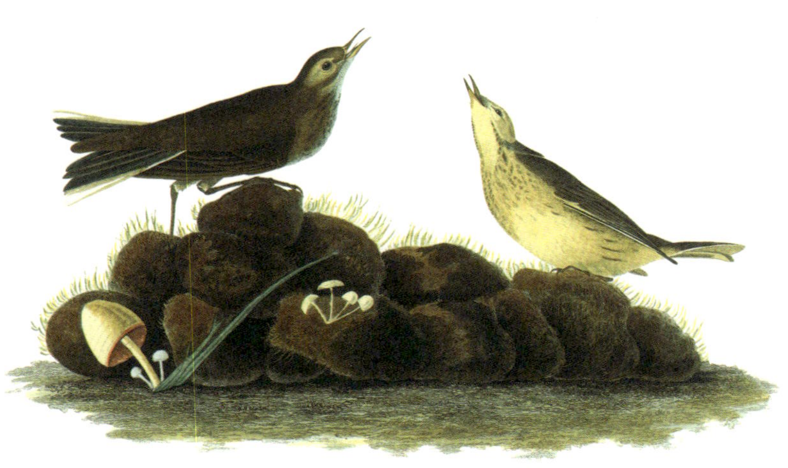

322  American Pipit [Brown Titlark]
*Anthus rubescens*

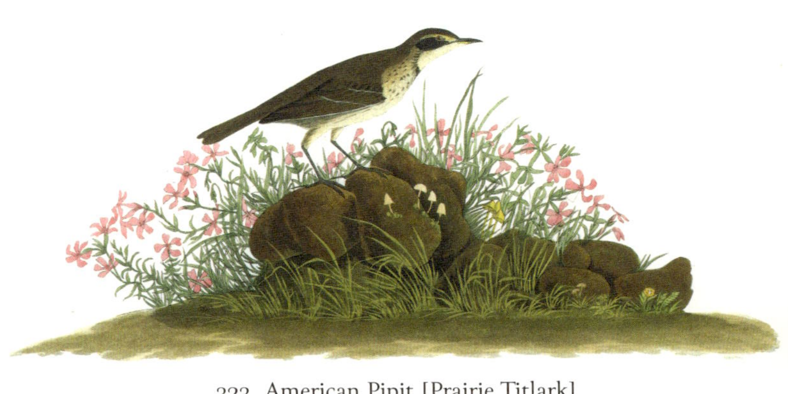

323  American Pipit [Prairie Titlark]
*Anthus rubescens*

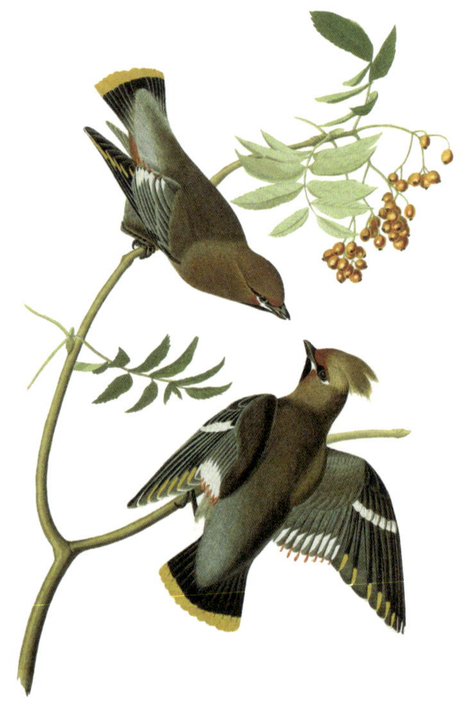

324  Bohemian Waxwing [Bohemian Chatterer]
*Bombycilla garrulus*

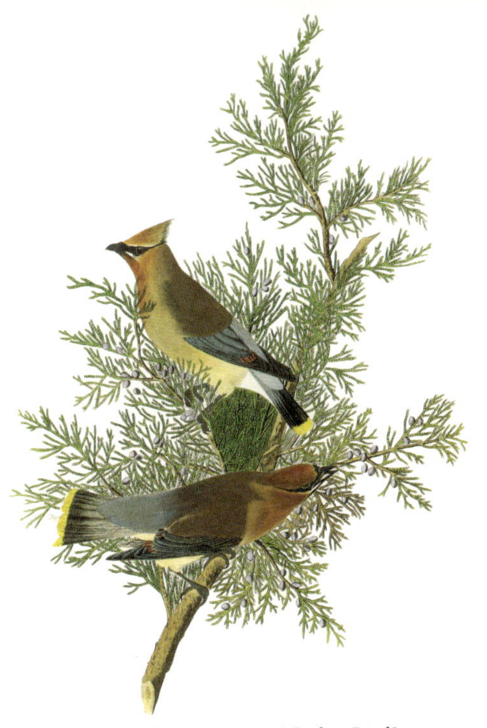

325  Cedar Waxwing [Cedar Bird]
*Bombycilla cedrorum*

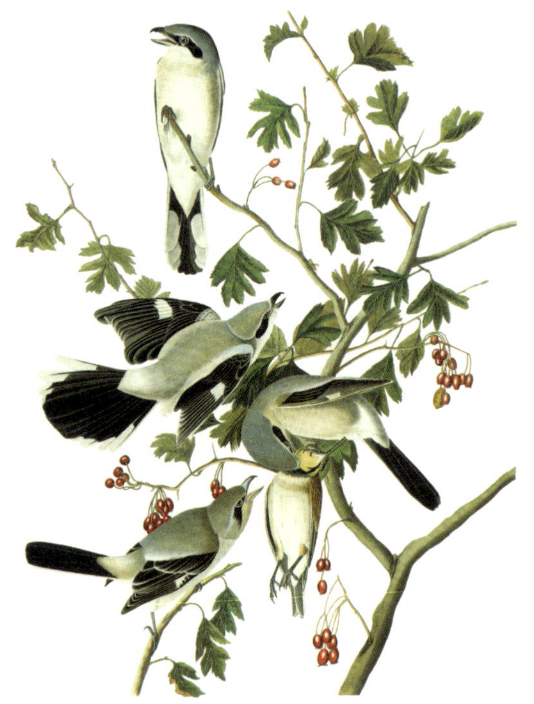

326  Northern Shrike [Great American Shrike or Butcher Bird]
*Lanius borealis*

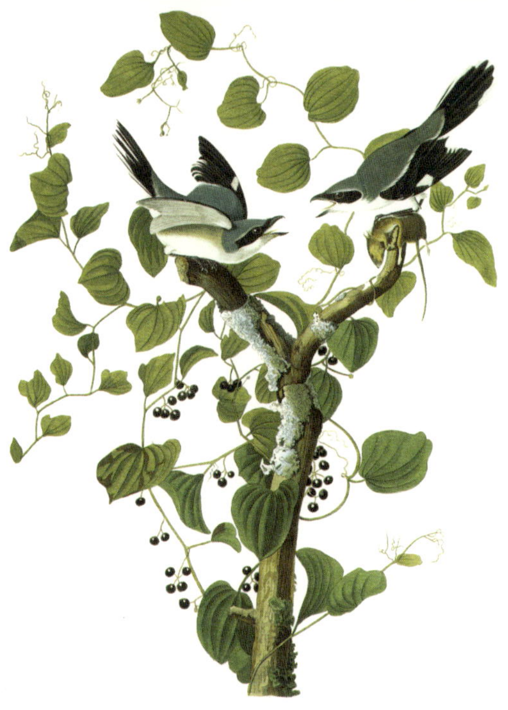

327  Loggerhead Shrike
*Lanius ludovicianus*

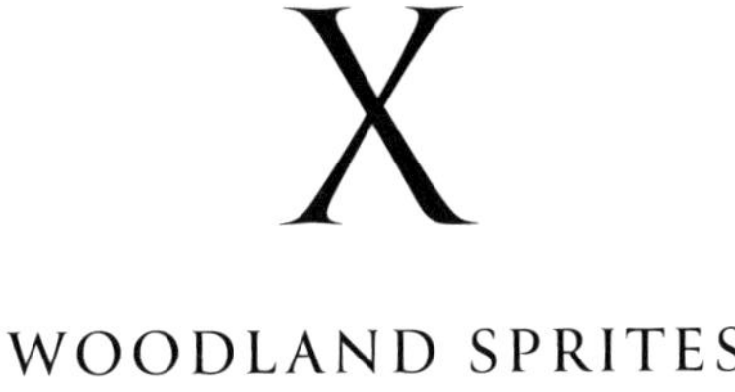

# WOODLAND SPRITES

Vireos and Warblers

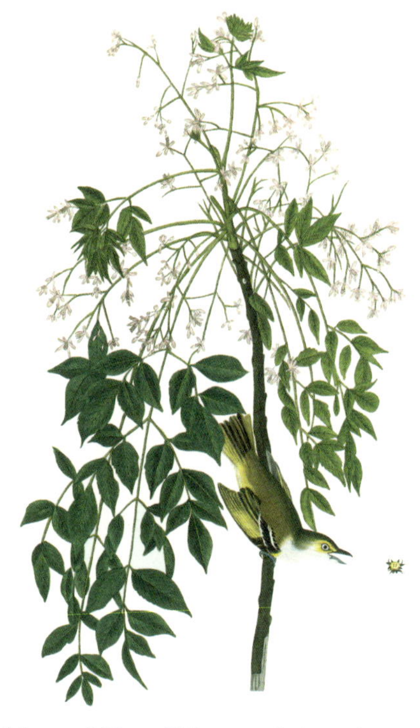

328  White-eyed Vireo [White-eyed Flycatcher or Vireo]
*Vireo griseus*

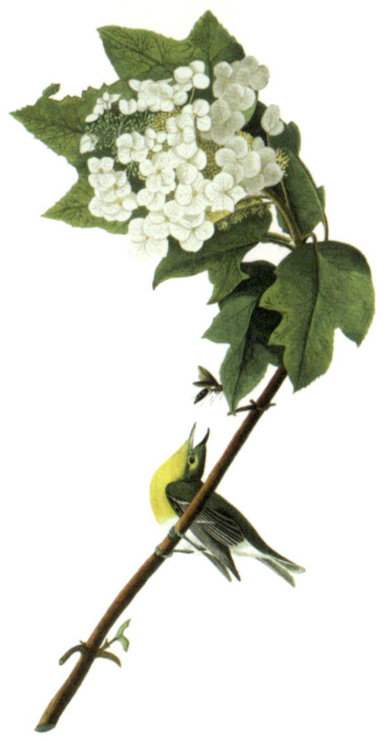

**329  Yellow-throated Vireo**
*Vireo flavifrons*

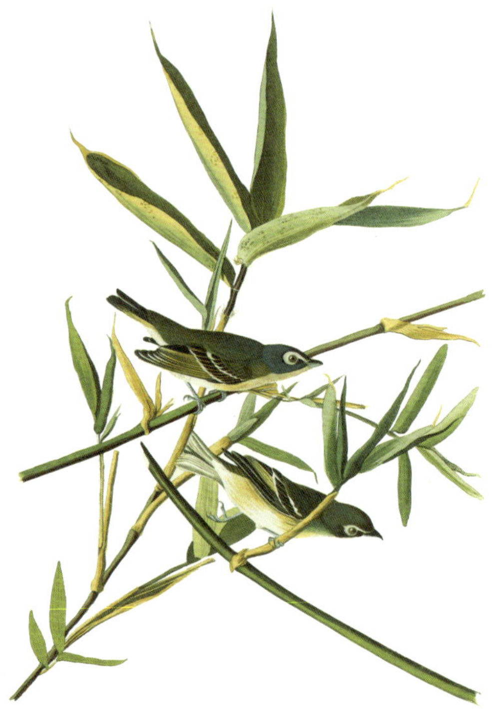

330  Blue-headed Vireo [Solitary Flycatcher]
*Vireo solitarius*

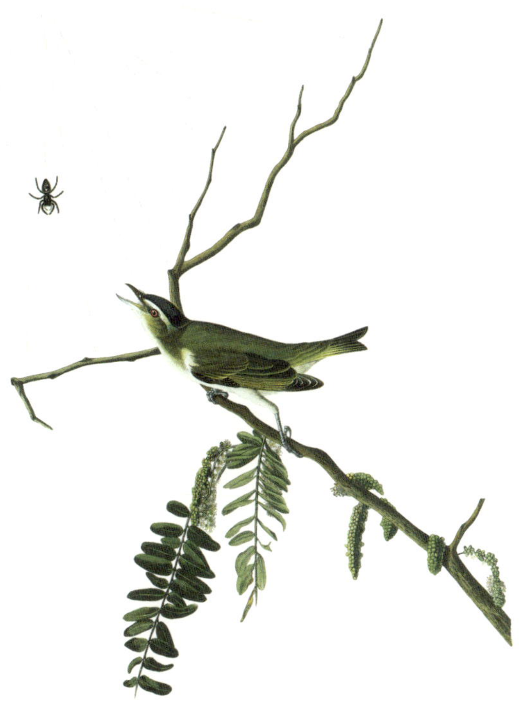

331 Red-eyed Vireo
*Vireo olivaceus*

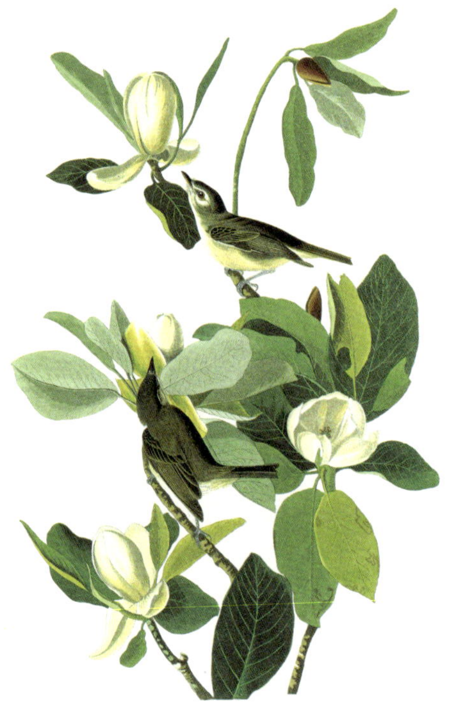

332  Warbling Vireo [Warbling Flycatcher]
*Vireo gilvus*

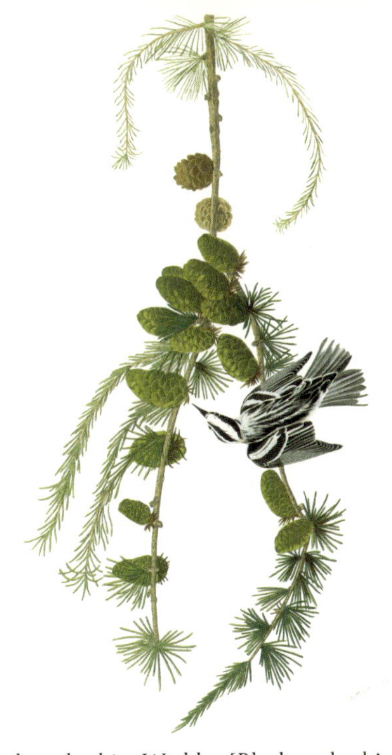

333  Black-and-white Warbler [Black-and-white Creeper]
*Mniotilta varia*

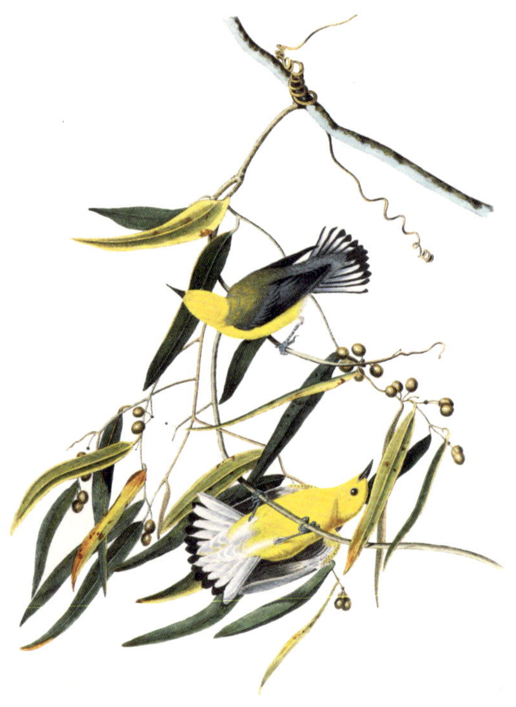

**334  Prothonotary Warbler**
*Protonotaria citrea*

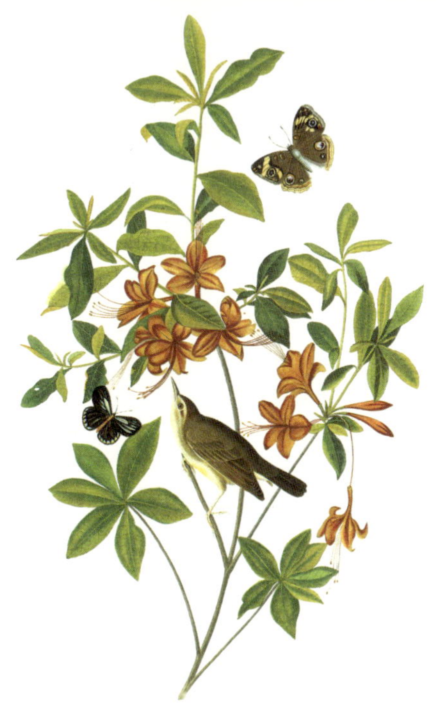

335  Swainson's Warbler [Brown-headed Worm-eating Warbler]
*Limnothlypis swainsonii*

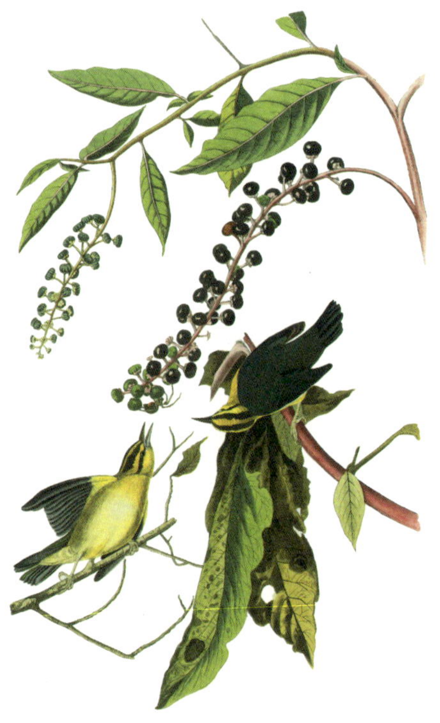

336  Worm-eating Warbler
*Helmitheros vermivorum*

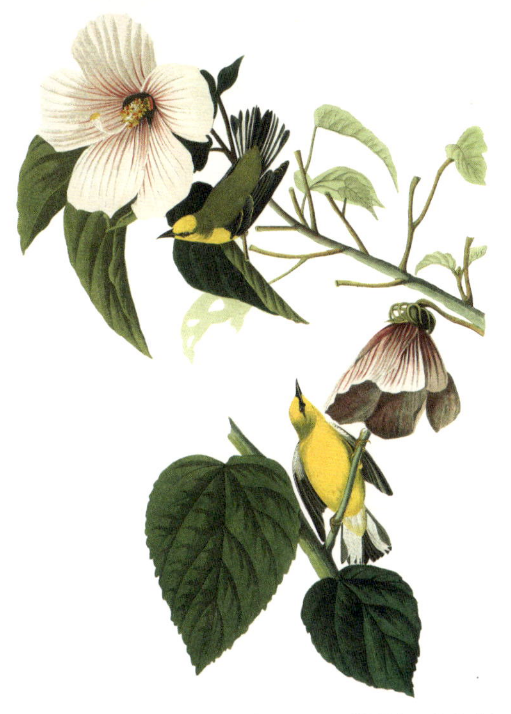

337  Blue-winged Warbler [Blue-winged Yellow Warbler]
*Vermivora cyanoptera*

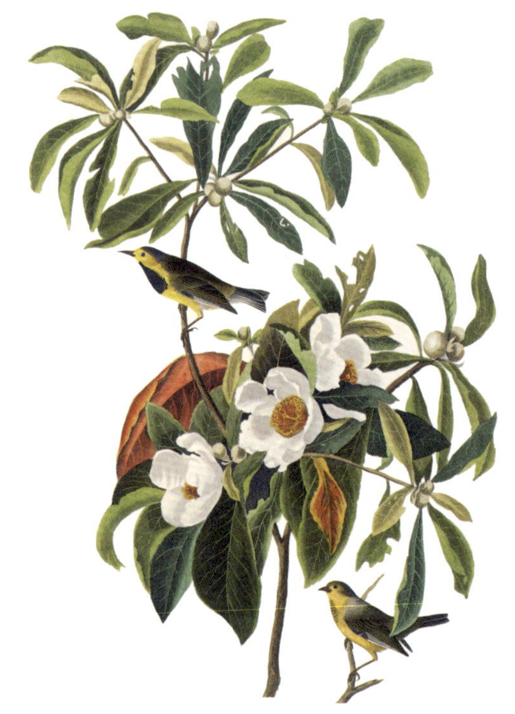

338  Bachman's Warbler

*Vermivora bachmanii*

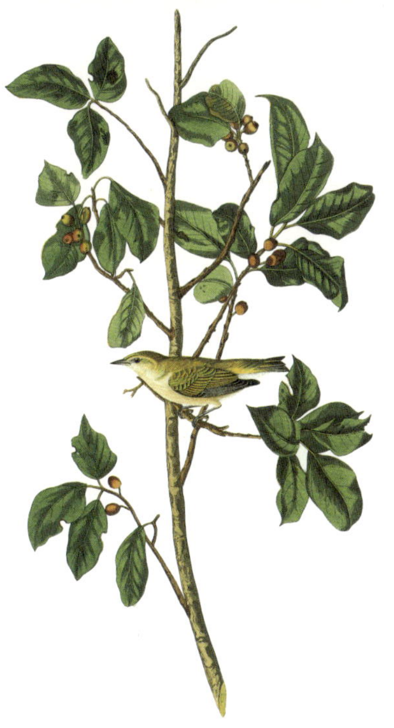

339  Tennessee Warbler

*Leiothlypis peregrina*

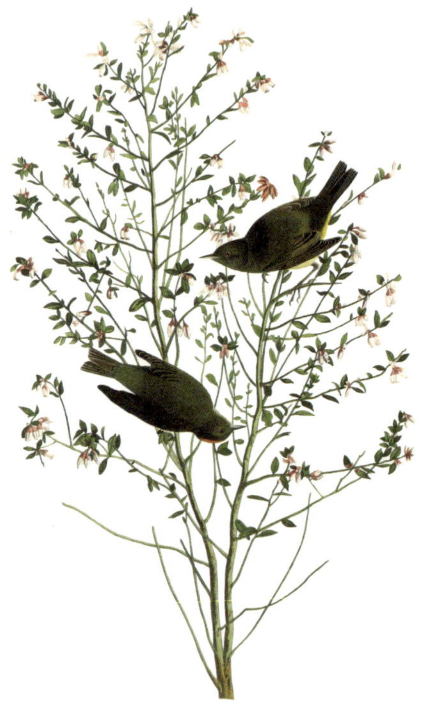

340 Orange-crowned Warbler

*Leiothlypis celata*

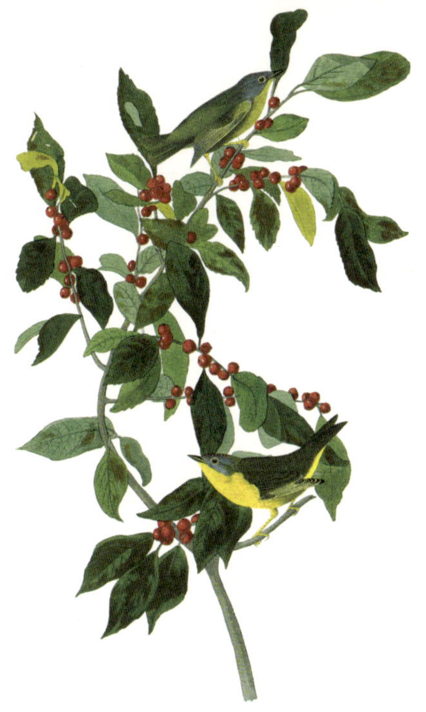

341  Nashville Warbler
*Leiothlypis ruficapilla*

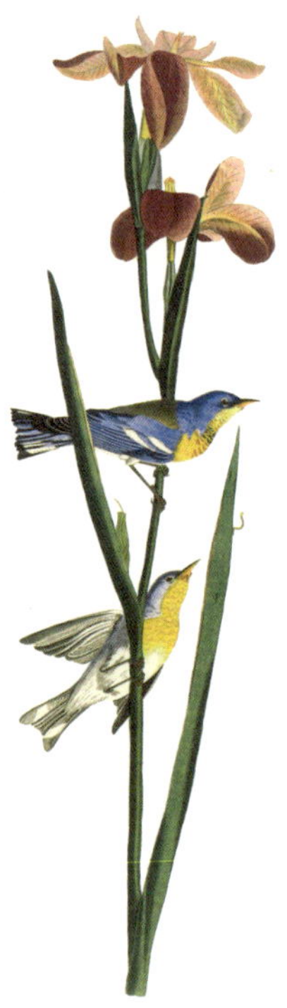

342  Northern Parula Warbler [Blue Yellow-back Warbler]
*Setophaga americana*

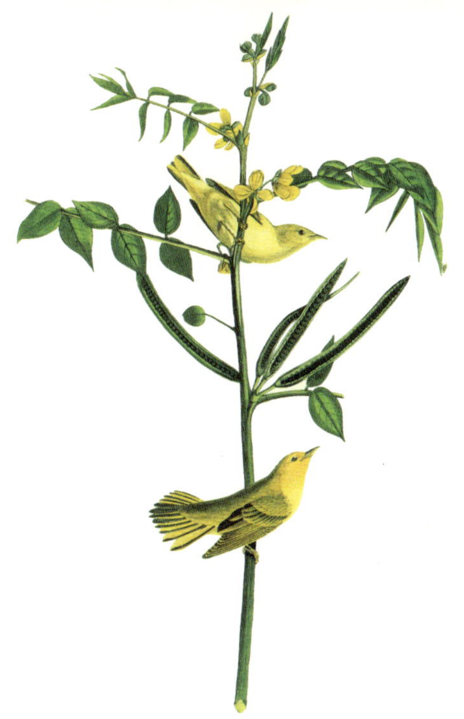

343  Yellow Warbler [Children's Warbler]
*Setophaga petechia*

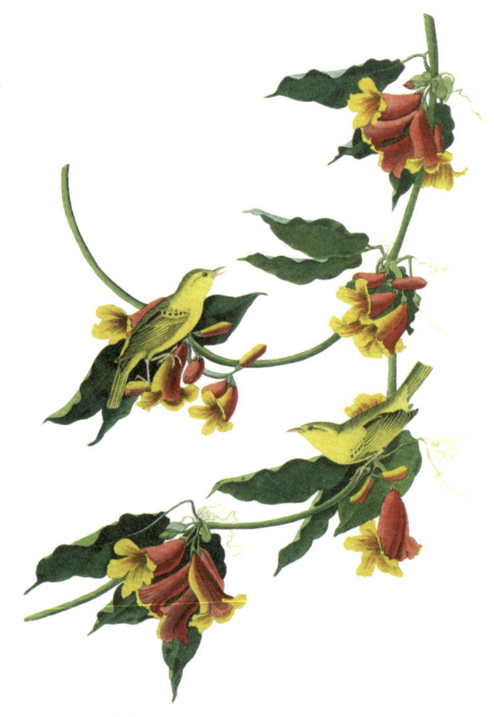

344  Yellow Warbler [Rathbone Warbler]
*Dendroica petechia*

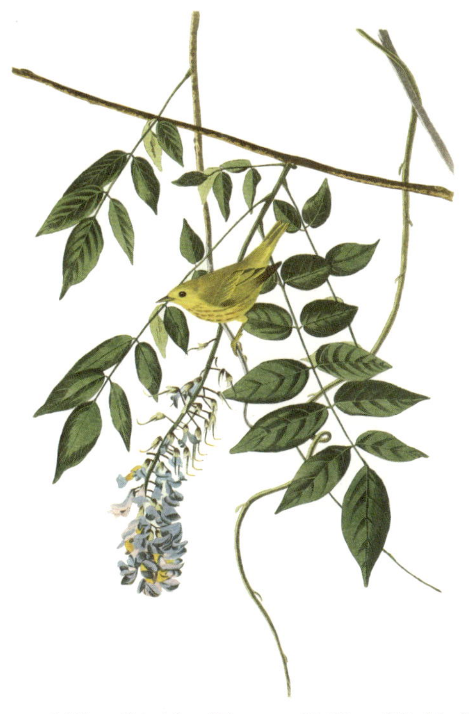

345  Yellow Warbler [Blue-eyed Yellow Warbler]
*Dendroica petechia*

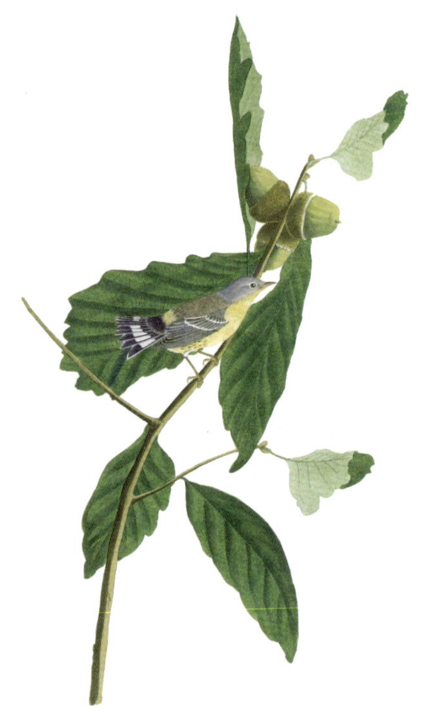

346  Magnolia Warbler [Black and Yellow Warbler]
*Setophaga magnolia*

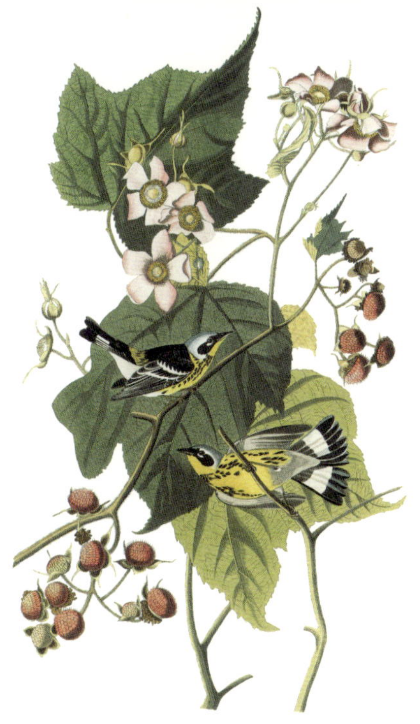

347  Magnolia Warbler [Black and Yellow Warbler]
*Dendroica magnolia*

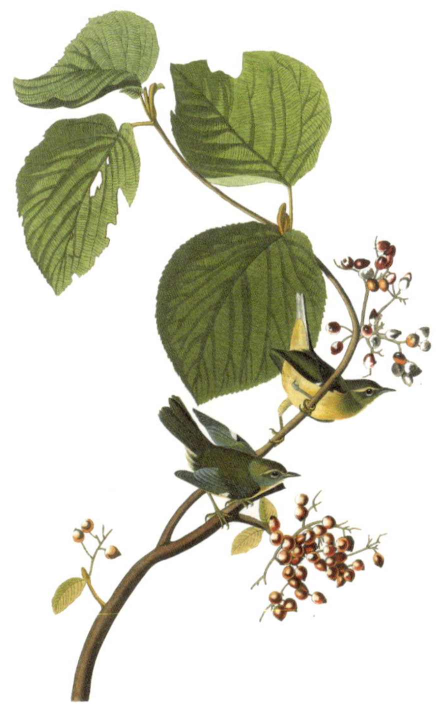

348  Black-throated Blue Warbler [Pine Swamp Warbler]
*Setophaga caerulescens*

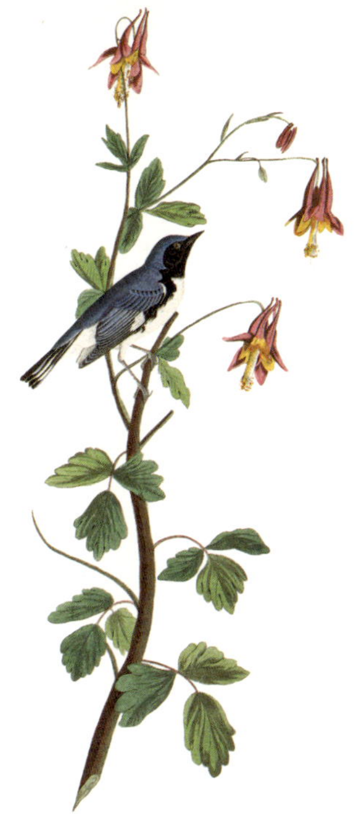

349  Black-throated Blue Warbler
*Dendroica caerulescens*

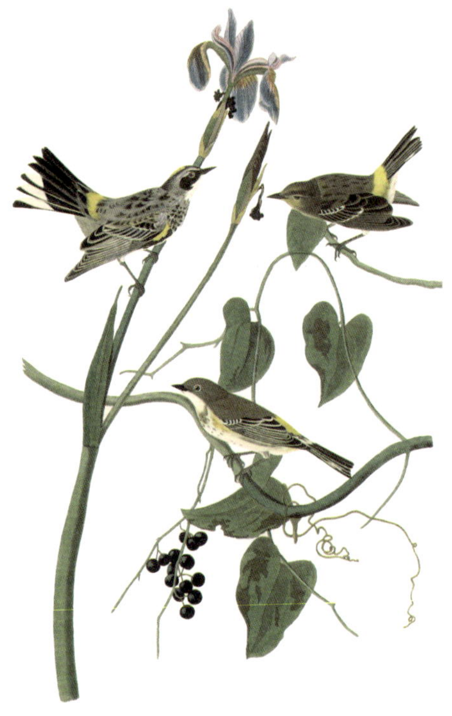

350  Yellow-rumped Warbler [Yellow-crown Warbler]
*Setophaga coronata*

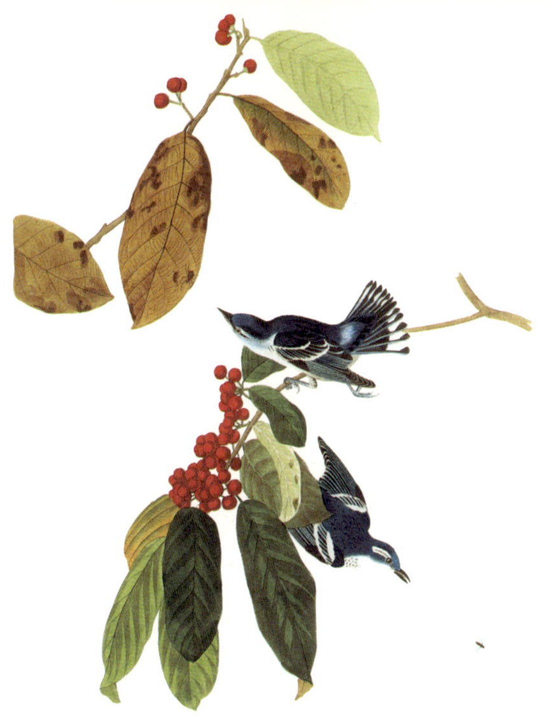

351  Cerulean Warbler

*Setophaga cerulea*

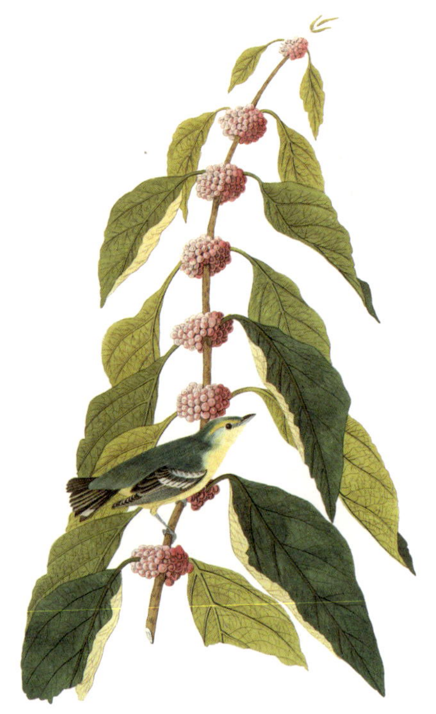

352  Cerulean Warbler [Blue-green Warbler]
*Setophaga cerulea*

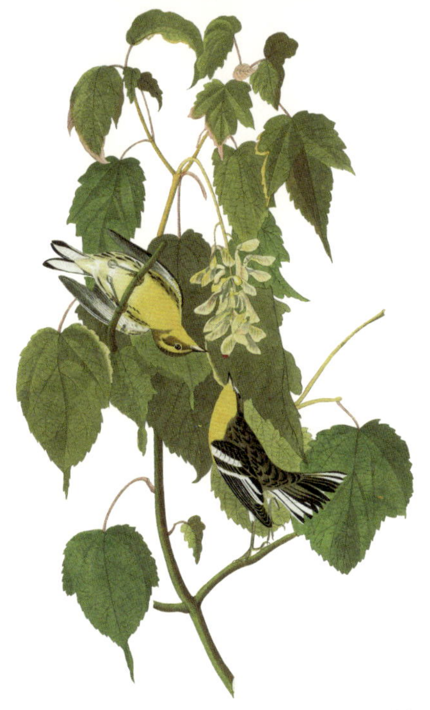

353  Blackburnian Warbler [Hemlock Warbler]
*Setophaga fusca*

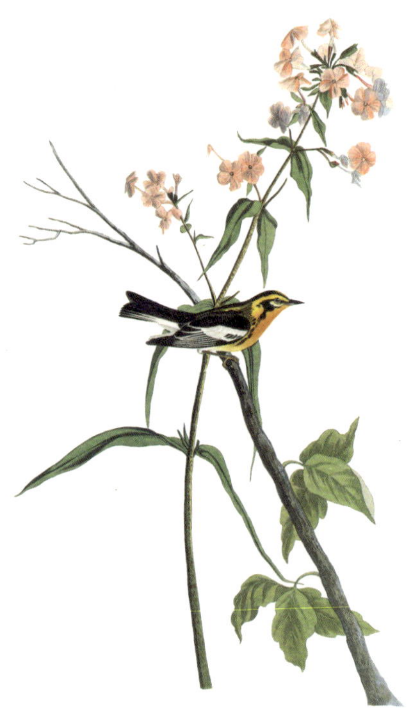

354  Blackburnian Warbler
*Setophaga fusca*

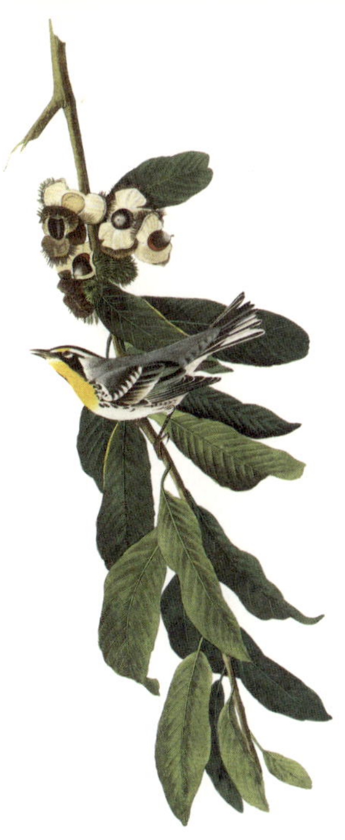

355  Yellow-throated Warbler [Yellow-throat Warbler]
*Setophaga dominica*

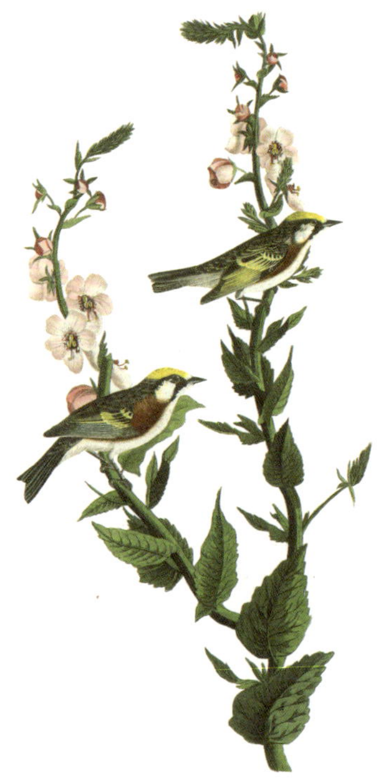

356  Chestnut-sided Warbler

*Setophaga pensylvanica*

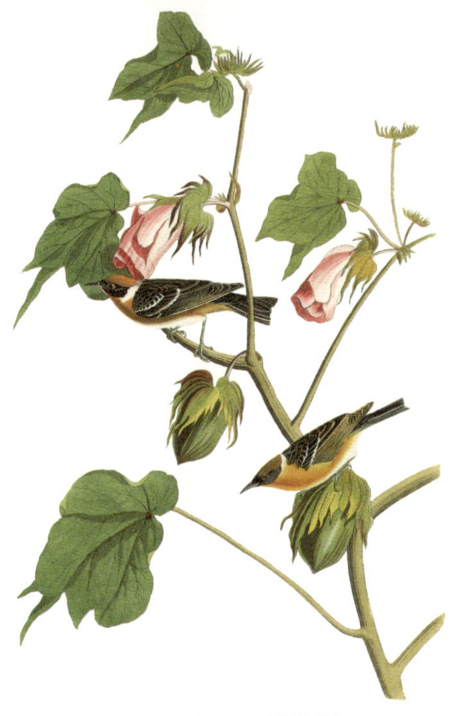

**357  Bay-breasted Warbler**
*Setophaga castanea*

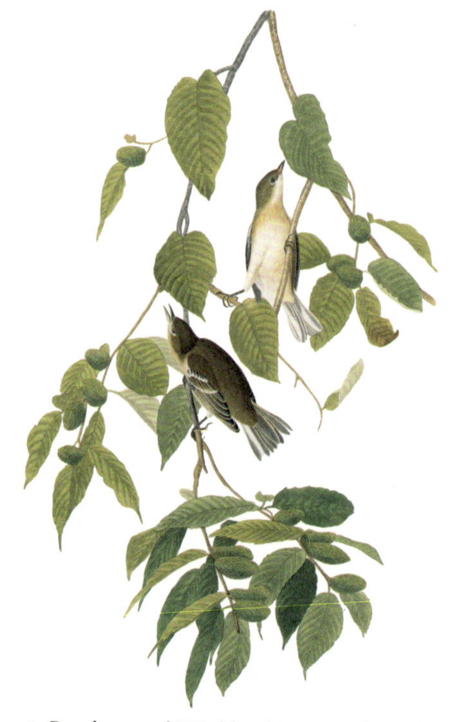

358  Bay-breasted Warbler [Autumnal Warbler]
*Setophaga castanea*

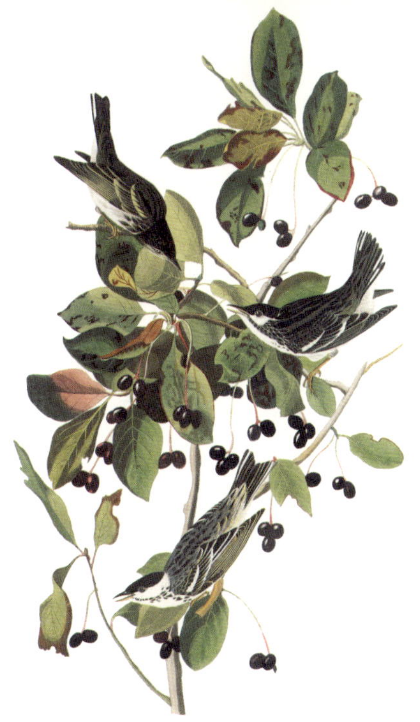

359  Blackpoll Warbler [Black-poll Warbler]
*Setophaga striata*

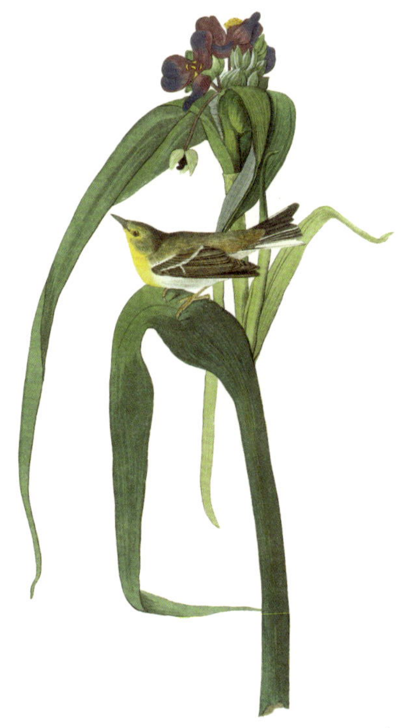

360  Pine Warbler [Vigors' Warbler]
*Setophaga pinus*

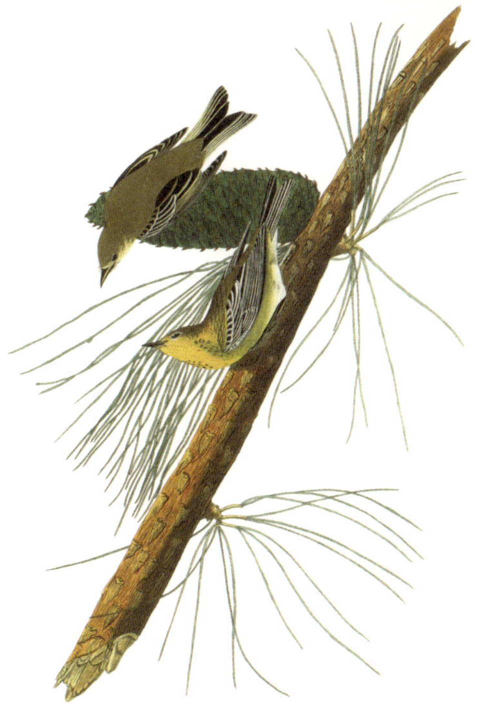

361  Pine Warbler [Pine Creeping Warbler]
*Setophaga pinus*

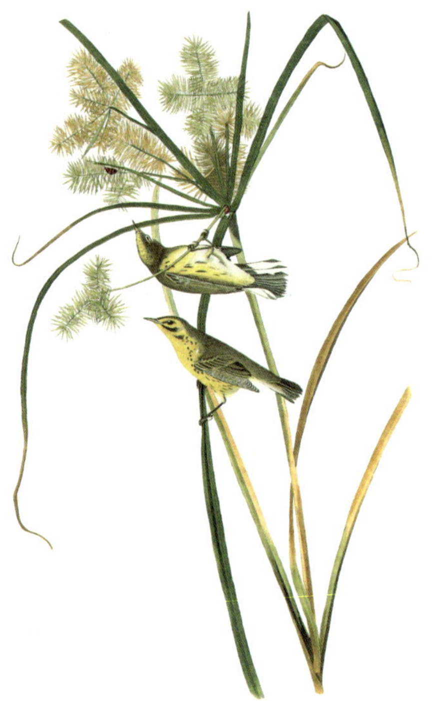

362  Prairie Warbler

*Setophaga discolor*

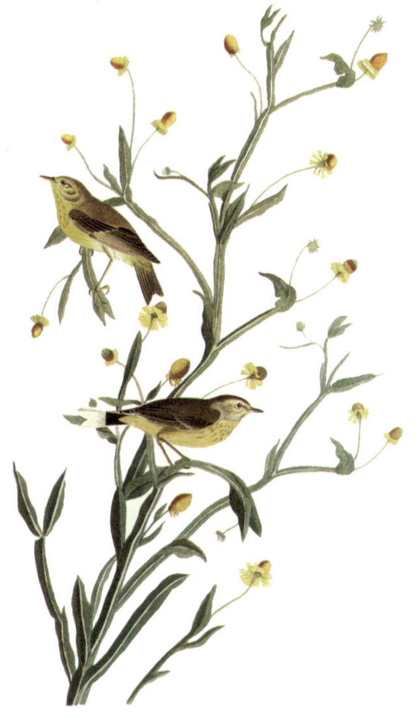

363 Palm Warbler [Yellow Red-poll Warbler]
*Setophaga palmarum*

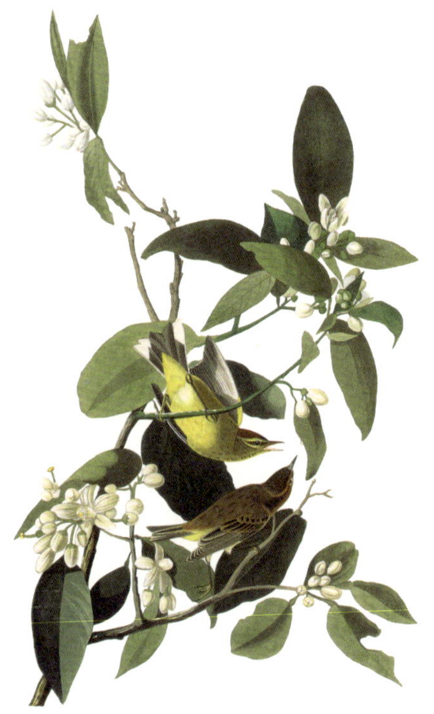

364  Palm Warbler

*Setophaga palmarum*

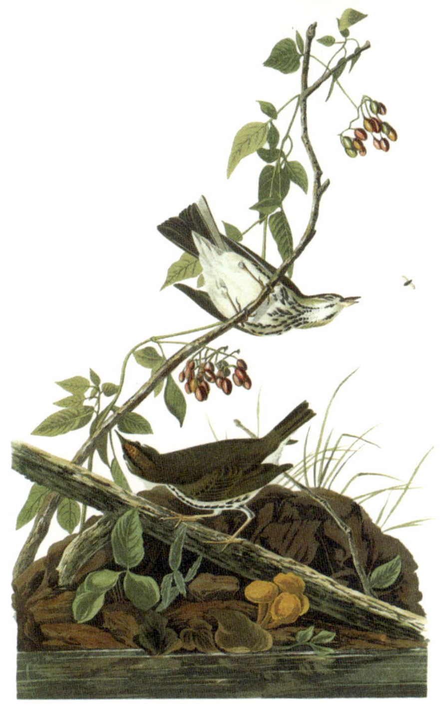

365 Ovenbird [Golden-crowned Thrush]
*Seiurus aurocapilla*

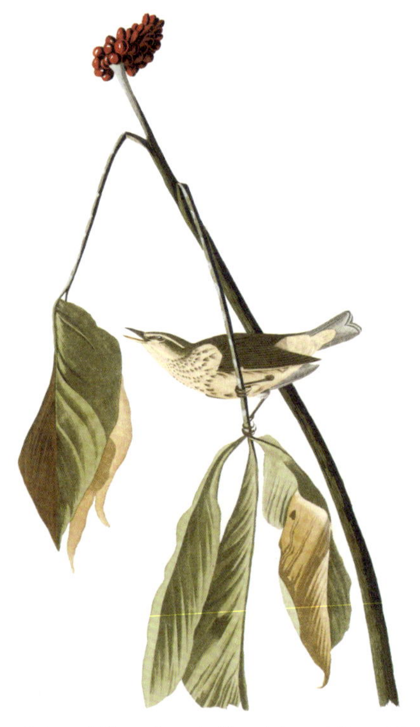

366  Louisiana Waterthrush [Louisiana Water Thrush]
*Parkesia motacilla*

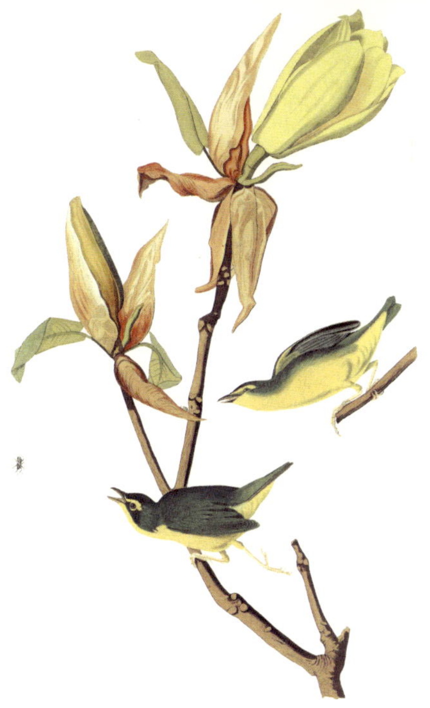

**367  Kentucky Warbler**
*Geothlypis formosa*

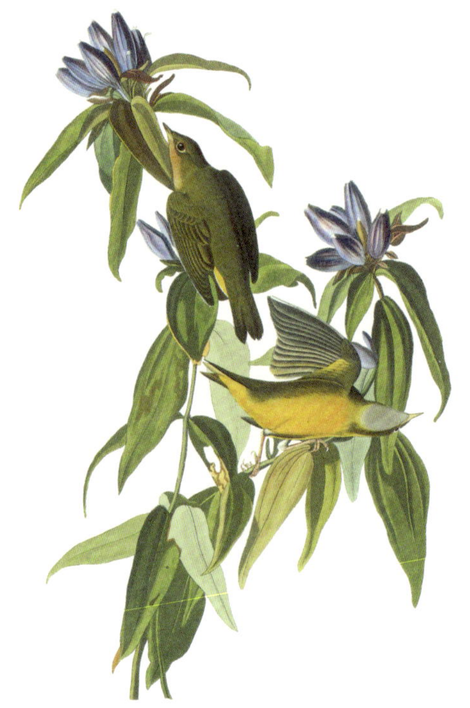

368  Connecticut Warbler

*Oporornis agilis*

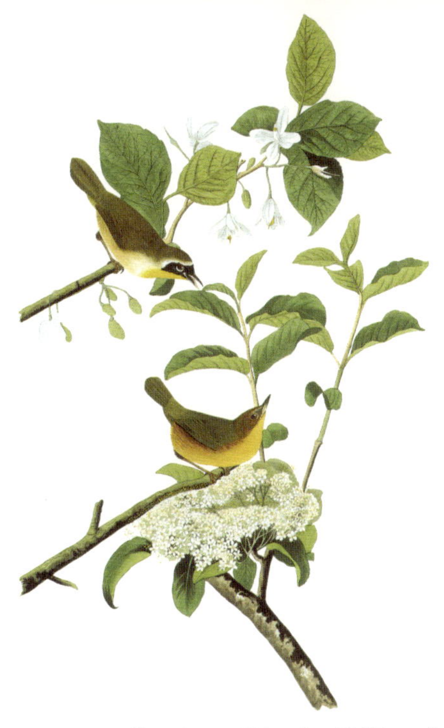

369  Common Yellowthroat [Maryland Yellow-throat]
*Geothlypis trichas*

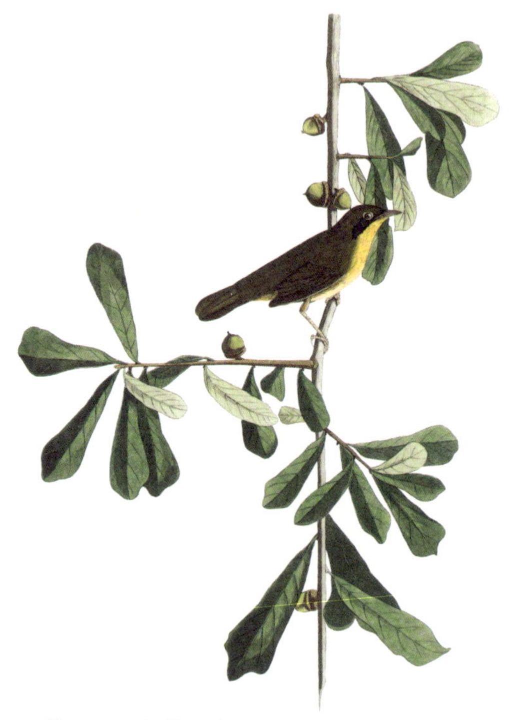

370  Common Yellowthroat [Roscoe's Yellow-throat]
*Geothlypis trichas*

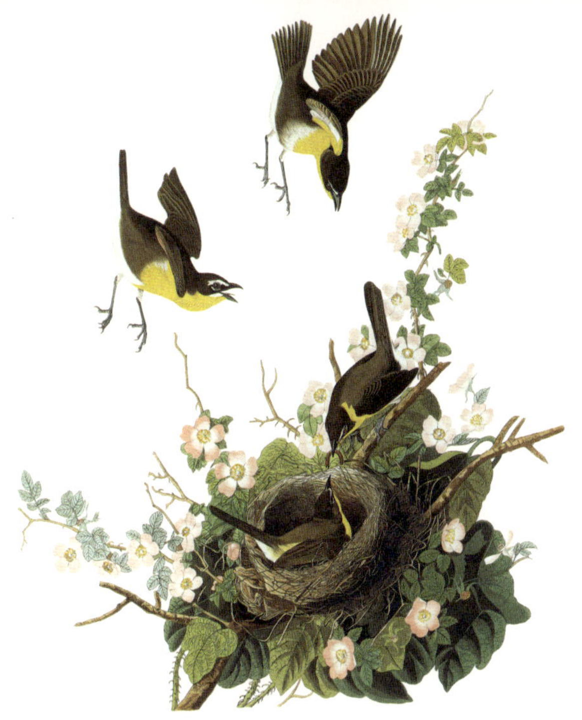

371  Yellow-breasted Chat
*Icteria virens*

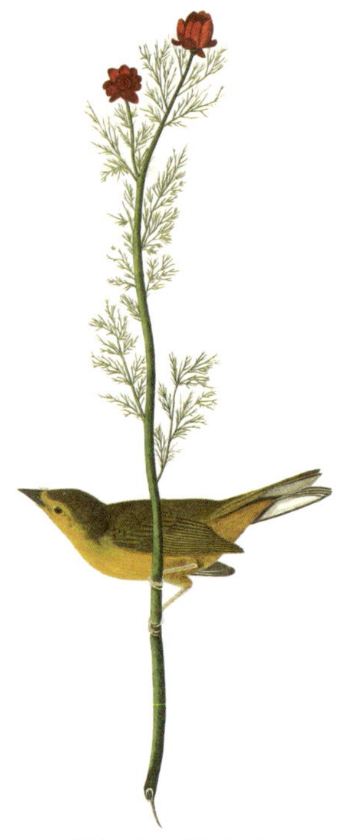

372  Hooded Warbler [Selby's Flycatcher]
*Setophaga citrina*

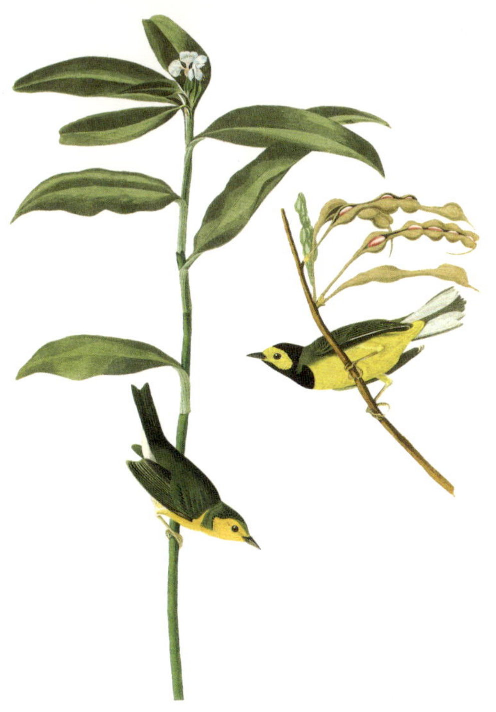

373  Hooded Warbler
*Setophaga citrina*

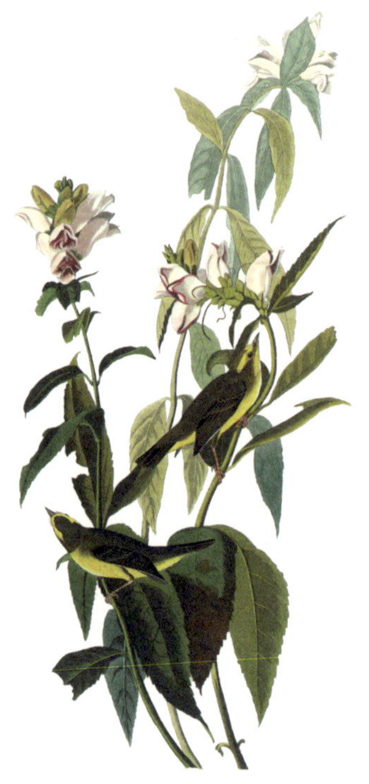

374  Wilson's Warbler [Green Black-capt Flycatcher]
*Cardellina pusilla*

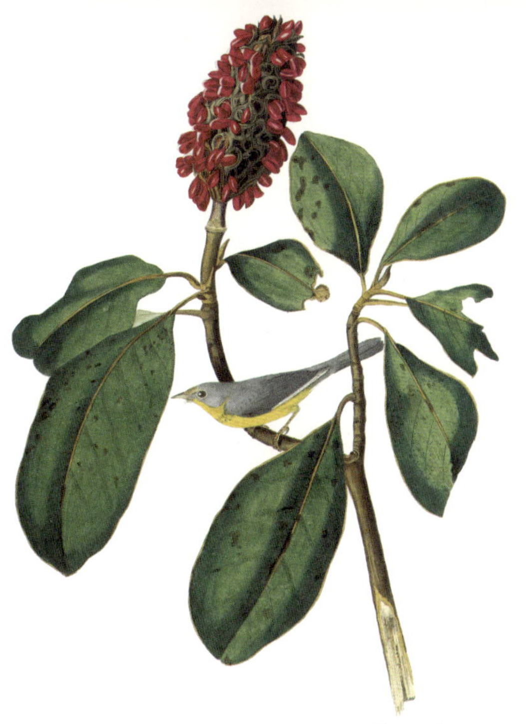

375  Canada Warbler [Bonaparte Flycatcher]
*Cardellina canadensis*

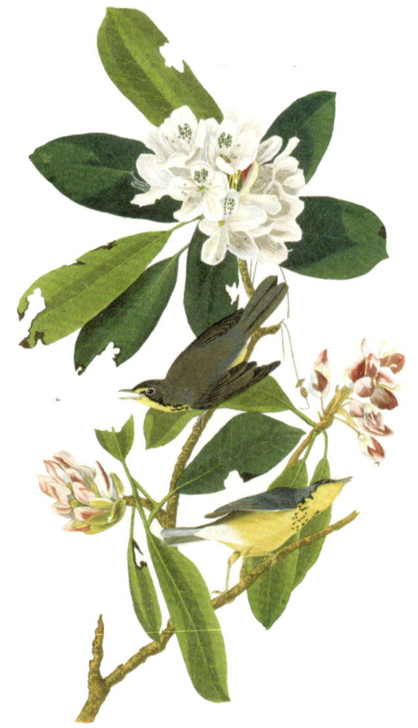

376  Canada Warbler
*Cardellina canadensis*

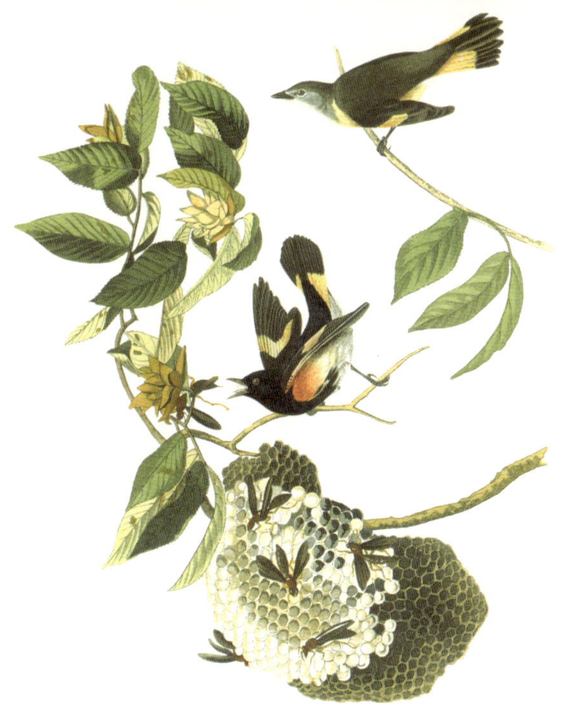

### 377  American Redstart
*Setophaga ruticilla*

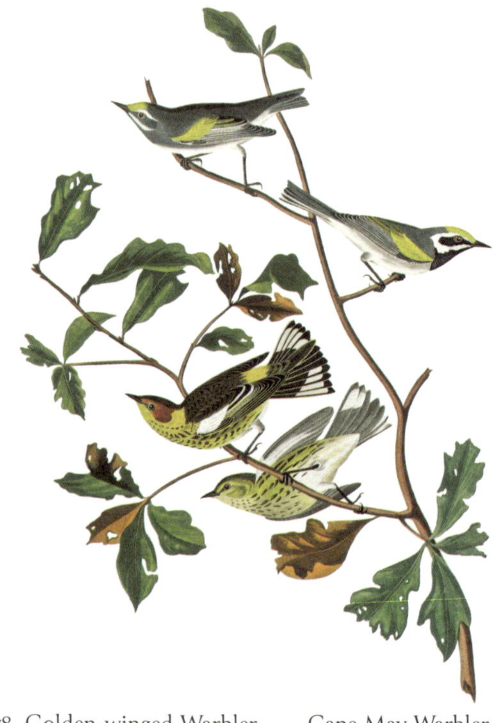

378  Golden-winged Warbler  Cape May Warbler
*Vermivora chrysoptera*  *Setophaga tigrina*

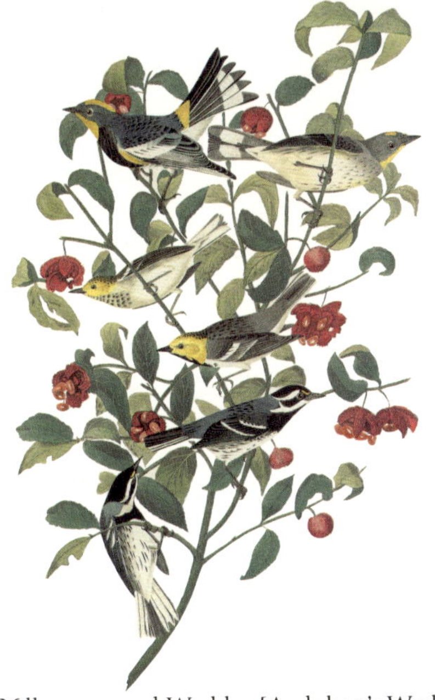

379  Yellow-rumped Warbler [Audubon's Warbler]
*Setophaga coronata*

Hermit Warbler
*Setophaga occidentalis*

Black-throated Gray Warbler
*Setophaga nigrescens*

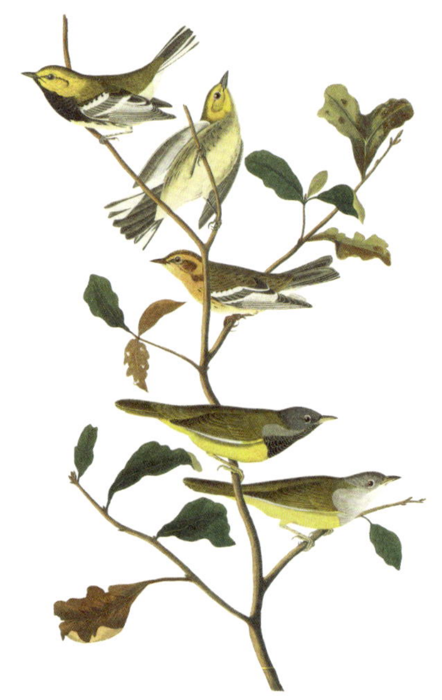

380  Black-throated Green Warbler
*Setophaga virens*

Blackburnian Warbler        MacGillivray's Warbler [Mourning Warbler]
*Setophaga fusca*                *Geothlypis tolmiei*

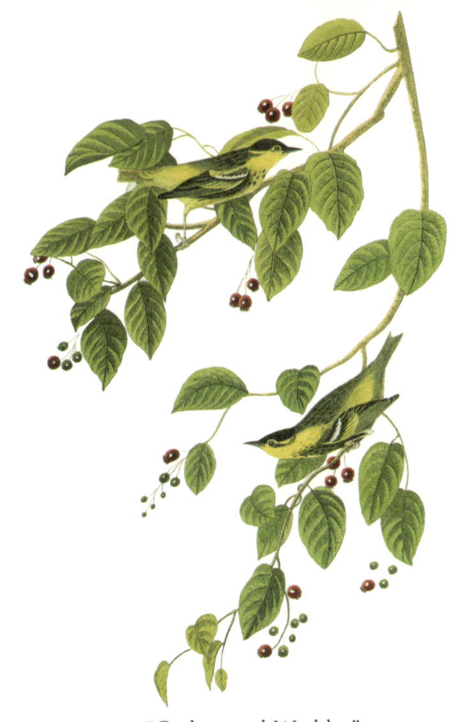

381  "Carbonated Warbler"
*"Dendroica carbonata"*

# XI

## FLOCKERS AND SONGBIRDS

Meadowlarks, Blackbirds, Orioles,

Tanagers, and Finches

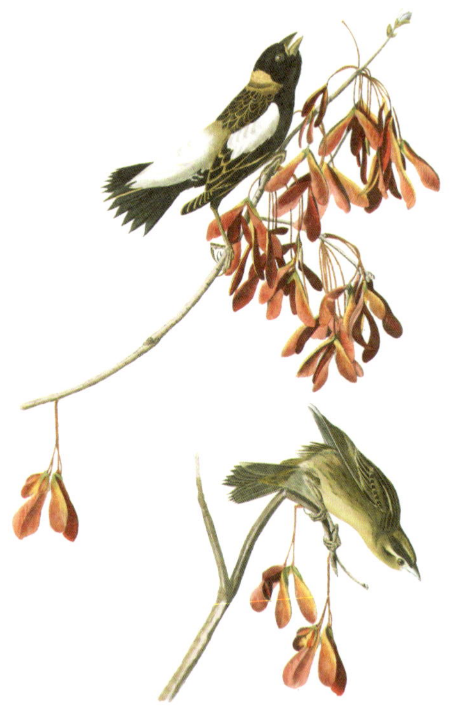

382  Bobolink [Rice Bunting]
*Dolichonyx oryzivorus*

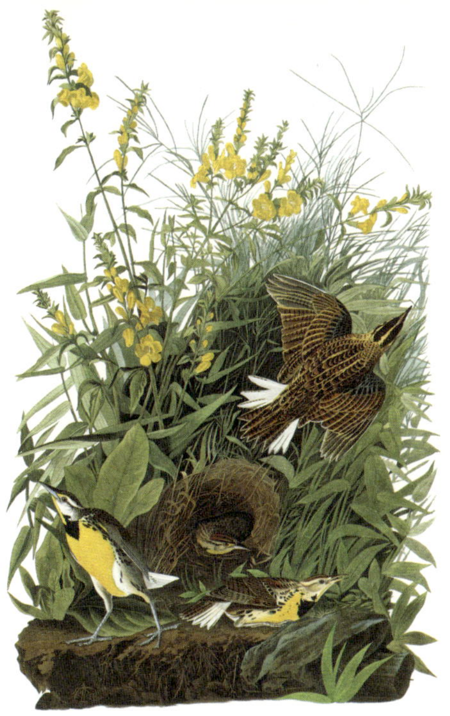

383  Eastern Meadowlark [Meadow Lark]
*Sturnella magna*

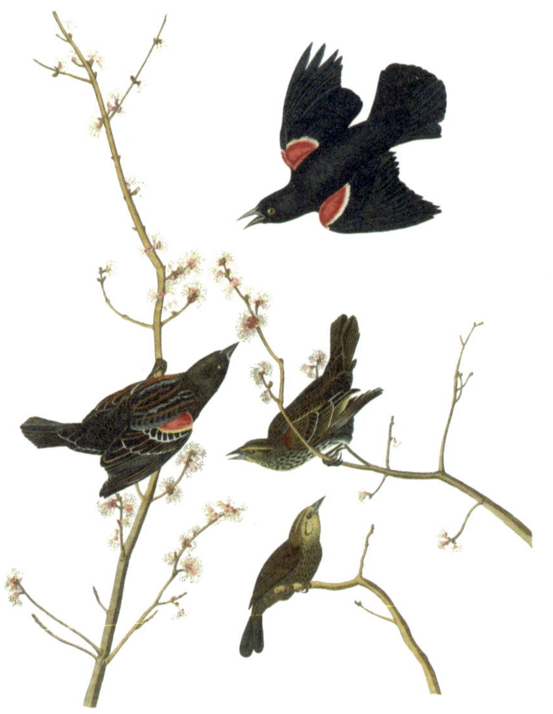

384  Red-winged Blackbird [Red-winged Starling]
*Agelaius phoeniceus*

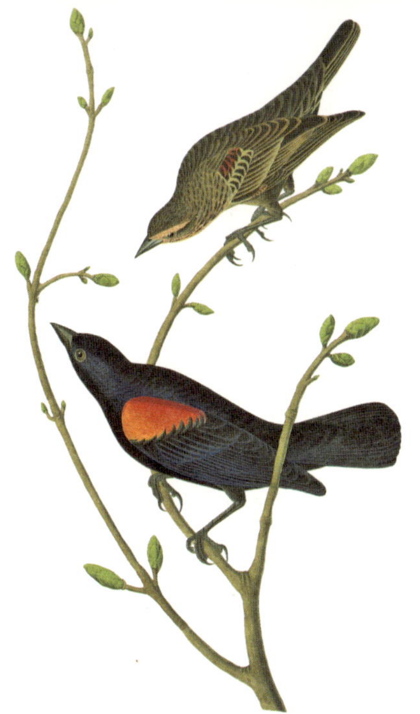

385  Red-winged Blackbird [Prairie Starling]
*Agelaius phoeniceus*

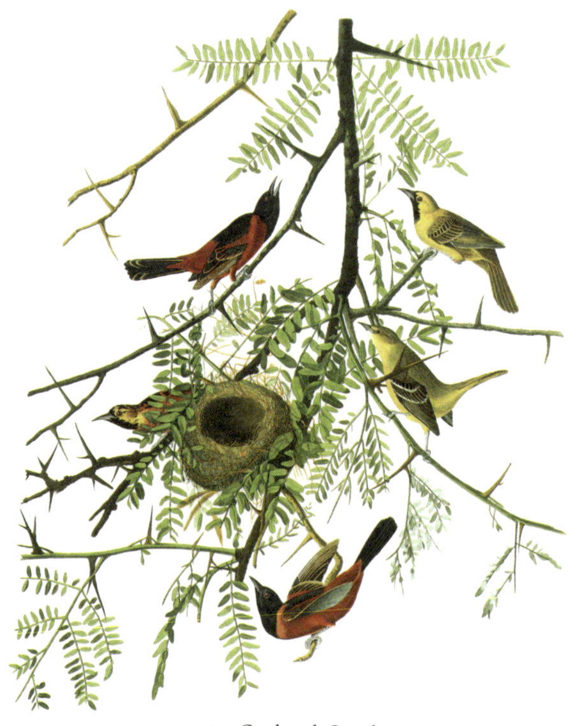

386  Orchard Oriole

*Icterus spurius*

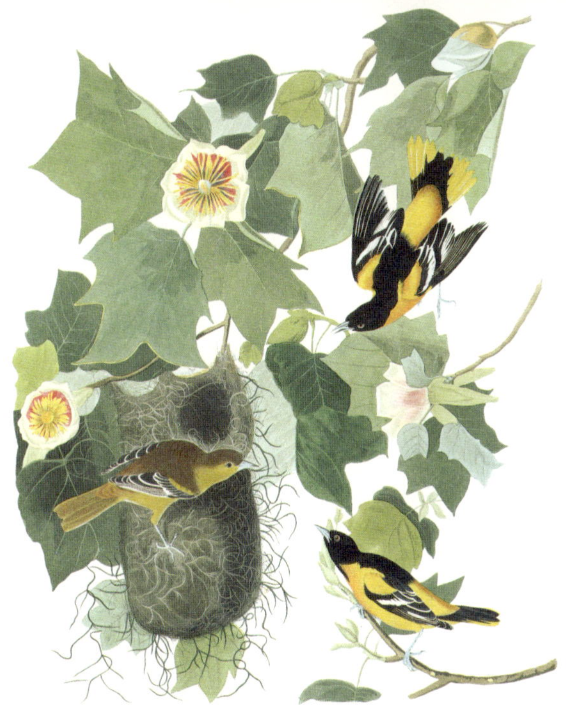

387  Northern Oriole [Baltimore Oriole]
*Icterus galbula*

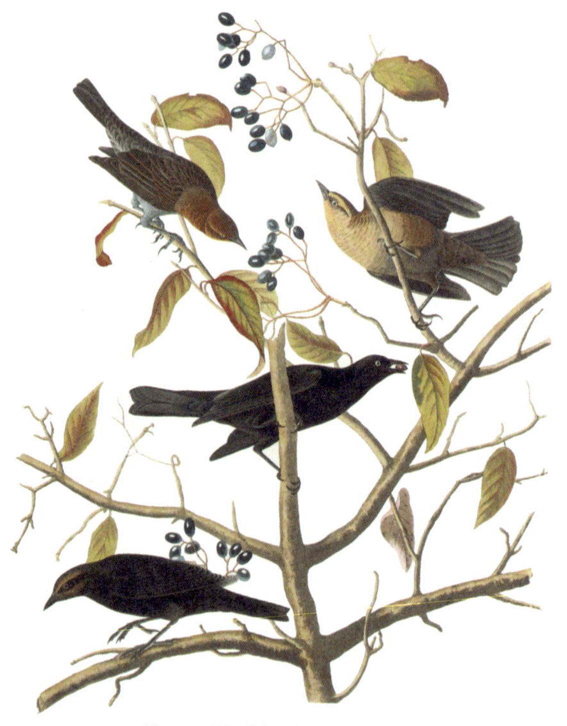

388  Rusty Blackbird [Rusty Grackle]
*Euphagus carolinus*

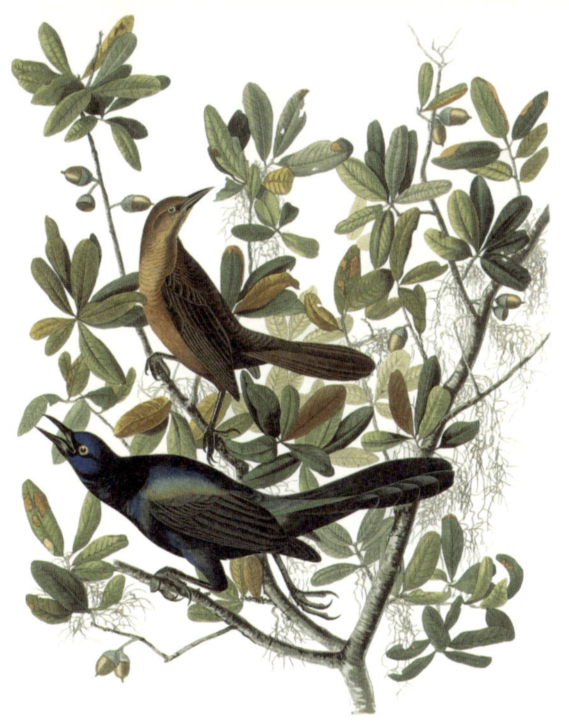

389  Boat-tailed Grackle
*Quiscalus major*

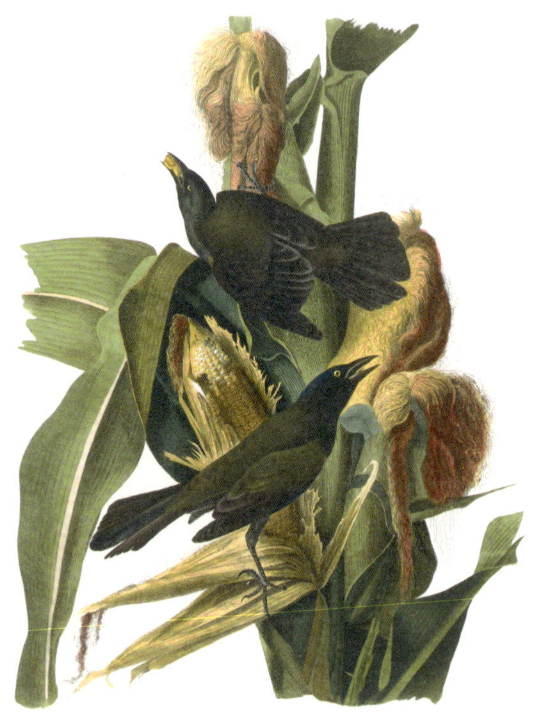

390  Common Grackle [Purple Grackle]
*Quiscalus quiscula*

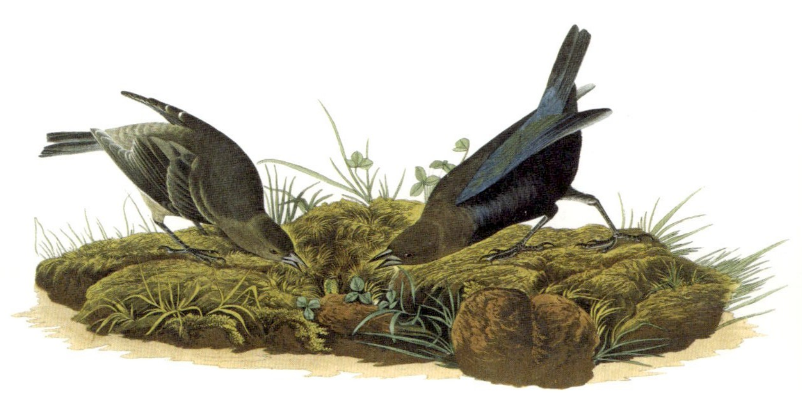

391  Brown-headed Cowbird [Cow Bunting]
*Molothrus ater*

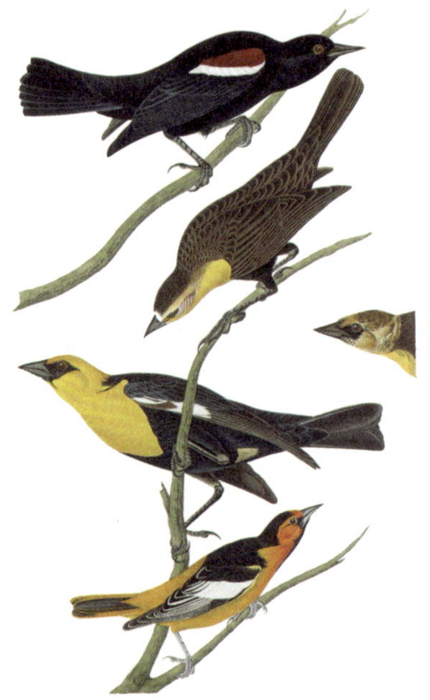

**392  Tricolored Blackbird [Nuttall's Starling]**
*Agelaius tricolor*

**Yellow-headed Blackbird
[Yellow-headed Troopial]**
*Xanthocephalus xanthocephalus*

**Northern Oriole
[Bullock's Oriole]**
*Icterus galbula*

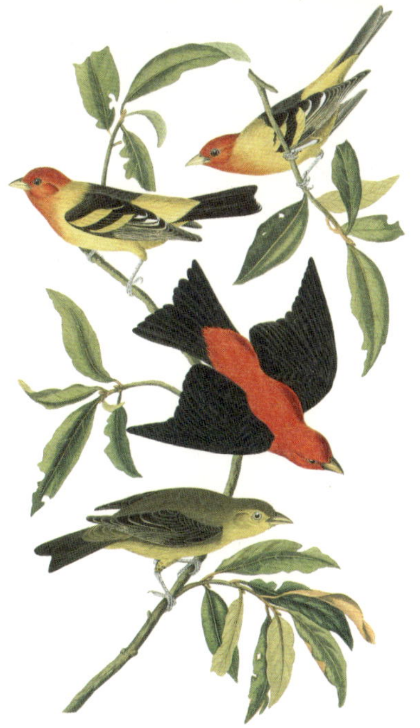

393  Western Tanager
[Louisiana Tanager]
*Piranga ludoviciana*

Scarlet Tanager
[Black-winged Red-bird]
*Piranga olivacea*

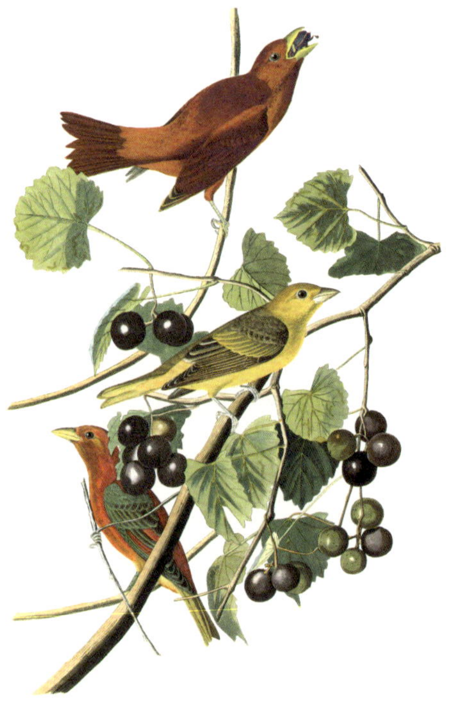

394  Summer Tanager [Summer Red Bird]
*Piranga rubra*

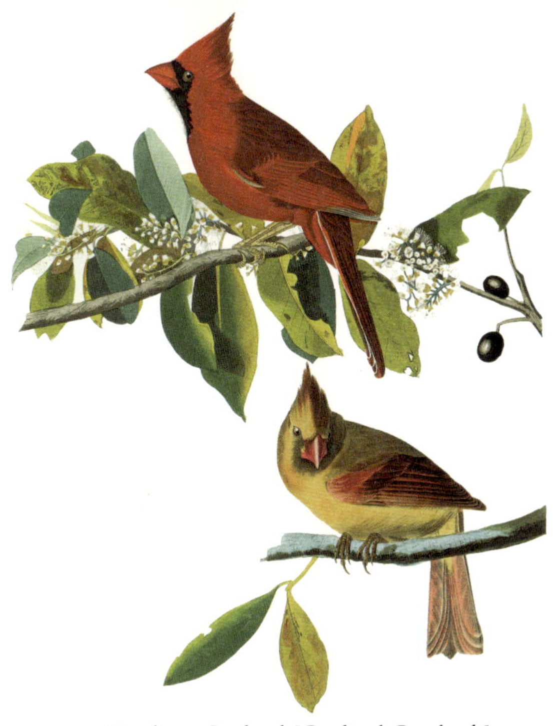

395  Northern Cardinal [Cardinal Grosbeak]
*Cardinalis cardinalis*

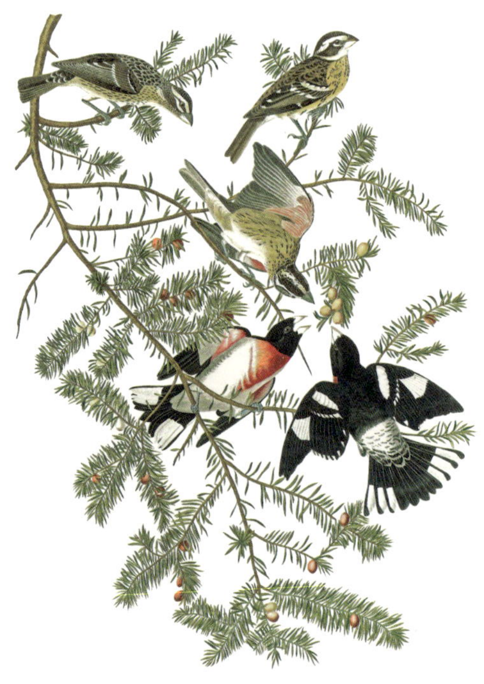

396  Rose-breasted Grosbeak
*Pheucticus ludovicianus*

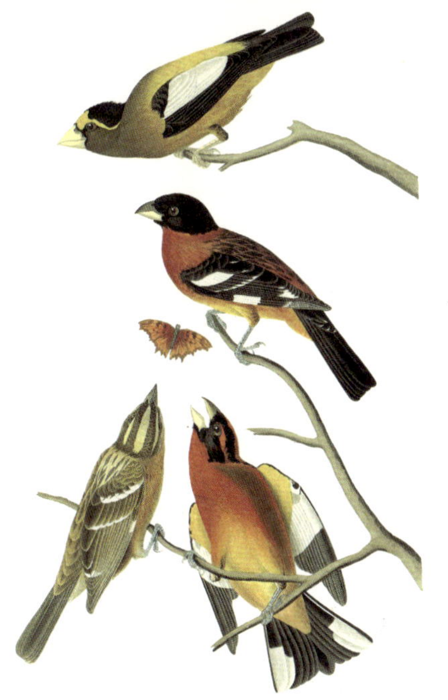

397  Evening Grosbeak
*Coccothraustes vespertinus*

Black-headed Grosbeak
[Spotted Grosbeak]
*Pheucticus melanocephalus*

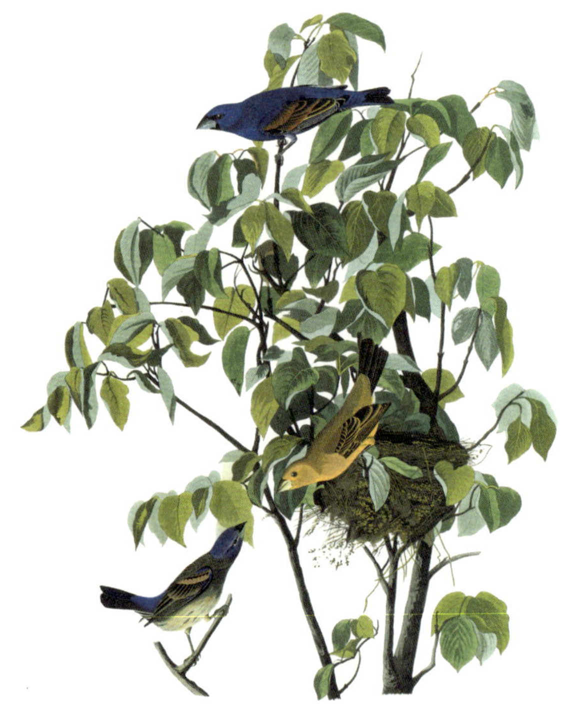

398 Blue Grosbeak

*Passerina caerulea*

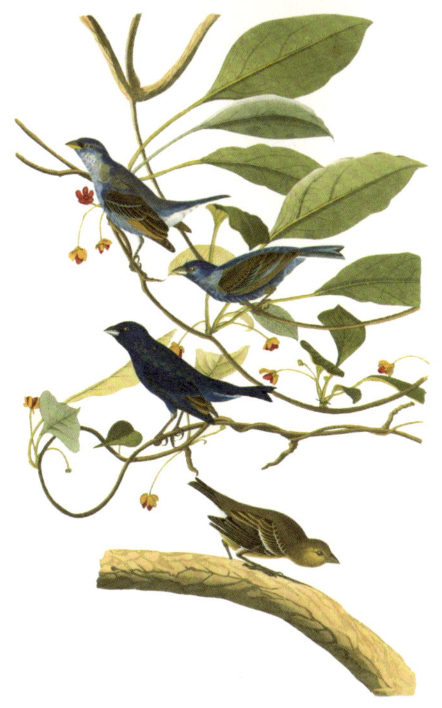

399  Indigo Bunting [Indigo Bird]
*Passerina cyanea*

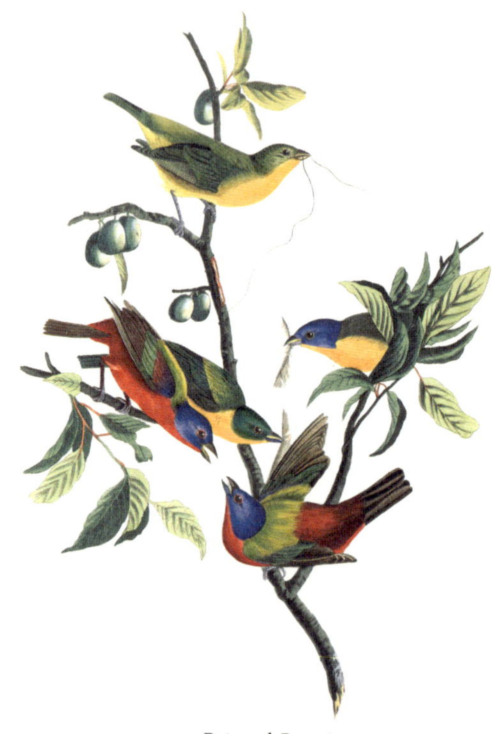

400  Painted Bunting

*Passerina ciris*

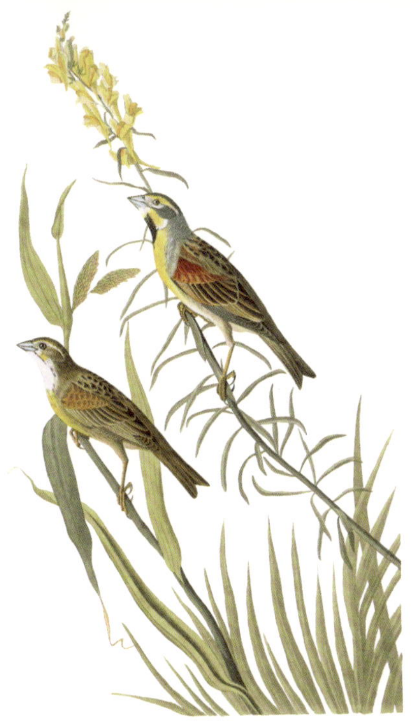

401  Dickcissel [Black-throated Bunting]
*Spiza americana*

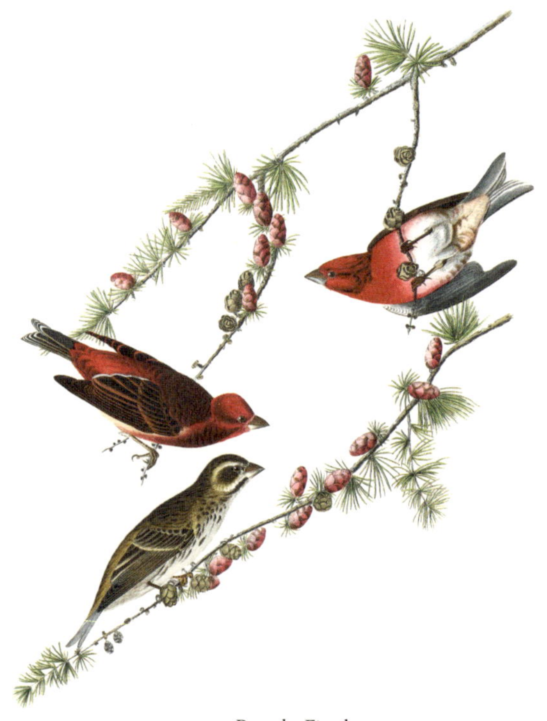

402 Purple Finch
*Haemorhous purpureus*

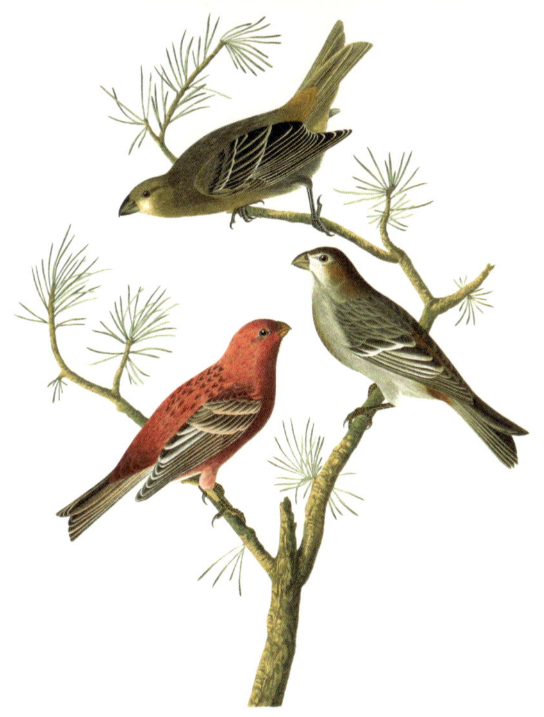

**403  Pine Grosbeak**
*Pinicola enucleator*

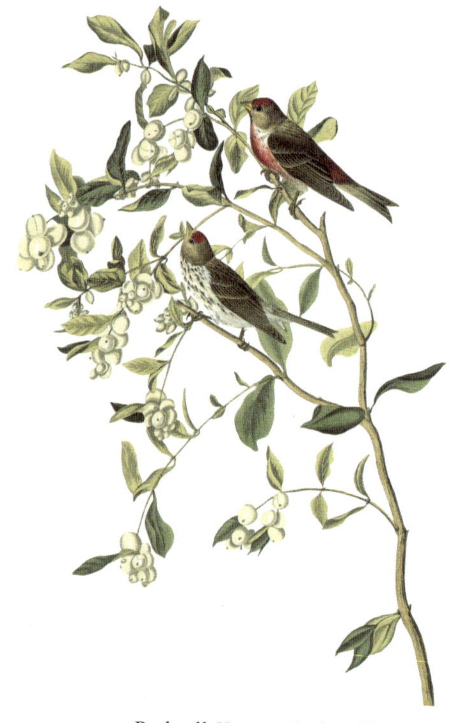

**404  Redpoll [Lesser Red-poll]**
*Acanthis flammea*

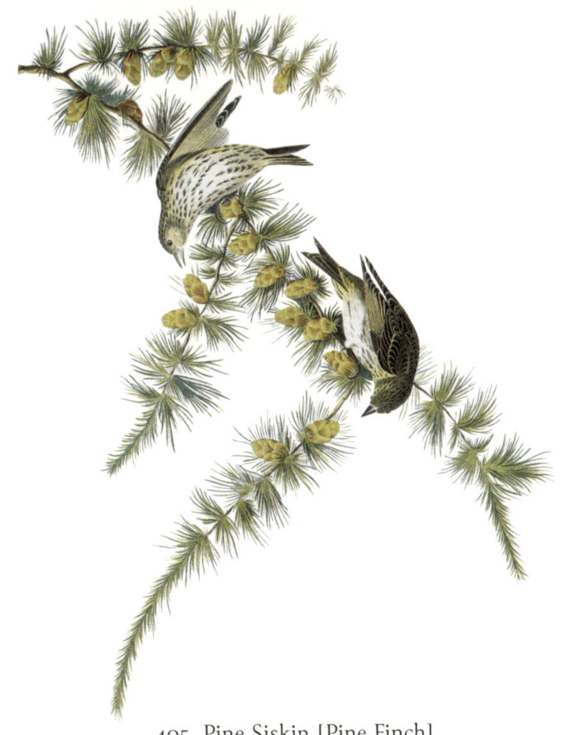

### 405  Pine Siskin [Pine Finch]
*Spinus pinus*

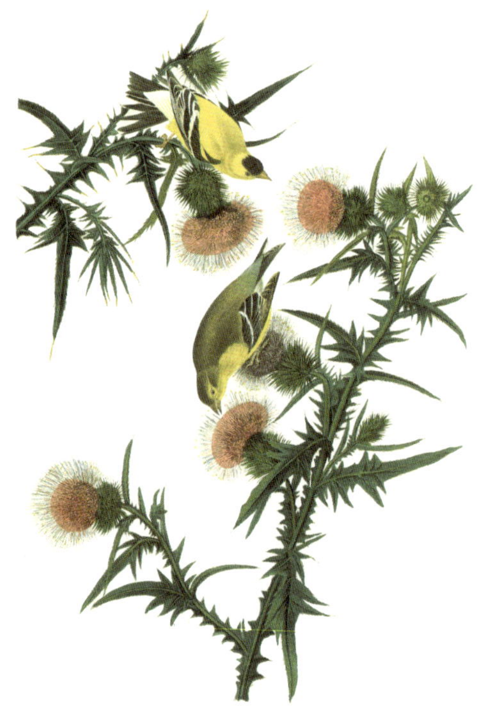

406  American Goldfinch [Yellow Bird]
*Spinus tristis*

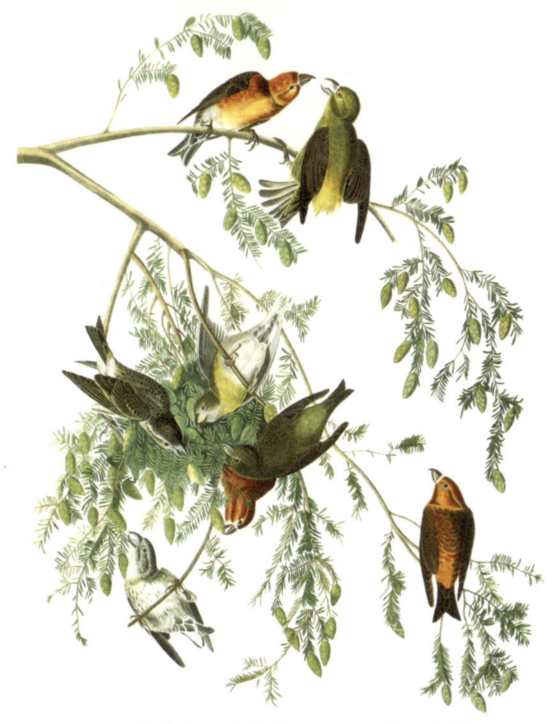

407  Red Crossbill [American Crossbill]
*Loxia curvirostra*

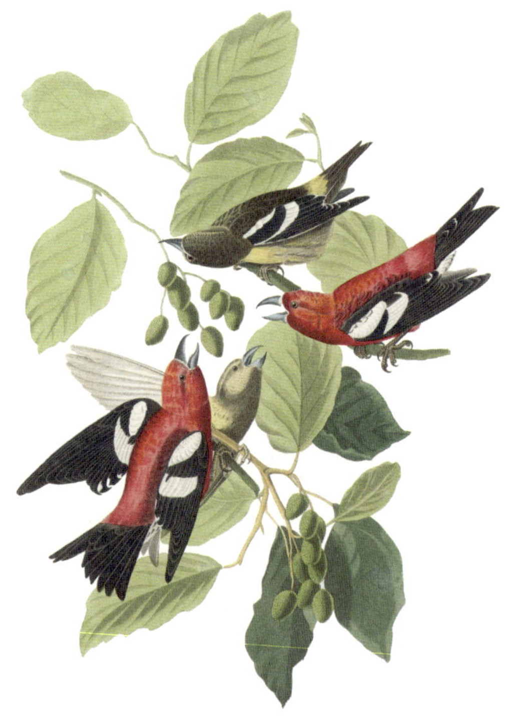

408  White-winged Crossbill

*Loxia leucoptera*

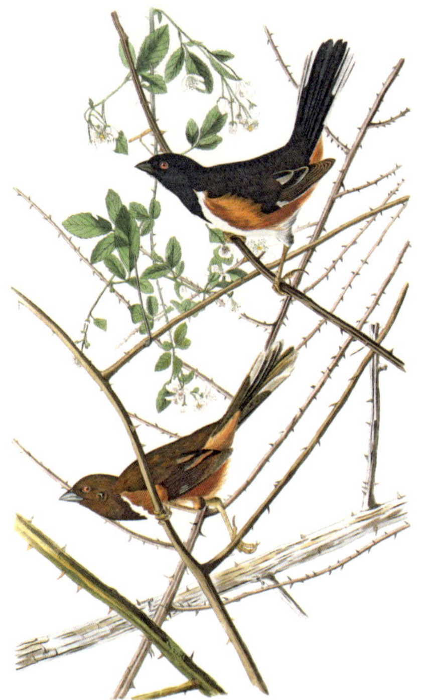

409  Eastern Towhee [Towee Bunting]
*Pipilo erythrophthalmus*

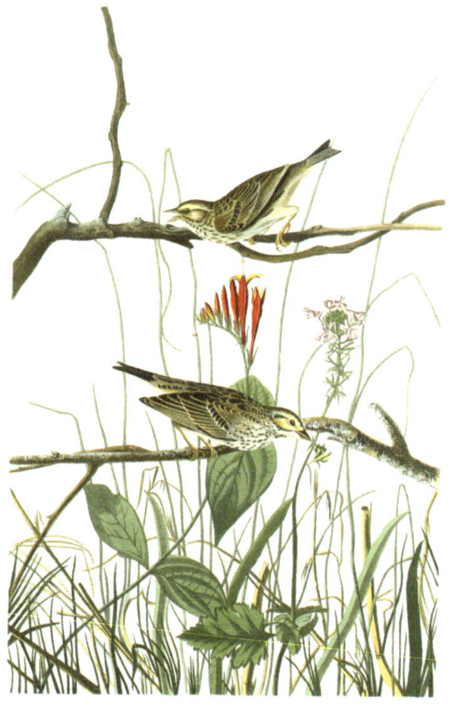

410  Savannah Sparrow [Savannah Finch]
*Passerculus sanwichensis*

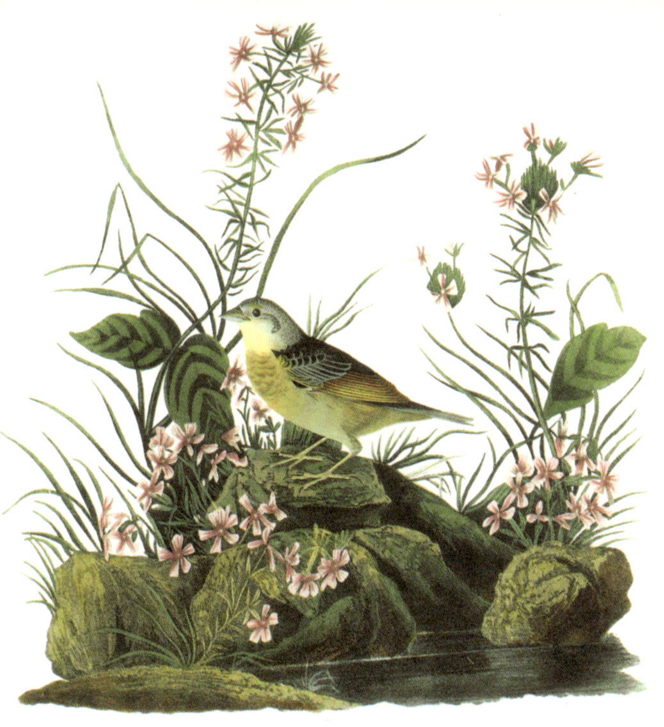

411 Grasshopper Sparrow [Yellow-winged Sparrow]
*Ammodramus savannarum*

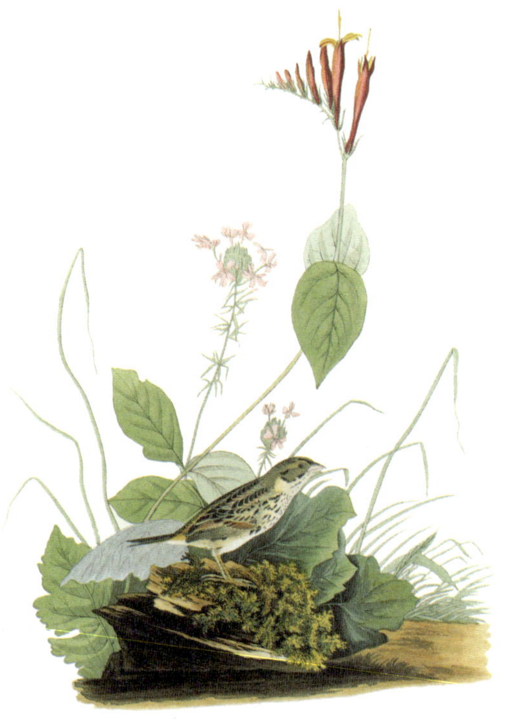

412 Henslow's Sparrow [Henslow's Bunting]
*Ammodramus henslowii*

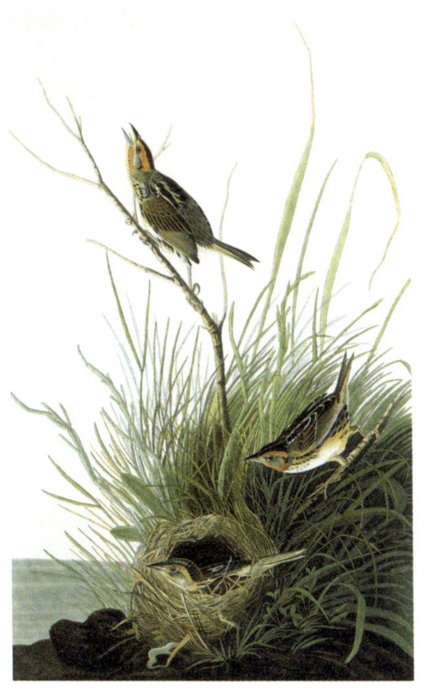

413  Sharp-tailed Sparrow [Sharp-tailed Finch]
*Ammodramus caudacutus*

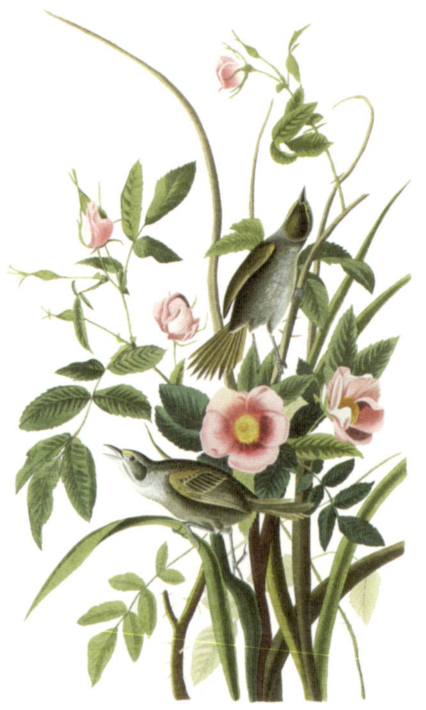

414  Seaside Sparrow [Sea-side Finch]
*Ammospiza maritima*

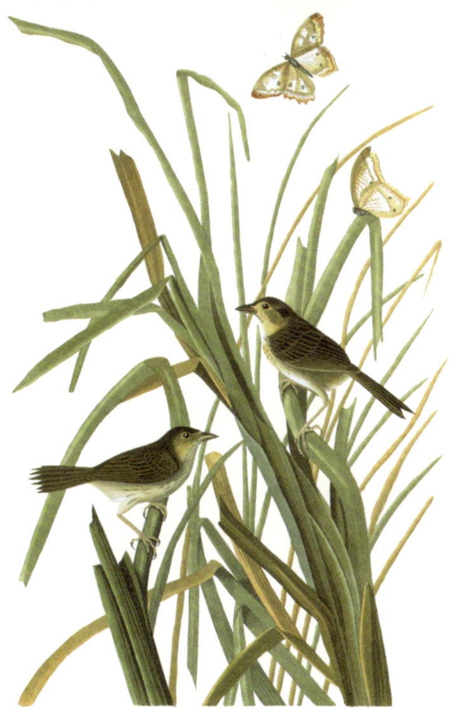

415  Seaside Sparrow [MacGillivray's Finch]
*Ammospiza maritima*

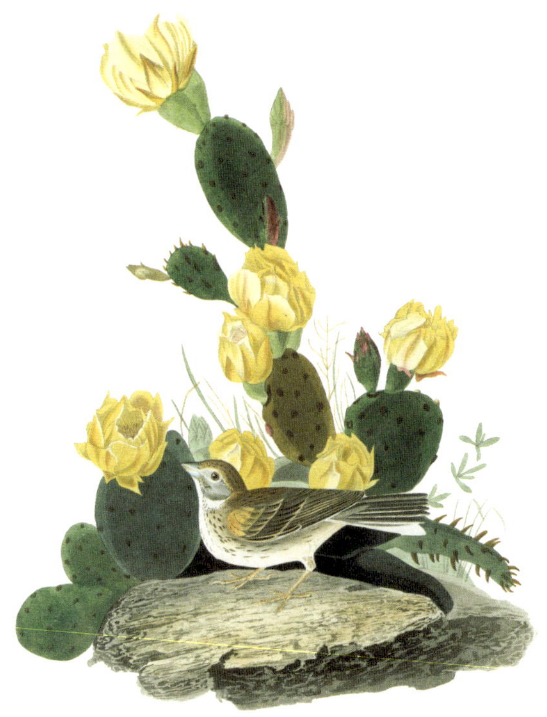

416  Vesper Sparrow [Bay-winged Bunting]
*Pooecetes gramineus*

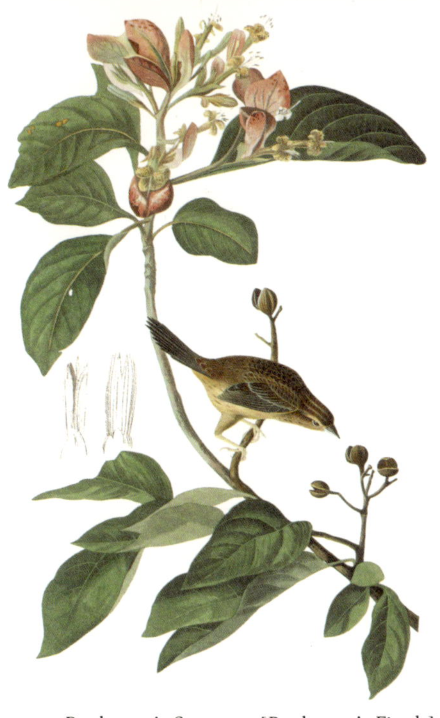

417  Bachman's Sparrow [Bachman's Finch]
*Peucaea aestivalis*

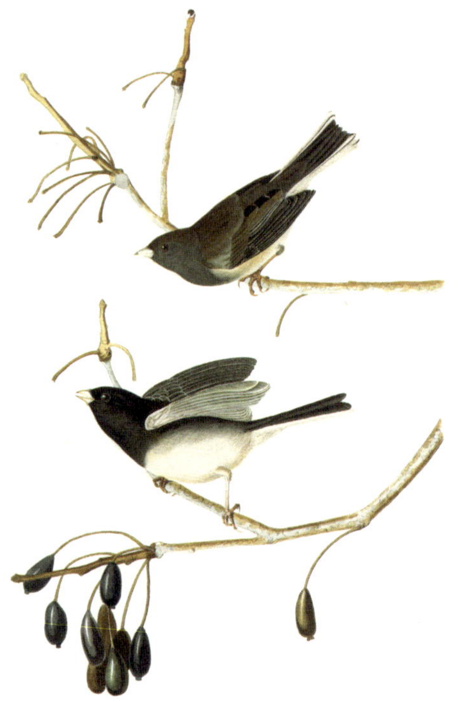

418  Dark-eyed Junco [Snow Bird]

*Junco hyemalis*

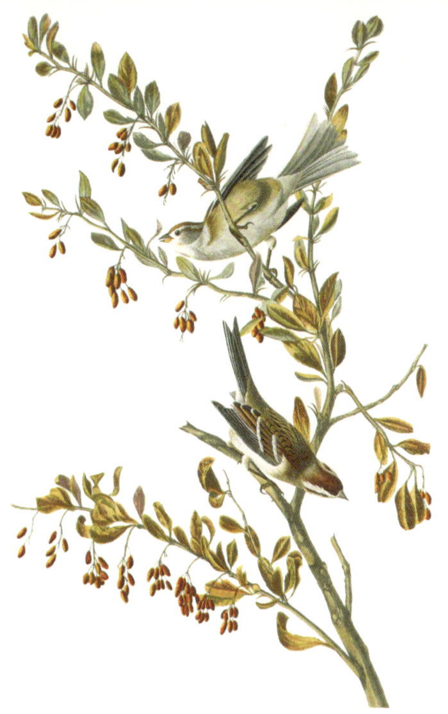

419  American Tree Sparrow [Tree Sparrow]
*Spizelloides arborea*

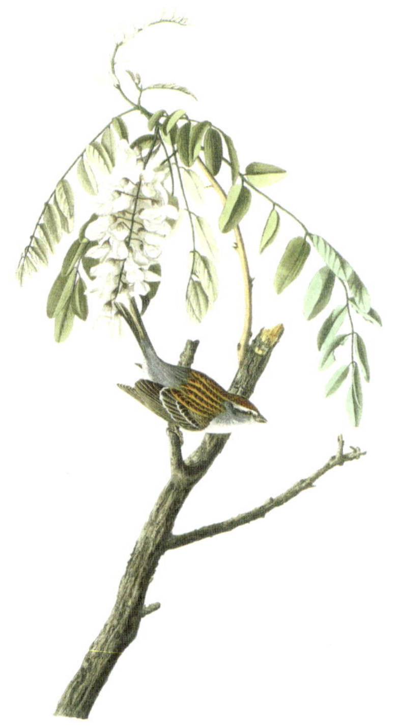

420  Chipping Sparrow
*Spizella passerina*

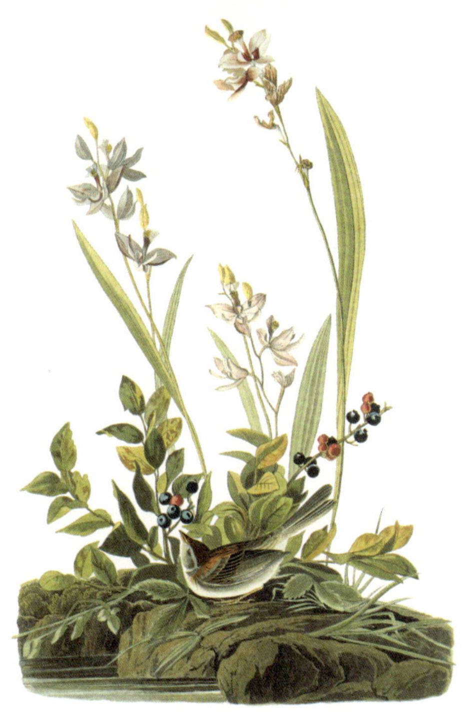

421  Field Sparrow
*Spizella pusilla*

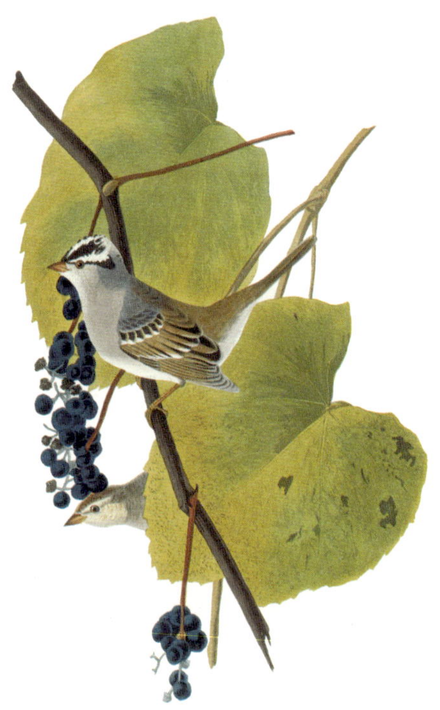

422  White-crowned Sparrow
*Zonotrichia leucophrys*

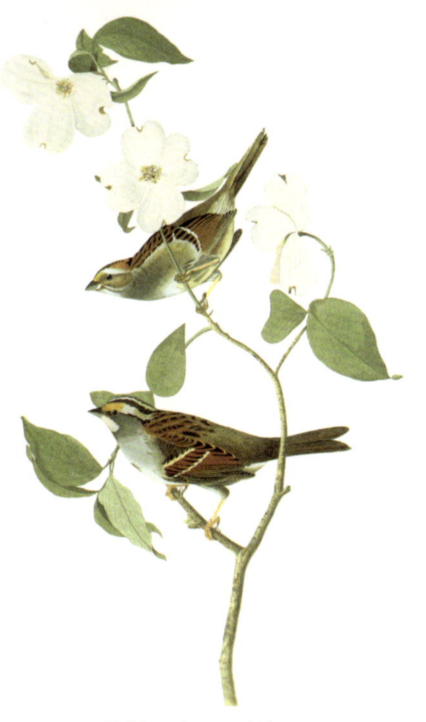

**423  White-throated Sparrow**
*Zonotrichia albicollis*

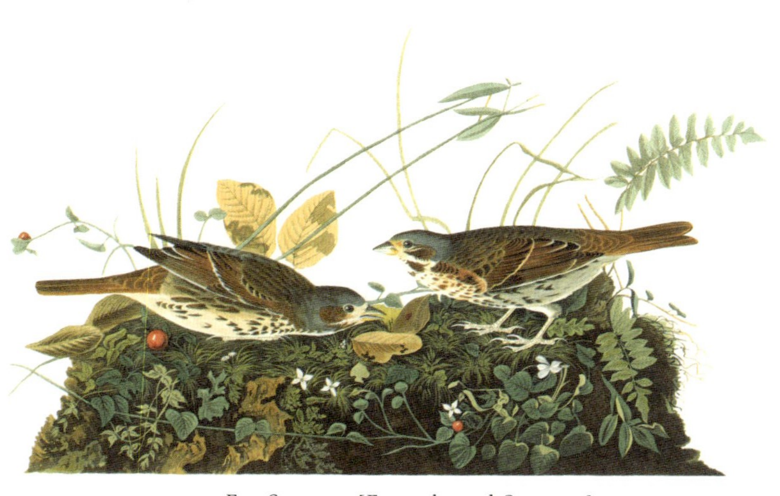

424  Fox Sparrow [Fox-coloured Sparrow]
*Passerella iliaca*

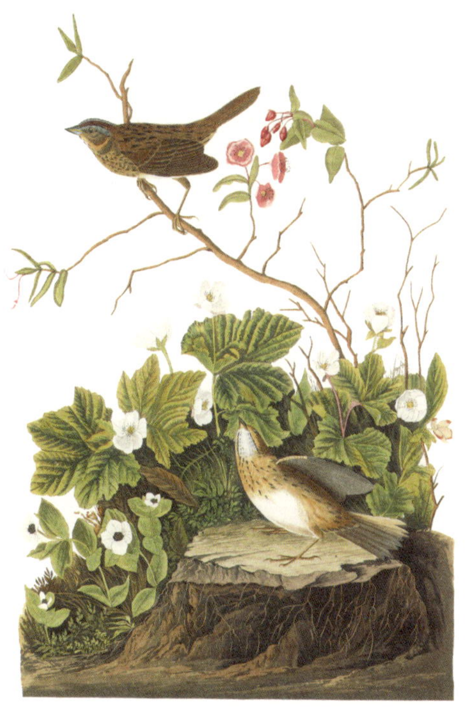

425  Lincoln's Sparrow [Lincoln Finch]
*Melospiza lincolnii*

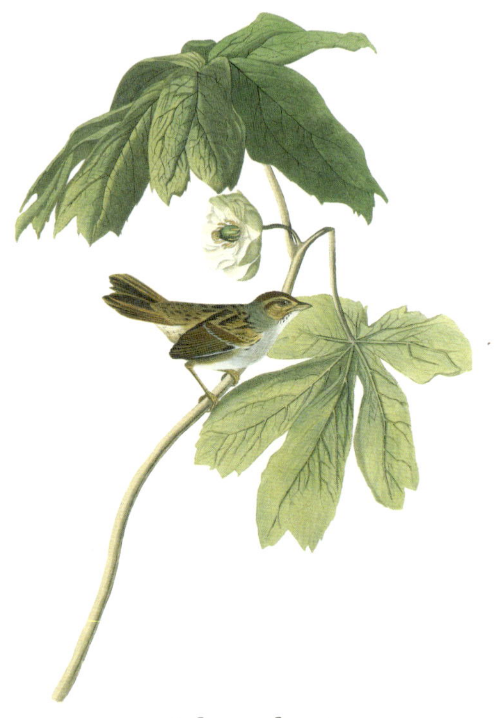

426  Swamp Sparrow
*Melospiza georgiana*

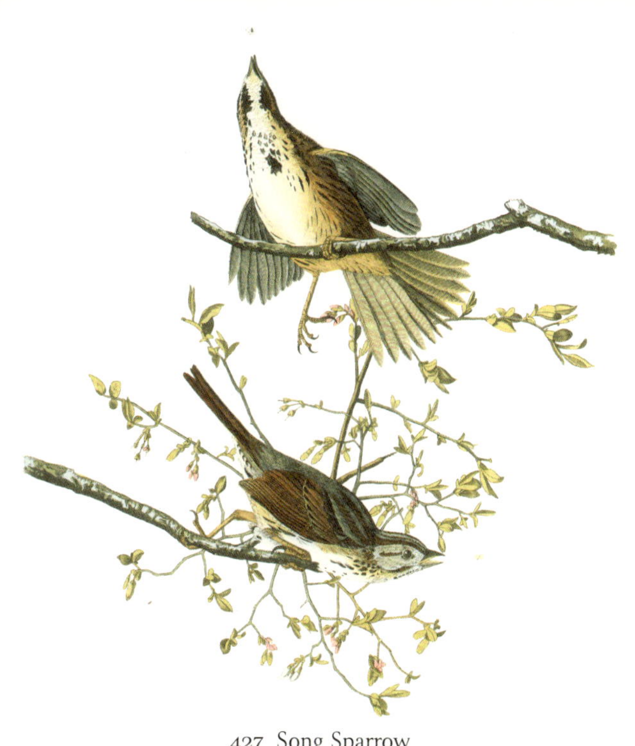

**427  Song Sparrow**

*Melospiza melodia*

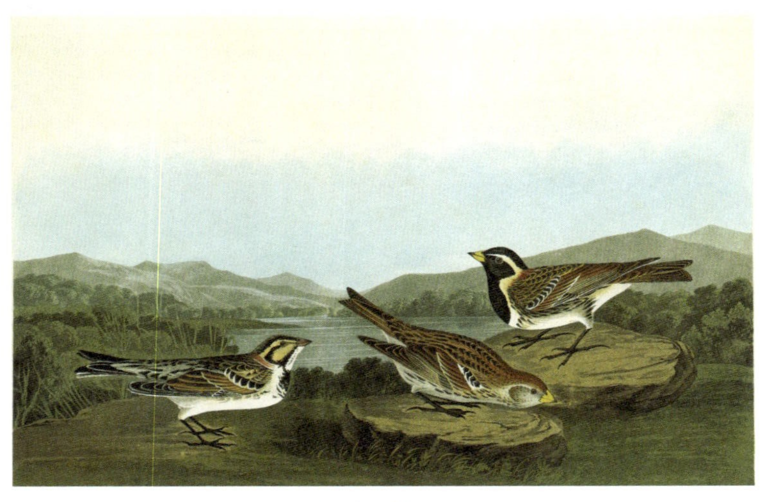

428  Lapland Longspur
*Calcarius lapponicus*

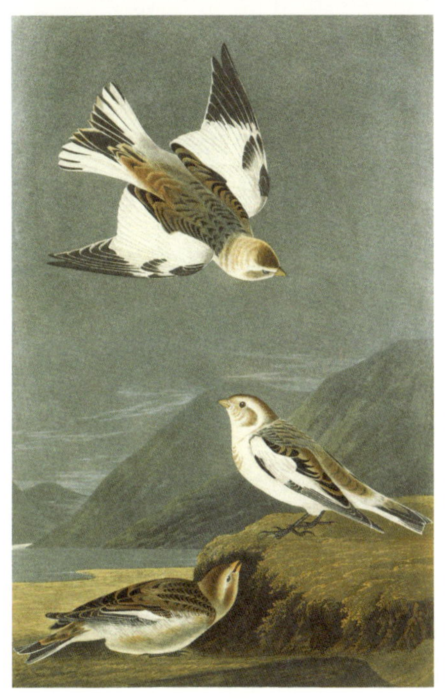

**429  Snow Bunting**
*Plectrophenax nivalis*

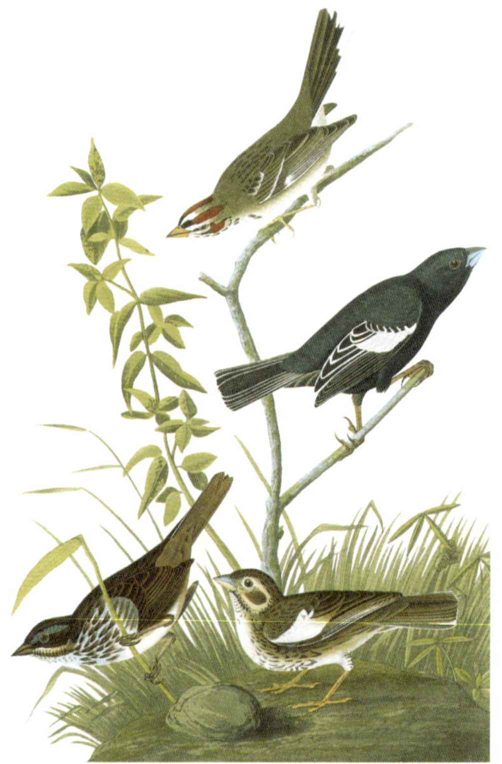

Left

430  Lark Sparrow [Lark Finch]
*Chondestes grammacus*

Lark Bunting [Prairie Finch]
*Calamospiza melanocorys*

Song Sparrow [Brown Song Sparrow]
*Melospiza melodia*


Following page from top to bottom

431  Chestnut-collared Longspur [Chestnut-coloured Finch]
*Calcarius ornatus*

Black-headed Siskin
*Spinus notatus*

Golden-crowned Sparrow [Black Crown Bunting]
*Zonotrichia atricapilla*

Spotted Towhee [Artic Ground-finch]
*Pipilo maculatus*

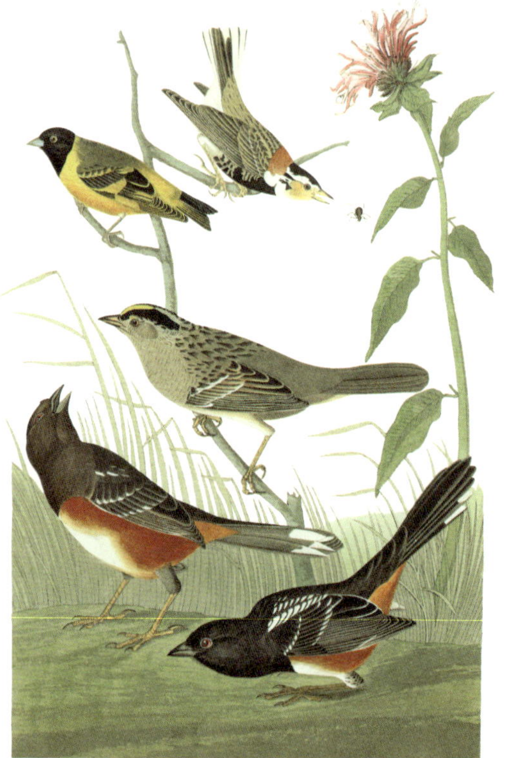

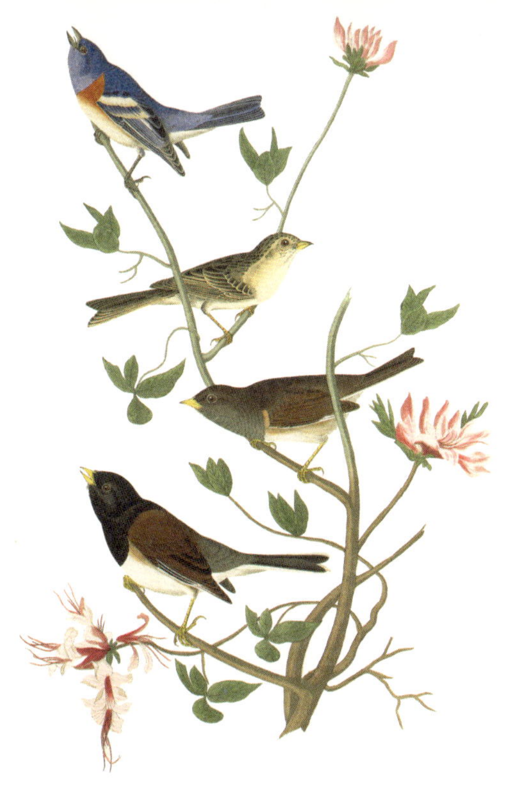

Overleaf

432  Lazuli Bunting [Lazuli Finch]
*Passerina amoena*

Clay-colored Sparrow [Clay-coloured Finch]
*Spizella pallida*

Northern Junco [Oregon Snow Finch]
*Junco hyemalis*


Clockwise from upper left

433  Lesser Goldfinch [Arkansaw Siskin]
*Spinus psaltria*

Hoary Redpoll [Mealy Red-poll]
*Acanthis hornemanni*

Western Tanager [Louisiana Tanager]
*Piranga ludoviciana*

Smith's Longspur [Buff-breasted Finch]
*Calcarius pictus*

"Townsend's Finch"
*Spiza townsendi*

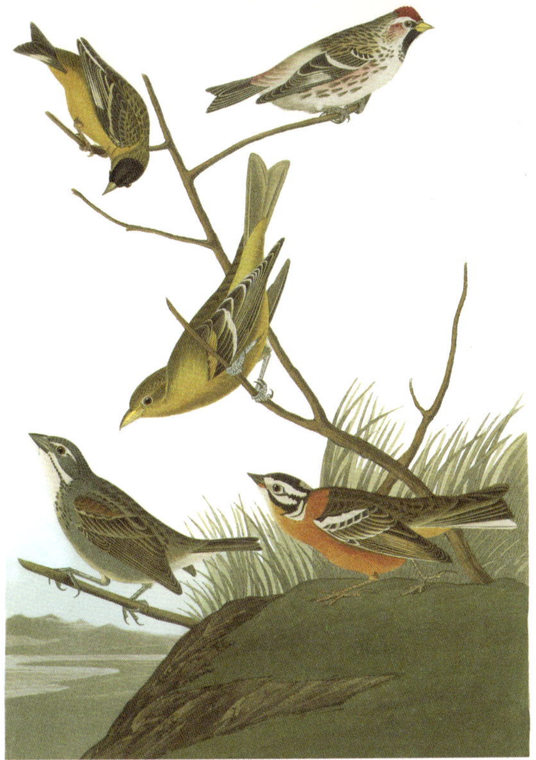

From top to bottom

434  Lazuli Bunting [Lazuli Finch]
*Passerina amoena*

House Finch [Crimson-necked Bullfinch]
*Haemorhous mexicanus*

Rosy Finch [Grey-crowned Linnet]
*Leucosticte arctoa*

Brown-headed Cowbird [Cow-pen Bird]
*Molothrus ater*

Evening Grosbeak
*Coccothraustes vespertinus*

Fox Sparrow [Brown Longspur]
*Passerella iliaca*

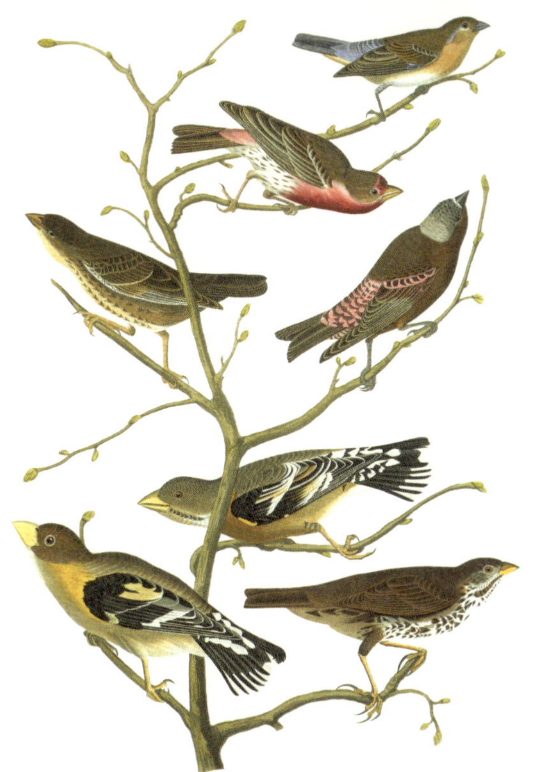

Clockwise from upper left

435  Northern Oriole [Bullock's Oriole and Baltimore Oriole]
*Icterus galbula*

Varied Thrush
*Ixoreus naevius*

Yellow-faced Siskin [Mexican Goldfinch]
*Spinus yarelli*

Northern Waterthrush [Common Water Thrush]
*Parkesia noveboracensis*

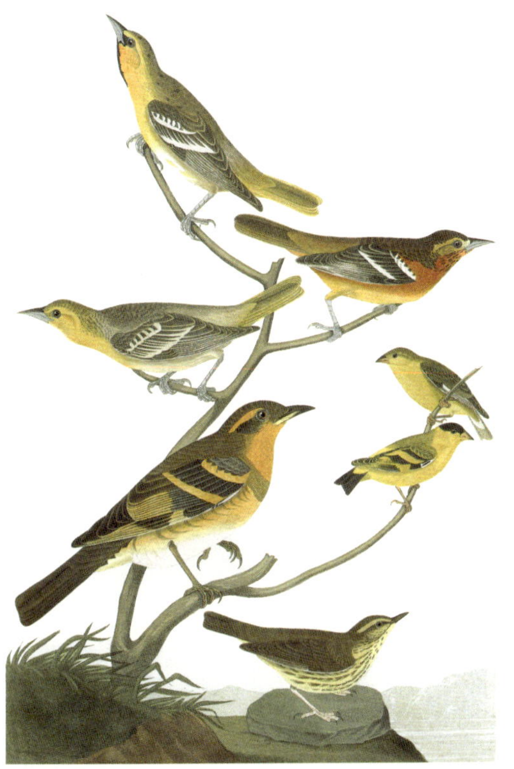